Praise for
MURDER ALONG THE WAY

Kenneth Gribetz has been district attorney of Rockland County, New York, where he has lived since 1974, and is currently serving his fourth term.

MURDER ALONG THE WAY

TRUE CRIME IN AMERICA'S SUBURBS

Kenneth Gribetz, D.A., and H. Paul Jeffers

BERKLEY BOOKS, NEW YORK

This Berkley book contains the complete text
of the original hardcover edition. It has been
completely reset in a typeface designed for easy
reading, and was printed from new film.

MURDER ALONG THE WAY

A Berkley Book / published by arrangement with
Pharos Books

PRINTING HISTORY
Pharos Books edition published 1989
Berkley edition / July 1991

ISBN: 0-425-12491-6

A BERKLEY BOOK ® TM 757,375
Berkley Books are published by The Berkley Publishing Group,
200 Madison Avenue, New York, New York 10016.
The name "BERKLEY" and the "B" logo
are trademarks belonging to Berkley Publishing Corporation.

PRINTED IN THE UNITED STATES OF AMERICA

10 9 8 7 6 5 4 3 2 1

To my Family
Florence, Dennis, Judy, Vicki, Tamar and Lisa
for all your love and support
. . . along the way . . .

ACKNOWLEDGMENTS

THIS BOOK IS a record of major murder cases prosecuted during my years of service in the office of district attorney in New York's Rockland County. Several received national attention in the media because of either their sensational nature or their significance. The successful investigations and prosecutions of all of them are attributable to literally thousands of individuals who have dedicated their lives, publicly and privately, to the rule of law and to the legal system itself. This book is also their story and a tribute to them.

Especially, I express my appreciation to the staff of the Rockland County District Attorney's office: secretaries, legal aides, detectives, assistant DAs, and others without whom the people's right to justice could not be assured. While it is not possible to recognize their individual contributions, I want the record to reflect my gratitude to them for all they have done and are doing. They, too, are the authors of this book.

Others to whom I can only express my gratitude in general are my friends as well as supporters in the political realm who by way of their personal support, financial assistance, and advice and counsel have made my career as district attorney possible.

Of course, none of this would have been possible without the support of my family.

Recognition is also due the people of Rockland County, who sometimes in conditions of extreme social and political difficulty and occasionally under a tremendous civic burden have been unflinching in their dedication to the American precept of equal justice for all under the law.

CONTENTS

1 | MURDER ALONG THE WAY

THE FACE OF the dead man had been beaten into meaty pulp.

"Who is he?" I asked.

"Arnold Sohn," said Cliff Tallman.

"My God, I know him!"

The head of the fully clothed corpse that lay before me on its back on a blood-soaked shag carpet was a mass of swollen and misshapen flesh with black and purple bruises, crusted scabs of congealed blood, eyes swelled shut, and a shattered chin. The split lips were parted by a bloody man's crew sock that had been used as a gag and knotted at the side of the jaw. The skull, crushed like an eggshell, oozed portions of lacerated gray brain tissue into dark hair matted with dried caked blood.

These lethal wounds were consistent with battering by a blunt object, possibly the butt of a gun. Yet, fragments of a broken kitchen knife were strewn near the body, indicating that some wounds to Arnold Sohn's head might have resulted from stabbing or slashing. Only an autopsy would provide the exact cause of death.

"Mrs. Sohn is in the bathroom," said Cliff. "She was gagged and held under water in the tub until she drowned."

Except for shoes, Elaine Sohn was fully clothed in a black sweater and purple stretch pants. The man's crew sock used as a gag was knotted at the back of her head.

Mrs. Sohn was a very large woman—well over two hundred pounds, I estimated—and dragging her to the tub and holding her down in it until she drowned was, it seemed to me, something that could not have been done by only one person.

Usually there were three residents at 38 Jill Lane—the Sohns and their daughter Sheryl—explained Cliff, but Sheryl had left a note on the kitchen table informing her parents that she would be staying with a friend. "Lucky for her," he said, adding that the Sohns' son Mark lived in Florida and was being notified of his parents' death.

"Who found the bodies?"

"Neighbors," said Cliff. "They got worried this morning and came over to investigate. We haven't been here very long. I was just about to call you. How'd you find out about this?"

"I just happened to be passing by."

I'd been driving my daughter Vicki to a friend's birthday party, taking Jill Lane because it was on the way, and had spotted the cluster of police cars and a vehicle belonging to the medical examiner. After dropping Vicki at her party, I'd rushed back.

It was Sunday afternoon, three days past Christmas 1980, when the homes in the comfortably middle-class neighborhood of Blueberry Hill in Spring Valley ought to have been a scene of serenity, but such a convergence of official cars meant there had been violent death, possibly a murder. Shocked and fearful residents congregated in hushed disbelief or peered from windows in horror at the terrible proof that something awful had happened in the modest split-level ranch of brick and blue shingles with neat lawns beginning to appear at the edges of a thin veneer of melting snow.

In the lives of most people murder is something that happens to someone else, in another place. It's the plot of a program on television—fictional death often being the stuff of prime time or the soap operas of daytime—or a puzzler printed on the pages of detective novels. The closest they might come to a genuine murder is a story on the evening news or in the paper, but even those real-life homicides always seemed to take place in locales that, even though they might be nearby, appeared distant and almost foreign and involved odd people and names that were unfamiliar and easily forgotten.

Murder did not fit into this Christmas-card setting on a sparkling day when everyone was still aglow with memories of a white Christmas and the tinsel-and-lights happiness of holidays Norman Rockwell might have illustrated. This place was far from the crowds and noise of New York City an hour's drive away, where violent death seemed to be the coin of life and the currency of the street, the place from which many of these people had fled for a better life (and, some believed, to preserve life itself).

I knew that Mr. and Mrs. Arnold Sohn of 38 Jill Lane had done just that. I also knew that their experience matched those of many families who were facing a vast array of serious new problems growing out of the rapid spread of a drug culture that seemed to be eroding the fabric of the nation itself. This crisis had grown so acute that bewildered and desperate parents frequently came to the district attorney seeking advice and assistance in dealing with out-of-control children. The Sohns had sought advice from me regarding drug-related problems involving their daughter Sheryl.

I also knew Arnold because of the coincidence of his being a very successful salesman in the furniture department of Bloomingdale's, the fashionable Manhattan department store of which my uncle, Lester Gribetz, was a senior executive vice-president.

Now, looking down at the crushed remains of Arnold's head, I could not help thinking about the bitter irony in the fact that the man I could no longer recognize had been a decent, hard-working, middle-aged family man who had moved away from the once predominantly Jewish neighborhood of the Grand Concourse of the Bronx and chosen to settle in Spring Valley in 1968 because he had wanted to get his kids out of the city to a place where it was safe.

For his neighbors the Thomases, this was another Sunday Arnold Sohn should have brought bagels and lox and cream cheese along with the Sunday papers. When he did not show up and no one answered the telephone, Leonard and Joyce Thomas became worried and went to investigate with their daughter Debra. It was she who made the awful discovery that Arnold and his wife Elaine had come back to their house after having spent a lively Saturday evening at a party marking the fiftieth birthday of their old and dear friend Alvin Zechnowitz and been brutally murdered.

This was the season for parties, the beginning of a week filled with the happy anticipation of the fast-approaching New Year's Eve, the culmination of a time for the exchange of heartfelt greetings. For the Sohns it had included a trip to Florida to visit their son, Mark. Three weeks earlier they had celebrated Hannukah, a period for Jews to commemorate miracles and mankind's age-old longing for peace on earth that both the Jewish people's candle-lighted Hannukah menorah and Christianity's Christmas star represent, each holiday festival being a joyous celebration centered on the children and the giving of gifts, each built around the family and the love between parents and their offspring, all anticipating the turning of the calendar to a new year.

I had been looking forward to 1981 with the hope that it would not be a repeat of the passing year, one of the most violent twelve months in the history of Rockland County and the most challenging of my six years as district attorney in the lovely rolling countryside west of the Hudson River dotted with quaint old villages and changing towns whose names—Pearl River, Tappan, Stony Point, Monsey, Nanuet, Nyack, New City, Suffern, Ramapo, Mount Ivy, Spring Valley—conjured visions of peacefulness and tranquil rural beauty.

Unhappily, like all communities across America in the waning hours of the year, those in Rockland were beginning to feel the effects of an increase in crime, once the hallmark of the cities but by then a bane of localities everywhere. My files in the Rockland County office building in nearby New City showed a blight of drugs, robberies, burglaries, rape, assaults, and murders, including thirty-four homicides since 1974, with ten of them in that year alone, five in 1979, four between May and November of 1980. And now this one.

So brutal and bizarre was this double homicide that it immediately evoked the hellish family created by the infamous Charles Manson a decade earlier, memories of that heinous string of murders stirring within the professional lawmen in the Sohn house the dark dread that we might be witnessing the horrible debut of a similar cult of killers in Rockland.

Spring Valley was by no means immune to violent crime in 1980, but until that moment the community's experience with homicide had been routine, if murder can ever be deemed routine—death dealt out between junkies, husband-and-wife homicides, lovers' stabbings, shootings associated with robberies. But here was a woman drowned in a bathtub and a husband whose life had been literally beaten out of him in their respectable middle-class home for no apparent reason.

To homicide investigators, the scene of the crime is a curious mixture of the strange and the familiar. Surroundings are usually new but the faces at the location are normally those of known associates, creating an atmosphere of familiarity. Underlying this feeling of new mixed with the old is an uneasy realization of intruding into the victim's privacy and taking into our hands all the intimate details of lives that had unfolded within those walls. But, of course, it is behind those doors, within the walls, in the closets, inside the bureaus, and enclosed in locked desk drawers that a solution to a murder may be found. So, into the inner sanctums of the murder victim must march an army of professional snoops—forensic specialists; experts in such weaponry of crime as guns, knives, ropes, and bludgeons; the medical examiner; crime photographers; fingerprint lifters; serologists searching for telltale bloodstains; white-gloved men looking like janitors lugging vacuum sweepers to sift dust and carpet fibers for clues; and a brigade of detectives who bring with them all their years of education, training, on-the-job experience, instinct, and (the most useful tool of all) their intuition.

Just beginning the detailed examination of the premises, inside and out, detectives Clifford Tallman and Edwin O'Neill were familiar and reassuring presences in the Sohns' house. Head of the Spring Valley detective bureau, Eddie was a rough and ready ex-marine and Cliff a handsome thirty-five-year-old six-footer with curly gray hair who'd had five years of experience as a plainclothes policeman and a decade in uniform on the streets where so many crimes are committed and so many are solved. Their boss was Spring Valley police chief Adam Krainak. Also there were the Rockland County medical examiner, Dr. Frederick Zugibe; Superintendent Thomas Sullivan, Assistant Superintendent Thomas Brown, investigators Vincent Winters, John Gaffney, Ed Starkey, and James Searle of the Bureau of Criminal Identification.

A fairly typical ranch-style dwelling in what had been both a pleasant town and a seasonal resort favored by Jews before the great postwar exodus from cities led to an explosion of what the sociologists quickly named *suburbia*, the Sohn residence had a garage at the front, a small porch, a deck, and rooms on two levels connected by a stairway. On one floor were bedrooms, including the master bedroom at the rear and two baths, the living and dining rooms, and a kitchen. On the next level was another bedroom and a recreation room. Doors led from a hallway to the front porch, to the deck from the kitchen, and to the garage.

An examination of the doors revealed that there were pry marks on one in the rear, but these appeared to be quite old. However, the glass of an outside aluminum door was broken, an indication that this was where the house had been forcibly entered.

The condition of the bedroom's furnishings indicated that Arnold Sohn had struggled desperately.

The spattering and splashing of blood had left patterns that, properly interpreted, would allow a reconstruction of the events in the room, the hallway, and outside the house—including a clear trail of bloodstains that left the house, crossed the snow, and disappeared in an area where the snow had melted. Other footprints found in the snow were believed to have been left by Debra Thomas.

In both the master bedroom and the master bathroom were numerous stains that appeared to be smears of blood, indications that attempts might have been made to wipe blood from various articles of furniture and to obliterate any fingerprints.

Cliff and Eddie pointed out that the wiping was not consistent with the general condition of the home. "This is a well-kept and cared-for home," Cliff noted. "The furniture all seems to be in place, except in the master bedroom, where there must have been a struggle. The surfaces appear to have been cleaned on a regular basis, so those wipe marks really stand out."

From my previous experience in cases in which there was the presence of so much blood I was quite confident that whoever had committed these horrendous brutalities couldn't have left that house without traces of it on themselves and on their clothing. The apparently blood-stained footprints in the snow seemed to justify that hunch; but, of course, a laboratory analysis would be required before it could be accepted that the red spots in the snow were, in fact, blood.

What puzzled me was that there appeared to have been no systematic ransacking of the house, as would have been expected if the intrusion had been burglary. Only the bedroom was disheveled. Of course, it was possible that panic had followed the killings and that burglary had been abandoned in favor of a hasty exit.

Only a detailed accounting of the Sohns' known possessions could tell us whether any items were missing. The son and daughter would be crucial to this aspect of the investigation.

If there had not been a burglary, what was the motive for these brutal murders?

Had someone been bent on revenge and lying in wait?

Were the Sohns the random victims of a Mansonlike family of homicidal maniacs?

A cursory look at the physical evidence made any of these scenarios plausible, but these were riddles for which there were no immediate or easy answers. Only painstaking, time-consuming, and persistent work of trained experts and the sleuthing of investigators like Cliff Tallman and Eddie O'Neill and the detectives I would assign to the case could come up with the evidence that would lead to answers and arrests.

Then it would be up to me to assemble the fruits of their labor and to place it in the hands of a jury for whom murder would suddenly become a profoundly personal human tragedy that had happened in their own backyard.

2 | THERE WAS A LITTLE GIRL

THE ROLE OF the district attorney at the scene of a crime differs from the job of the police. The police look at a crime and the crime scene from the vantage point of "probable cause" for an arrest; that is, whether there is sufficient evidence connecting a particular person to the crime to support and justify his or her arrest. The DA, on the other hand, must look beyond that solitary, albeit important, event. He or she has to consider the quantity and quality of the evidence with a view toward whether there is sufficient proof to persuade a jury of the defendant's guilt "beyond a reasonable doubt."

Therefore, aside from making himself and his resources available to the local police to assist in their investigations, the DA at the scene is always looking for ways to develop new evidence, to locate new witnesses, and to ensure that no legal mistakes are made in the gathering of that evidence to avoid losing a case on a so-called technicality. For a DA this is not just a matter of crystallizing the evidence the police turn up; it is an ongoing process. There can never be too much evidence. His work does not end until he rises in court to announce "The People rest."

Fortunately for me, Cliff Tallman and Eddie O'Neill had always demonstrated as deep a commitment to winning convictions as they showed in making collars, so they were eager to confer with me from the start. From the moment they came on the case they'd had no pause, accumulating a vast and growing record of the details of the physical evidence adding up to the surmise that the Sohns had been surprised, probably by more than one person, then gagged and robbed of valuables on their persons within their home and murdered.

An intact .32-caliber bullet was discovered in the bedroom where Arnold Sohn had been beaten to death, leading to speculation that the weapon used to beat him was probably a gun, although one or more other blunt objects might have been employed, perhaps a wrench or a tire iron. A search of a wide area on both sides of Jill Lane had been made but no weapons had been found. The fingerprints discovered appeared to be those of members of the Sohn family. Casts of footprints had been made. One had been identified as that of Debra Thomas; others had flecks of red that appeared to be bloodstains.

Questions had been asked, including a brief interrogation of Sheryl Sohn, but none of the interviews provided any breakthroughs.

Late Sunday evening in the detective bureau of the Spring Valley police headquarters, no closer to solving the murders than they'd been that afternoon, Cliff and Eddie could only go over the evidence again and again, discussing it and speculating about it in the hope that they might hit on something new. From time to time each would take a moment to answer a phone. Most of the calls were routine stuff, including a call from the police in North Plainfield, New Jersey, asking if there were any warrants filed in Spring Valley for a James Sheffield of Spring Valley, who'd been picked up for being in a park after hours. "The kid had a bag of clothing with him," the police reported, "and some of the items have what could be bloodstains."

There was a rap sheet on Sheffield, including at least one charge involving violence, but he was not on a wanted list at that moment.

James Sheffield could therefore not be held, a distressing fact that registered clearly in the faces of Cliff and Eddie in my office the next morning. They had come for a meeting that I hoped would become a brainstorming session for sifting clues, asking questions, weighing answers, challenging assumptions, thinking the unthinkable, and postulating theories: what if? what about? who? what? where? when? how? why?

Why? Why would anyone kill Arnold and Elaine Sohn?

That had been the question nagging at all of us from the moment we'd set foot in their home.

The first detective to arrive, Cliff had noticed on entering the house the note that had been left on the table by Sheryl to inform her parents that she would be sleeping at Jody Stich's house.

He knew Jody Stich, and what he knew about the girl could be summed up in a word: *drugs*.

As he read Sheryl's note, Cliff's detective training reminded him to keep an open mind until all the evidence was in and to accept the note for what it seemed to be on its face: a stroke of luck for Sheryl to have been absent when her parents' murders were being committed in her home. Even so, he couldn't ignore the fact that Sheryl Sohn was a girl with a long-standing and serious drug problem and, as he proceeded through the house and surveyed the carnage, his instincts stirred, crying out "Drugs! Drugs are at the root of this."

Subtly but surely there grew in his mind a suspicion that it was more than a remarkable coincidence that this young woman who had known associations in Spring Valley's seamy underbelly of drugs and druggies had been away during the commission of a crime that was easily within the capabilities of the sordid people Sheryl Sohn kept company with in two of the known locations of drug activity in Spring Valley—a dive called the Camelot and a section of town known as the Hill.

In a gentler and more civil era, the Hill had been the site of numerous small hotels and rooming houses nestling among shade-giving groves of trees. A breeze-cooled place of respite and relaxation, the area had catered to the Jewish clientele for whom Spring Valley was both a pleasant resort and a place to settle permanently: closer to their roots in New York City, less expensive than the Catskills. In recent years it had become a mixture of blacks, Hispanics, and whites who had only one thing in common—poverty.

Drugs inevitably make an appearance in such an environment, and by 1980 they were rampant. Everywhere on the Hill there were users and dealers.

These same people frequented the Camelot, a bar and disco on Main Street, the once-prosperous and flourishing "downtown" of Spring Valley whose stores and businesses had seen customers flock to shopping centers and malls, leaving economic decline and desolation behind—the breeding ground of crime and the drug world.

Cliff and Eddie knew the Hill and the Camelot well and, like policemen all over the world, had developed relationships with some of its patrons from Spring Valley's population of drug users—professional relationships of mutual benefit in which they provided information and tips and the detectives reciprocated, sometimes with money and at other times with promises of assistance if they were in trouble. This help generally included assurance that their cooperation would be made known to higher authorities such as the district attorney or the courts.

Was it not possible that someone at the Camelot bar or on

the Hill had overhead Sheryl's plans to stay at Jody's? Wasn't it possible that someone heard the Sohns were fairly well-to-do? that they might have money on hand? that there were valuable possessions in the house that might be fenced for a handsome payoff? Wouldn't Elaine Sohn, a lively and sociable woman, have jewelry? Might Sheryl have let it slip not only that she would be staying with Jody but also that her parents had plans to attend a party? Wasn't it a possibility that someone had seen a chance to pull off a very profitable burglary?

Cliff also asked himself "Had Sheryl taken a hand in the crime herself?"

The same question had been on my mind as well as I'd moved from the master bathroom of the house where Elaine Sohn's head had been held under water until she drowned to the bloody bedroom where Arnold Sohn lay bludgeoned beyond recognition, then to a thin veil of tramped and blood-spotted snow outside and to a broken pane in a storm door.

In everything I saw, sensed, and felt instinctually, I said as we sat in my office going over the case, "I keep coming back to drugs and to Sheryl Sohn."

"There was a little girl," goes an old poem. "When she was good She was very, very good, But when she was bad She was horrid." That was Sheryl Sohn, but in a father's eyes a daughter is always beautiful, and so Sheryl must have seemed to Arnold Sohn, but the sad reality was that the twenty-three-year-old girl who had trained as a beautician lacked the headturning, stunning looks she had been trained to create for others and had never been successful at attracting attention from young men. Painfully plain and overweight, she often appeared unkempt and slovenly, but everyone who knew the Sohns knew that Arnie adored her.

Mothers often are harder, more vigilant and critical,

and—the Catskills-resorts comedians contend—it's even more so when the family is Jewish. Lifelong comedic careers have been built on the premise, but anything amusing to be found in the tensions between Elaine and Sheryl had disappeared between the joyous occasion of Sheryl's birth in Queens, New York, on January 3, 1958, and the tragedy on Jill Lane in the largely Jewish tract-home neighborhood of Blueberry Hill on December 28, 1980. The promising and happy child who had been moved to the safer and more wholesome environment of Rockland County in 1968, who had graduated from Spring Valley High School in 1976, and earned an associate degree in business administration from Rockland Community College the following year had gone awry.

In 1977 she was asked to leave home by her father at her mother's insistence.

Taking a small apartment in Garnerville, she had little contact with her parents but she did come into contact with law enforcement officials: arrest and conviction on attempted petty larceny charges for stealing groceries from a supermarket in West Nyack and cash from the purse of a co-worker at the Letchworth Village Development Center in Thiells, where she worked five months as a therapy aide trainee.

During this troubled time she began to frequent the Hill and the Camelot.

Heartbroken and desperate, in the summer of 1980 the Sohns had come to my office for advice and assistance and Sheryl was enrolled in the drug rehabilitation program of Phoenix House. Eventually she moved back to the comfortable home on Jill Lane, but her problems with drugs continued. So did her visits to the Camelot and the haunts of narcotics abusers on the Hill.

Cliff Tallman and Eddie O'Neill were familiar with the

tragic but increasingly common story of a girl who went wrong, but immediately after the discovery that her parents had been murdered Sheryl had not been questioned. Although she had been summoned to the house, she had been left alone to grieve in a room on the lower level while the police search for physical evidence was being conducted.

That afternoon she was interviewed by Cliff and Eddie at the Spring Valley Police Station. "We asked about her whereabouts on the evening of December 27 and into the early-morning hours of December 28," Cliff recalled for me. "She told us that she had spent the twenty-seventh with Jody Stich at the mall and that she and Jody dropped in at the Camelot around nine o'clock. Around eleven, she said, she returned to her house to get some clothes and then went back to the Camelot until the early-morning hours. From there, she told us, she went to Jody's house to spend the night. Maybe it's all true, but. . . ."

As Cliff's thought dangled unfinished, I knew that had he completed the sentence it would have been to express a doubt, based on Sheryl's history, that she'd given the whole story. For me as for Cliff, Sheryl Sohn was a flashing light, a bell that was ringing.

She had to be questioned further.

Our preference was to arrange for the interview to be conducted at the state police facility at Middletown by Investigator Jeremiah O'Leary, an expert in the use of the polygraph, commonly called a lie detector.

I believe the polygraph is not so much a machine to catch people telling lies as it is a means to get them to tell the truth. It's not a lie detector. It's a truth-provoker.

The value of this controversial apparatus is not in its ability to register whether a person is not being truthful but the psychological atmosphere in which it places a subject. Fear of the polygraph and the personal confrontation with the examiner is what works on the individual. If a person is guilty and knows he's going to be "on the box," he is quite likely to come clean at any point during the procedure and sometimes before the test even begins.

Our hope was that the polygraph would shake Sheryl up and dislodge whatever she might know about the murders.

It was psychological warfare.

The opening salvo was fired that afternoon—Monday, December 29.

At 12:20 P.M., Cliff Tallman and Eddie O'Neill pulled up in front of the Thomas residence next door to the Sohn house, asked if they might speak to Sheryl, then asked her if she'd accompany them to the police station.

Sheryl consented, but in the car Cliff turned abruptly to her and said "You have the right to remain silent."

The assertion of her constitutional rights against self-incrimination was required, but it was also a useful psychological tool. "Do you understand, Sheryl?"

"Yes."

"Anything you say can and will be used against you in a court of law."

Did she understand this?

Yes, she repeated each time Cliff read her rights to her and asked if she understood them.

Next he requested her consent to be taken to the state police barracks at Middletown. An hour later she was being introduced to Investigator Jerry O'Leary, a soft-spoken gentleman whose experience in five hundred cases had taught him the subtleties of conducting polygraph examinations. Presently he explained the entire process to her, making it clear that she could stop the procedure at any point and again asserting all of her constitutional rights. "I am telling you if you don't want to take this polygraph test, you should refuse it," he said. "I will be happy to test you if you want me to, and if you don't want me to, tell me and I will not test you."

"I want to," Sheryl said.

"You must sign a consent form."

"I'll sign it."

In a dimly lighted adjacent room, Cliff Tallman and Eddie O'Neill observed everything through a window that allowed them to see all that went on in the examining room and to hear all that was said but remain unseen and unheard themselves. Behind the glass they watched and listened as Jerry prepared for the interview, first by testing the machine and then testing Sheryl's reactions with questions designed to create a record of how she reacted and how the machine recorded her reactions to those queries. Next he allowed her to know the nature of questions that would be put to her and, if she desired, to refuse to have them included or to alter their phrasing.

"In any way did you take part in your parents' murder?"

She would answer, she said, if the question were "Did you *knowingly* take part in your parents' murder?"

In the darkened room, Cliff Tallman gave Eddie O'Neill a gentle nudge.

"Did you set up yesterday morning's burglary?"

The question she'd answer, Sheryl indicated, ought to be "Did you plan yesterday morning's burglary of your parents' house *with anyone*?"

Cliff and Eddie smiled.

Unwilling to admit direct involvement, they figured, Sheryl was prepared to implicate others, to name names, to tell the whole story—to confess.

To a point.

Now came the painstaking intricacies of administering the actual polygraph test—the questions regarding the crime that she had agreed to answer asked once and then again, a technique known as double verification.

Studying the results, Jerry pronounced solemnly, "In my opinion, Miss Sohn, you haven't told the entire truth about what happened."

Tensely, Cliff and Eddie leaned toward the glass and waited for her response.

"I have told the truth," Sheryl said sharply.

"I'm sorry," said Jerry gravely, shaking his head as he studied the scrawled lines on the long roll of polygraph paper, "but you haven't."

Fidgeting and with a nervous sigh, Sheryl said, "You're right. I'm afraid to tell the truth. I know who murdered my parents but I am afraid to tell the police. I'm scared for my life."

Softly, sympathetically, gently, Jerry said, "You'll have to tell sooner or later. You do see that, don't you?"

Slowly nodding, she said "Yes."

"Tell me who did it."

"His name," she muttered, "is . . . Panama."

3 | A NIGHT IN CAMELOT

BELTON LEE BRIMS.

Street name Panama.

His entire life was a police rap sheet.

Born in Selma, Alabama, on January 29, 1955, one of six children in a broken family raised by his mother, Dorothy Gabriel, on North Main Street near the Hill, he first got into trouble with the law at eleven for having set fires in five occupied homes. He'd spent four years in a state training school, where apparently the only thing he had learned was how to be a better criminal.

At least ten convictions with time served, above and below the Mason-Dixon Line. Violent, too. In 1977 he was convicted of the $1400 armed robbery of an Allendale, New Jersey, supermarket and assaulting four Ramapo police officers who questioned him about the stick-up of a delicatessen in Spring Valley.

In the mid-1970s he reportedly told a police officer who arrested him "I am dedicated to the cause of crime and I will leave you dead in the streets."

Sentenced to the Rahway State Prison in New Jersey, he served less than three years and had come back to Spring Valley on November 18, 1980.

Muscular and strong, he possessed the deadly power needed to wrestle a heavy middle-aged woman to a brimming bathtub and to hammer her husband's skull into fragments.

Now, in the quiet of Jerry O'Leary's polograph room with Cliff Tallman and Eddie O'Neill listening behind the one-way glass, a girl whose parents had been dealt those horrifying deaths began pouring forth a confession—a bursting of damning details of years of pent-up hatred for her mother, of spite, of selfishness, envy, and greed and, ultimately, of an uncaring daughter's cunning, calculating, and cold-blooded plot to have them robbed.

Killed?

Never!

On December 11, 1980, she was up on the Hill. There she met a guy who introduced himself to her as Panama, his real name being Belton Brims. The two of them had a general conversation. She told him that her mother had a ring she wanted. This ring was her grandmother's diamond ring and she wanted it.

She saw Panama on Christmas Eve, also on the Hill.

The next time that she met him was on December 27.

That night her parents were going out to a party.

When she left the house she intentionally left the garage door open.

She was with her girlfriend, name of Jody Stich. They'd arrived at the Camelot bar around 9:00 P.M.

Panama came in and she then went to the back of the bar.

She told Brims her parents had gone out and her mother was wearing the ring.

If Brims waited in the house, he could rob them when they came home.

If Brims got the ring for her he could have all the money and jewelry that he found, but she wanted the ring. That, Panama said, was no problem.

Her father had a heart condition and wouldn't resist and he would probably tell her mother not to resist and would give him whatever he wanted.

If Panama brought a gun, neither one would resist.

Then Brims left the bar and got into a dark-colored car with another guy, named Sheffield.

Behind the glass Cliff Tallman grunted bitterly, "James Sheffield!"

"Son of a bitch," grumbled Eddie O'Neill.

A little later, Brims returned to the bar and complained that the door was not unlocked.

At that time, she left the bar with Jody, saying she had to get some clothes. She went home, wrote a note telling her parents she'd be sleeping at Jody's that night and left the house, making sure that the door was unlocked.

Returning to the Camelot, she assured Brims that he'd have no trouble this time and Brims left.

A while later Brims came back and asked "Why did you do that to me?" For some reason he hadn't been able to get the door open.

She couldn't leave the bar again, she said, because it would make Jody suspicious.

Brims then asked about other back doors and windows on the ground floor. She told him that the windows were high and that they would be difficult to get into. The only other doors were the front door and the kitchen door in the back of the house.

Did she still want the ring?

Yes.

No problem, said Brims.

Leaving the bar again with Sheffield, he got into a dark-colored car and sped from the rear parking lot.

• • •

Switching off the polygraph, Jerry O'Leary walked out of the room, leaving Sheryl alone.

A few moments later, the detectives came in and Cliff asked, "Are you willing to tell us everything?"

Yes, she said, all of it.

"This guy Sheffield," asked Cliff Tallman. "What was he wearing?"

"A long tan coat. Not sure what color pants. Sneakers."

"What did Panama Brims have on?"

"A blue bomber-type jacket. White-colored pants. Light sneakers."

"Would you be willing to give us a written statement?"

"Yes."

Eddie O'Neill typed it.

The following statement is being given by Sheryl Sohn, 23, residing at Number 38 Jill Lane, Spring Valley, New York.

This statement is in reference to Spring Valley Police Case involving a double homicide. . . .

Murders? Death was not her plan, she insisted. Murder had not entered her mind that night in the Camelot—not perched on a stool next to her friend Jody at the long bar, not a little later at one of the tables at the rear planning a burglary with Panama Brims, not when she might have dropped a coin in the jukebox or in a cigarette machine knowing he was on his way to carry out the scheme. Not even when he came back angry because he'd found the door locked did murder cross her mind, nor while returning home with Jody to pick up clothes and leave a note for her parents and make sure the door was left unlocked, nor while describing for him how her parents would act if he took a gun along.

Amid the blaring music and thick smoke inside that dive named Camelot while dreaming about a fabulous heirloom diamond ring that soon would come to be hers, it *definitely* did not occur to her that the price of it would be the death of her parents.

Following Sheryl's statement, the question before us was the appropriate time to pick her up and charge her, because the moment we arrested her it would become known to Brims.

"She's not going anywhere," suggested Eddie O'Neill. "She's got the funerals to go to. If she skipped out on them it would be as good as a confession. Besides, she's probably thinking that since she hasn't been arrested, she won't be."

"You didn't promise her she wouldn't be?"

"Nope. No promises of any kind," said Cliff.

"She made a statement, that's all," said Eddie. "And she understood that's what it was. I'm sure she's convinced she is not about to be arrested."

"If we arrest her now," I stressed, "we send a clear signal to Panama Brims that he's next. Do you know his where-abouts?"

"He's in town," replied Eddie.

"What's the story with Sheffield?" I asked.

"He's long gone from North Plainfield," Eddie said. "And running hard, I imagine. It's too bad we hadn't had Sheryl's statement before we got that call from New Jersey, but that's the breaks. We'll spread the word nationwide that we'd like to talk to him. A guy like him's bound to go wrong wherever he goes and when he does we'll collar him."

"Is Jody Stich a suspect?"

"She'll lie to try to help her friend Sheryl," said Cliff,

"but Eddie and I don't think she had anything to do with this directly."

"We want Brims off the street as soon as possible," I said, "but I'd be happier if we had more evidence tying him into this than Sheryl's statement. I'm willing to wait a day or two to see if we can turn up something else. On the other hand, we don't want Brims skipping out on us. Let's give it just a little more time, and if nothing turns up, we collar him. Just keep in mind that this is the guy who once bragged 'I am dedicated to the cause of crime and I will leave you dead in the streets.' "

"And a Happy New Year to you, too," Cliff said as he and Eddie left my office.

The murders of the Sohns had dimmed prospects for a joyous welcoming of 1981 by the shocked and frightened residents of Spring Valley, especially in the neighborhood of Blueberry Hill and along Jill Lane, where fear was most acute.

Newspapers had headlined the crime, of course, and it was on TV and radio newscasts.

Along with those stories were published and broadcast the reactions of residents that seemed to be clichés—how nice the Sohns were, how quiet and untroublesome they were, how no one ever expected anything like this to happen around here. "They were good-natured and kind," one of the neighbors told a newspaper reporter. "They were happy people," said another. "Arnold Sohn was just like the rest of us," said a third to radio reporter Fran Schneidau. "He only wanted what was best for his family."

Clichés, perhaps, but nonetheless true.

Also there were familiar sidebar articles concerning the impact of the killings on the residents of the area, a picture of terrified homeowners rushing to protect themselves in their houses. "Since the gruesome deaths, locksmith trucks have joined police cars and film crews as common sights along the quiet residential streets surrounding 38 Jill Lane," reported *The Journal-News*, Rockland's countywide paper.

"We're really shook by this," a neighbor said.

"It's so close, it's a nightmare," another observed to a reporter.

"You can't sleep," said a woman quoted by *The New York Daily News*, which added that she had answered her door accompanied by a Doberman pinscher. "Everybody is talking about putting in burglar alarms." An increase in calls had been noted by the owner of a New City locksmith business, who told an interviewer, "Understandably, some of the people are frightened."

Accounts like these always appear in the aftermath of a terrible crime, but they are the genuine expression of the stunning effect a murder next door can have on ordinary, law-abiding people.

When there is crime, the community is also a victim.

The result is most obvious when people take actions like those of the scared residents of Jill Lane, Blueberry Hill, and all of Spring Valley, but victimization of a community ranges far beyond people's concern for personal security. It has an economic effect and sometimes it is disastrous.

Crime and punishment costs.

To be paid for are the expenses during the investigations of crime in the form of salaries of the law enforcement people involved and the cost of their increasingly sophisticated and expensive equipment and laboratories, the expenses associated with the prosecution of cases and trials: court facilities, judges, court personnel, and all the vital record-keeping and paperwork required to ensure justice. Finally, there is the cost of incarceration.

For small towns and rural counties these accumulated costs of crime can threaten bankruptcy.

While society must be concerned about the costs of locks for private doors and prison gates, they are not the real measure of the toll crime extracts. The highest price paid is found in the fear rampant crime has instilled in all of us and that the reaction of the people of Spring Valley illustrated, but there is no way to calculate the deep psychological and spiritual scars left on the people who loved Arnold and Elaine or knew them as friends or who had never heard of them until what happened to them raised the terrifying reality that in this day and age crime can strike anywhere, at any time, and against anyone. In that context there is no way to figure the cost of crime like the murders of the Sohns.

An architect's vision of how to realize a social engineer's dream of enlightened urban design, 244 North Main Street was a complex of low-rise apartments planned as a garden-like setting of open space admitting cooling breezes and shade-giving trees, but by January 1, 1981, the vision and the dream were rapidly becoming the nightmare of blight that already had consumed the surrounding Hill area.

Eating at the foundations like relentlessly voracious termites was an infestation of drugs, users, and peddlers, in the ranks of which no individual surpassed Belton Brims for sheer accomplishment.

Big deals. Big money. Big shot.

A braggart, too. Almost anyone hanging around on the Hill or any patron at the Camelot could recount Panama Brims' boasting about his big dope-dealing operation.

Well, I wouldn't call it an operation. I would call it—I had some people that knew about drugs and knew where to go to get the drugs, and I would furnish the money.

• • •

The financier. The money man. That was Panama.

He had lots of others to do the legwork.

James Sheffield was one.

Before launching his drug enterprise, Brims was a financial whiz kid in prison. Football pools. Baseball pools. Boxing. It was called "running the store." There was loan-sharking. Cigarettes.

On the books the day he'd walked out of Rahway Prison he had $190, most of it given to him by his mother, but off the books he brought with him $13,000 earned running the store.

They search you going into prison, not coming out.

Thirteen grand was used to get his dope business going.

It took him all of two days to set it up.

There were lots of customers.

One of them was Jody Stich.

Another was Sheryl Sohn.

When had been the last time Panama had done business with Sheryl?

As far as Cliff Tallman and Eddie O'Neill knew as they left the Spring Valley Police Department in an unmarked car a little before 9:00 P.M. on January 1, 1981, turning right toward North Main Street, the last time Panama and Sheryl were together had been on the night of December 27, at the Camelot.

The last time Cliff and Eddie had seen her was the night of December 30, the day after she'd dictated and signed the statement at the Middletown Barracks.

Seeing her on the thirtieth had been a surprise.

And a little upsetting.

Cruising on the Hill, they were spotted by Sheryl and

Jody Stich. The girls flagged them down. Nervously Sheryl approached the car and exclaimed, "The word all over the street is that as soon as my parents' funeral's over, I'm going to be arrested."

"That's bullshit," Eddie replied.

It wasn't going to happen, Cliff said emphatically.

Whether Sheryl believed them was a question.

In any case, she hadn't been picked up and wouldn't be until Panama Brims was under arrest.

Not for murder.

Not yet.

There wasn't sufficient evidence for that. Yet. But the time had come to get him off the streets and locked up.

Our immediate cause to arrest him was a couple of outstanding warrants, one based on a misdemeanor complaint filed in Spring Valley alleging that Brims had pulled a gun on a Charles Moore on December 23, the second a New Jersey warrant in connection with the robbery of a Hilton hotel and valid enough to take Belton Lee Brims out of circulation for a good long time—enough time to gather the evidence to provide probable cause to charge that he had been inside 38 Jill Lane in the early hours of December 27, 1980 . . . and to prove that at that place and time he had participated in two homicides. Proof that would be sufficient to eliminate from the minds of twelve faired-minded jurors any reasonable doubt that Belton Brims killed Mr. and Mrs. Arnold Sohn.

Detectives Tallman and O'Neill were not going after a man as dangerous as Belton Brims unaccompanied. From all directions on that crisp, cold, and quiet night an armada of police vehicles converged and parked, their occupants prepared to wait as long as necessary for Brims to appear. Beside them on the seats were shotguns. Pistols were strapped to their belts or tucked into shoulder holsters. None regarded Brims' words "I'll leave you dead in the streets" an idle threat.

They didn't have to wait long.

With a nod toward a figure emerging from the shadows of a small wooded area into a parking lot, Cliff Tallman muttered "That's him."

"He's got someone with him," whispered Eddie O'Neill. "A woman." Moving slowly as if they were out for a stroll and unaware that they were being observed, Brims and the woman approached the apartments. "Do you recognize her, Cliff?"

"Mary Curtis. She hangs around the Hill a lot. She wouldn't have any part in this."

"Well, she's about to get the surprise of her life," said Eddie, flinging open the car door.

Bristling with guns, police officers swarmed from cars.

"Panama!" shouted Cliff. "Freeze! Police!"

Aghast, Mary Curtis jerked away from Brims.

With his hands flung upward Brims demanded indignantly, "Whatchoo want from me? What's this all about?"

Holstering his gun, then reaching for Brims' hands and cuffing them, Cliff said, "We have a warrant for your arrest."

4 | CRITICAL MASS

CLIFF TALLMAN LOOKED Belton Brims in the eyes.

"You killed Sheryl Sohn's parents."

It was worth a shot. A bit of bluster. A flourish of confidence. A not-so-veiled suggestion that the police had Brims dead to rights and he might as well come clean.

Unfazed, Brims replied, "I didn't kill nobody."

A confession would have made the case stronger, but Brims didn't confess; therefore our case would be built on the physical evidence we could collect, starting with the clothes Brims was wearing—a blue jacket with a snorkel hood, a pair of light-colored pants, low-cut white sneakers with brownish stains that could be blood.

"Strip."

In the pocket of the jacket—deep inside—a slip of paper with writing on it. A name: Jackie Shoulders. An address in Chesapeake, Virginia. And a couple of phone numbers.

A key, possibly to a hotel or motel room.

Around Brims' neck: gold chains and a medallion.

Studying an inscription on it, Cliff asked, "When did you win an English award, Brims?"

"What?"

"English. Did you win an award for scholarship in English?"

"Not that I remember."

"You're not on the faculty of any university?" Cliff showed Brims the medal. "It says 'A date to remember. English Department, June, 1969.' What English department was that from?"

"It was given to my mother from my brother and my mother gave it to me because I seen it lying in her jewelry box and I asked her could I have it."

"Your brother was on the faculty of a university?"

"He could have been."

"Was it Harvard?"

"I don't know."

"Did you steal this medallion?"

"No."

"Of course you didn't," said Cliff, turning away. "And you didn't kill the Sohns either."

Picking up a phone, he dialed my home number. "Ken, we've arrested Brims. I guess we ought to have a meeting. What time's convenient?"

"Now."

With an arrest made, I now brought in officially a pair of detectives from my own staff, Jim Stewart and Phil Burden. Eager, energetic, and young, they would be as tireless and tenacious as Tallman and O'Neill when it came to digging out every bit of evidence and pursuing witnesses and the circumstances needed to get convictions.

What the arrest of Brims gave us was breathing room— the time to investigate without worrying that Brims would flee, a likelihood erased by the warrant issued in New Jersey, meaning that Brims would have to be locked up in the Garden State to await trial for the Hilton hotel robbery.

We began with Sheryl's account of the events of the night of the murders and focused our attention on two facts: that a dark car, probably a Cadillac, was used by Brims that night and that Sheryl had been in the company of Jody Stich.

A slender, attractive twenty-two-year old, Jody lived on Buckman Place near the Sohns. She'd attended Rockland Community College for a year and a half, was now an employee at an auto dealership in Tarrytown, and had been a familiar face to Cliff Tallman and Eddie O'Neill during investigations or other police business that took them to the Camelot and the Hill.

On January 6 she sat down with them and in the course of a long interview told him about visiting the home of her friend on Christmas Day. "There was a loud argument between Sheryl and her mother. They were upstairs. I was downstairs. After about fifteen minutes, Sheryl came down and began punching doors and saying she was going to kill her. I said, 'What's the matter? Who are you going to kill?' She said her mother. I told her to calm down. I said, 'Come on, you can only be kidding around.' She said, 'No. If you think I'm kidding, I have somebody doing something for me.'"

"Did she say who?"

"No."

"Now tell me everything you know about the night of December twenty-seventh," said Cliff.

"At nine o'clock I left my house and had gone down to her house where she did my makeup for me and around nine-twenty we left to go down to the Camelot Bar. I parked my car in the rear. In the bar I spent some time talking with a man I knew who had just come back from Germany. He asked me if I wanted to go outside. I said yes, I would. We were talking for a while and I decided to go back inside. Sheryl wasn't standing at the bar when we went back in but I saw her sitting in the back with a large black male."

"Did you see his face?"

"No, I didn't."

"Did you see what he was wearing?"

"It was a blue snorkel jacket."

"Then what happened?"

"Sheryl said she had to go back to her house to get her pajamas so she could stay overnight at my house."

"What happened at the house?"

"She was rummaging through the drawers for her clothing and then she went upstairs to the kitchen and she wrote her mother a note stating that she was staying over at my house and that she would see her tomorrow."

"You went back to the Camelot?"

"Yes."

"What happened then?"

"I saw Sheryl talking again to that black male with the blue snorkel jacket, but later she was alone. Then we went out and were talking for a few minutes by my car when a large black sedan pulled up alongside the curb. Sheryl said 'Excuse me' and got into the back seat. They drove around the parking lot and then stopped again and Sheryl got out and came back to my car. I asked her what was going on and she said 'Never mind, it was nothing.'"

"Were you and Sheryl together the rest of the time?"

"For a while I couldn't find her, didn't know where she was."

"How long was that?"

"About twenty to forty minutes. Finally, when I found her, I said I was tired and wanted to go home. That was about three o'clock."

"What happened then?"

"I was almost asleep when Sheryl nudged me and said, 'If anybody asks you if you were with me all night, just say yes.' I said all right and went back to sleep. The next morning I heard a banging at the door. It was Debbie Thomas asking if Sheryl was there. She screamed that Sheryl's parents had been murdered. We told Sheryl and she ran out of the house."

"Was she crying?"

"No."

"About that long black car at the Camelot. Is there anything else you remember about it?"

"It had dark windows—black-tinted windows."

Memory is a policeman's best tool: faces, facts, old cases.

Cliff Tallman's cop's memory always served him well, and it delivered that day an image of a black Cadillac with dark-tinted windows that belonged to Katherine Brims, Belton's aunt, but was usually driven by Willis Brims, called Cuz by Panama, known to his family as Willie and on the streets by the monicker Moo Moo.

"Eddie, you bring the kid in," said Cliff, "and I'll get a search warrant for the Caddy."

On January 7, while conferring with me in my office, Cliff got a phone call from Eddie O'Neill informing him that Willie and the car had arrived at the Spring Valley Police Department and that Willie had given a statement.

Looking into Cliff's beaming face as he hung up the phone, I asked, "Has there been a break?"

Despite the smile, Cliff was restrained and cautious. "Maybe."

A former soccer star at Ramapo High School, Willis James Brims had a boyish face, oval-shaped and framed by a short Afro haircut. Living with his mother in the apartment next door to his cousin Belton, he was a familiar character around the Game Room (a poolhall on the Hill) and was famous for scouting for the prettiest dancing partners among the girls at the Camelot and other Main Street discos. Never in any serious trouble with the law, he was employed as the supervisor of a staff of seven cooks at the Burger King in Monsey.

The tale he had to tell began a week before the Sohns were murdered, said Willie, and it started in Willie's house at 244 North Main Street. "Panama asked me how would I like to make three thousand dollars. 'How?' I asked him. 'Don't worry,' he said. 'I'll get twenty thousand and you will get three.' In thirty to ninety days I'd get three thousand."

He'd heard nothing more about it and had just about forgotten the proposal until the night of December 27.

He'd been at work until 9:00 P.M., after which he went home and cleaned up before going out for the evening in his mother's Cadillac. In the course of the evening he connected with his cousin Belton and a friend of Panama's by the name of James Sheffield.

At one point during the evening, Willie said, he drove his car into the parking lot behind the Camelot and stopped near a gray Pinto. "Panama rolled down the rear window," he went on, "and Panama said, 'Yo, come over here,' so a fat white female with long brown hair came over and got in the car. She stayed for a couple of minutes."

"Did you hear any conversation?"

"No."

"Then what happened?"

"A little later, Sheffield is driving cause he knows how to get to the friend's house that Panama wants to visit, so we drove up Maple Avenue to the Jewish school and Sheffield made a right-hand turn up to Blueberry Hill and up the hill to 38 Jill Lane, where he parked next to some hedges by apartments across the street where Panama and Sheffield got out."

"And you?"

"Panama told me to stay in the car and stay down."

"How long were Panama and Sheffield gone?"

"A couple of minutes. When Panama came back, he said, 'The bitch lied. I don't play games.' He said, 'We're goin' back to the Camelot.'"

"Go on."

"We parked my car in the rear and Panama told me to wait and after a while the fat white girl came out, got into my car and says to take her to the same house we just came from, so I drove her to the blue house on Jill Lane and she went in the house."

"For how long?"

"By the time I got the car turned around she was outside waiting. She got in and I asked her who lived in that house."

"What was her reply?"

"She said, 'Some people.'"

"Did you know who lived there?"

"No."

"Had you ever been there before?"

"About three weeks before I went past there with Panama and a guy named Greg Norfleet and a guy named Anthony. Panama said, 'That is where she lives.'"

"What happened after the fat white girl got back into your car?"

"We went back to the Camelot and some time went by and Panama came over again and said to take them back to the house. I drove with Sheffield in the passenger side and Panama in the rear. At the house they got out and I was told to stay in the car and stay down. So that's what I did for about forty-five minutes."

"What happened then?"

"I seen a gray car pull up to the blue house and a white

male got out, lifted up the garage door, got back into the car and drove the car into the garage. I saw a white female get out also. He closed the garage door and that was the last I seen of them."

"Then what?"

"After another forty-five minutes I seen Panama and Sheffield come walking very fast toward my car. As they were approaching to my car, I seen that Panama had two socks. He had one sock on his hand and he was carrying a sock with a heavy object in it and he had a ski mask. Sheffield also had a ski mask."

"How did they act?"

"They were very nervous, very nervous and excited, so they threw themselves into the car and stayed down."

"What was the time, do you recall?"

"Approximately two-thirty or three."

"Where'd you go after that?"

"I drove Sheffield to his apartment on the Hill. Panama told him not to get in touch with him; he'd get in touch with Sheffield. Then I drove Panama to 244 North Main Street and he got out and told me 'Wait.' His pants were soaking wet."

"What else was he wearing that night?"

"A snorkel type of jacket."

"And Sheffield?"

"A long tan jacket."

"What happened next?"

"Panama came out in different pants. He had a lot of items in his hands, balled up, and he got into the car and told me to take him to Rose Avenue."

"What's there?"

"There was a big dumpster on the side of the road by the shopping center. I stopped and he rolled down the window and I seen him rip up a ski mask and throw it into the dumpster. Then I drove beside a building and he got out and threw something. It was dark, so I couldn't see what it was. Then I drove to a second dumpster on Rose Avenue and he got out and threw some items into it."

"When he finally got back into the car for the last time did he have anything in his hands?"

"Nothing."

"What happened after that?"

"I drove to Harvey's Lounge on Main Street and after about fifteen minutes I drove him and a girl named Cassandra to the kosher pizza place on Maple Avenue and then to the apartment complexes where they got out. I went back to the Camelot for about fifteen minutes and then home. I slept until late, late Sunday and then I seen specks of blood on the windshield of the car, so then I went to a self-service car wash and cleaned all the windows and the seats."

"When did you next see Panama?"

"Thursday. New Year's Day. The day he got arrested. I drove down to 244 North Main and Panama was outside. I stopped and he said to take him to a lady's house. In her apartment he told me he'd done some serious business. He said he made Sheffield beat the guy's brains out with the butt of a gun. He said that he, Panama, drowned the bitch. That he took some jewelry and he was going to have it appraised by a woman he knew from Virginia. Then he tells me be cool and live your everyday normal life and do all the things you usually do, and in thirty to ninety days I'd get paid that three thousand."

Break indeed!

Thanks to Willie, our investigation had split wide open.

We knew that a car had been used, whose car it was, and that bloodstains had been left in and on it; and we had the car and a search warrant to examine it. We'd learned about ski masks and we knew where one of them had been discarded. We knew that a gun had been used to beat Arnold Sohn to death and that James Sheffield had done it. We knew Belton Brims came out of the Sohn house carrying a weighty sock. We knew that jewelry had been taken and arrangements made to dispose of the loot. We had a statement about Sheryl's contacts with Belton Brims and James Sheffield that night and of Sheryl returning to the house with Willie Brims. We knew that Belton had confessed everything to his cousin and we knew that he had expected to make a lot of money from his deeds.

All of this we knew based on Willie's statement, but not a shred of it was sufficient to convict Belton Brims of murder. It was the word of Willie Brims against that of his cousin. It was a story that was not substantiated by any independent or corroborative evidence—unless we turned up the blood from the car and linked it to Mr. Sohn's; located the ski mask; found the gun; retrieved the stolen jewelry; and/or located, arrested, and obtained a full confession from James Sheffield, who had not been heard from since he walked away from the North Plainfield police.

Under New York's criminal procedure law, except in sex crimes the testimony of an accomplice in a case could not be used against another person without independent evidence to support the word of the accomplice. It was a rule that had been opposed by the New York State Law Enforcement Council, an advocate for the law enforcement community in legislative matters. New York State differed in this rule from other states, including adjoining New Jersey, asserted the council, pointing out "New York has placed itself in a distinct minority of American jurisdictions" and noting that "no such impediment exists in federal prosecutions." The effect of the Accomplice Corroboration Rule in New York in some cases was unsuccessful prosecutions and hindrance of law enforcement in high-level narcotics crimes, white-collar crimes, and government corruption cases, in which the word of accomplices may constitute the major evidence. Consequently, the Law Enforcement Council (representing the state's associations of district attorneys, sheriffs and chiefs of police, and the attorney general, the New York City criminal justice coordinator, and the Citizens Crime Commission) was working to repeal that section of the law.

Since under the Accomplice Corroboration Rule Willie's statement was inadequate to convict Belton Brimes, our only hope of succeeding was in obtaining either eyewitness testimony (an unlikely prospect) or as much physical evidence as possible to substantiate Willie's statements.

The next day, bright and early Cliff Tallman drove to the Rose Avenue shopping center described by Willie and located the dumpster in which Willie had said his cousin had disposed of a ski mask. It took only a few moments for Cliff to find it, photograph it and its surroundings, tag it and mark it with his initials, bag it, and secure it as evidence.

Willie had spoken of another object that had been thrown away, flung into the darkness, but locating it would be impossible at the moment, Cliff decided, because the area behind the shopping center was blanketed with five inches of snow. A search for that object (Cliff suspected and hoped that it was the gun) would have to wait for a thaw.

There was no need to wait to inspect Willie's mother's Cadillac, however, and soon, despite Willie's attempts to scrub away the blood spots he'd discovered late in the afternoon of Sunday, December 28, our experts found traces of blood in the car. They and the stained sneakers taken from Belton Brims, along with the spots of blood found in footprints in the snow at the Sohn house, would be tested by technicians in the crime laboratory to ascertain if they matched the blood of Arnold Sohn.

Next?

The jewelry, the booty from this horrible crime.

To trace it we had to locate and question the woman to whom, according to Willie Brims' statement, Belton might have shown the items and whose name, address, and phone numbers, we believed, were those on the slip of paper fished out from the depths of the pocket of Belton Brims' blue jacket with the snorkel hood.

For this purpose Juan Rocha, a detective on my staff, and Detective George Gibson of the Spring Valley Police Department traveled to Virginia, and, accompanied by a pair of local detectives, visited the residence of Jacqueline Shoulders.

An attractive twenty-two-year-old who had attended Old Dominion College and was now studying at Norfolk Business College, she lived with her husband and their year-old daughter.

Clearly shaken by the sudden appearance of detectives seeking to question her, she cooperated readily.

During the week between Christmas and New Year's Day, she stated, she had traveled to Spring Valley to visit her mother for the holidays and had been introduced to Belton Brims at her mother's apartment across the street from the apartments where Brims resided. He was introduced to her as Panama and she to him as Jackie. This first meeting on Saturday, December 27, was casual and brief, but on the following evening Panama came for dinner and stayed several hours.

At some point, she said, Panama went upstairs briefly

and returned, sat beside her, held out his hands—palms down—and placed two rings in her hands. "Take these in the bathroom and have a look at 'em," he said with a smile.

Rocha asked, "Can you describe the rings for us now?"

"One was a woman's diamond ring," she said. "A large diamond in the center and two diamonds on the side. The other was a man's gold ring with a dark stone. When I returned, I handed them back and told him they were pretty. He told me he'd given another one to his mother."

"Was there any further conversation about jewelry?" asked Rocha. "Did he show you any other jewelry?"

"Yes. He also showed me a gold chain with bar links on it. Another was a rope chain, gold chain, and another was a gold chain with a pendant with Hebrew writing, like an open tablet or something. There was another with a heart. He asked me how much did I think they were worth. I told him I didn't know. He said the heart alone was worth over five hundred dollars and if I didn't believe him he would take me somewhere to get it appraised. Then he said, 'Do you like it?' I said, 'Yes.' So, he said, 'Well, it's yours if you want it.'"

Calmly, although he barely could contain his excitement, Rocha asked, "Do you still have it?"

"Yes."

"Where is it?"

Nervously, Jackie said, "When my husband told me there were detectives at the door I panicked, so I threw the necklace behind the bed."

Rocha retrieved it, explaining that it was believed to have been stolen and that at a later time Jackie might be asked to look at photographs to see if she could identify the jewelry in the pictures as the same jewels Panama had given to her. Then he asked, "Did you see or talk to him at any time after he gave you jewelry?"

She had seen him briefly on Wednesday, she said, and later that evening—New Year's Eve—he'd telephoned her. "I told him I'd be leaving the next day and asked if he could go to the bus station with me. He was saying that he liked me and asked could he come to Virginia to see me, and would I give him my address and telephone number."

"Did you?"

"Yes. The next day I seen him when I went to pick him up before we went to the Port Authority Bus Terminal in New York City. I wrote my telephone number and everything on a piece of paper and gave it to him."

"What did he do with it?"

"He put it in his jacket pocket."

There comes an instant in any criminal investigation that is like the moment known as critical mass in a nuclear reaction, when energy is released and either is contained or explodes—a time when all the diverse elements of statements of witnesses, the physical and circumstantial evidence, corroborative testimony, the experience, judgment, and instincts of investigators and everyone else involved fall into place and the case crosses a threshold. Sometimes it happens almost instantly—murder in a fit of passion with a confession blurted out by a dazed, terrified, and remorseful killer; the culprit caught standing over the corpse and holding a smoking gun; the robber nabbed red-handed with the stolen goods; a suspect cracking during questioning; a crime-lab expert making an almost immediate match of prints or blood types or fibers; a tip—but most of the time the moment of truth is reached only by painstaking, laboring investigators who spend days, weeks, months, and occasionally years chasing clues, interviewing, studying and restudying files, and just plain thinking.

At this point we did not have the gun.

We did not have fingerprints.

We did not have James Sheffield.

Those negatives notwithstanding, what we had was enough evidence to bring the Sohn case to such a critical juncture, ample evidence that went beyond a policeman's "probable cause" to the "beyond a reasonable doubt" a DA requires. That material consisted of the statements of Sheryl Sohn, Jody Stich, Jacqueline Shoulders, and Willie Brims; the blue snorkel jacket and stained sneakers taken from Belton Brims; bloodstains in a car and in the snow: the ski mask; and the jewelry provided by Jackie Shoulders with its provable direct links from the Jill Lane home of Arnold and Elaine Sohn to the hands of Belton Brims.

After reviewing all of this, weighing it, evaluating the case one more time, I decided we had a solid enough case with which to seek indictments.

A grand jury agreed and on January 14, 1981, voted true bills accusing Belton Brims, James Sheffield, and Sheryl Sohn of the murders of her parents.

Brims was in custody.

Sheffield was on the lam.

Sheryl Sohn was still at liberty.

On the basis of the indictment an arrest warrant was ordered and, happily handing it to Cliff Tallman, I said "Arrest her."

After his capture, Belton Brims had been transferred to the Bergen County Jail, arriving there on January 5.

A jail was hardly an unfamiliar surrounding for him, nor were the routines a new experience, so he adapted immediately to his accommodations, a cell shared with others. It was the last one on the right side of a tier with two rows of ten cells, each separated by a wide corridor at one end of which was a dayroom with recreational equipment and phones that were available to any inmate. He'd been in similar lockups before and had expected no more than he got although, he complained to a prisoner in a cell diagonally opposite his, the lightbulb had burned out and there wasn't a lot of heat.

The other prisoner replied that when it came to a lack of heat his cell was worse because it had a broken windowpane that let in the cold. "My name's John Riegel," he said.

"Panama," Brims replied. Then, as was his custom in a new jail—and that of nearly everyone who winds up in a cell—he asked Riegel what he was in for.

Riegel's tale must have seemed alien to Brims. A graduate of Bucknell University and, after that, an employee of Irving Trust Company, Riegel had served as a second lieutenant in the army. Following military duty, he said to Brims, he became an assistant vice-president of Peoples Trust Company in New Jersey, where for ten years he had been in charge of commercial loans. Leaving the bank for a position with a large trucking company in North Bergen, he became comptroller. Next he went into business for himself—fast food. Then he got into a financial bind and to get out used stolen securities to obtain loans in the amount of $265,000. From that moment, life had been a fast skid downward: forfeited home; wrecked marriage; convictions for forgery, bad checks, fraud, theft by deception, and possession of stolen property.

These crimes were on a level that made Panama's record of robbery, assault, and drug-dealing seem penny-ante, or so it must have seemed to the erudite and sophisticated Riegel as Panama spelled out his past paltry misdeeds, but soon Panama started boasting to his congenial jailmate that he had pulled off a truly daring escapade—*two* cold-blooded murders.

As Panama began to spin his story about a pair of

slayings in Rockland County, Riegel had doubts, but as details spilled out of Panama's mouth, Riegel recalled reading about the murders—an item in *The New York Times* written in the restrained style that had made *The Times* Riegel's newspaper of choice.

He'd never talked with a murderer before and was amazed by the ease with which Panama spilled out the confession, a carefree admission of direct responsibility for a double homicide, the easygoing manner with which he described getting rid of evidence—a ski mask, a gun, clothing—and his forthright way of explaining his plans for disposing of the jewelry he'd stolen during the killings, of giving an attractive woman from Virginia a necklace in a room in a Howard Johnson motel in Spring Valley, of an alibi he'd arranged in which he would say he couldn't have done the murders because he was helping out his mother cleaning up at the movie theater where she worked, and of a male accomplice he could trust, a friend who wouldn't talk and who was in a safe place.

This friend was the one who actually killed the man, Panama said, but, of course, Panama said, he had insisted that the friend do one of the killings just to be sure that friend could never talk. "I gave him a gun and he just beat him over the head and knocked the shit out of him," Panama said.

It all happened, he stated, because of the junkie daughter of the murdered people who had hated her mother and wanted to get a valuable ring off her mother's finger.

For a week during hour after hour of conversation in their cells, in the corridor, and in the dayroom, Panama parceled out the details to his newfound jailhouse buddy.

Everything he had been told by Panama Reigel repeated to the lawyer Riegel had hired to try to get him out of jail and out of the mess his life had become.

The lawyer began that task by contacting my office.

On January 21, from 2:30 to 4:07 P.M. in the Bergen County Jail, Riegel repeated Panama's story again to Detectives Cliff Tallman and Phil Burden.

5 | "THIS IS NOT PERRY MASON"

THE ROCKLAND COUNTY courthouse is a gem. Built in 1928, it sits atop a hill in Art Deco splendor and the imposing chambers within its sturdy walls are grand expressions of the solemnity and dignity of our system of justice.

Rarely had the courthouse attracted so much attention from the general public and the news media as it received on Monday, September 28, 1981—the day Sheryl Sohn and Belton Brims went on trial, exactly nine months after Arnold and Elaine Sohn were murdered.

The Constitution of the United States guarantees to persons accused of crimes—and demands of those whose duty it is to prosecute—a "speedy and public trial." Why, then, did it take nearly a year for Sohn and Brims to reap the benefits of rights to which they were entitled under the Sixth Amendment?

The answer is to be found partially in the amendment itself. After bestowing on the accused the right to a swift trial, it declares that the accused must have "an impartial jury" and also "be informed of the nature and the cause of the accusation; to be confronted with the witnesses against him; to have compulsory process for obtaining witnesses in his favor; and to have the assistance of counsel for his defense."

Bolstering those protections is an immense body of law

and rulings by many courts, especially by the Supreme Court of the United States.

In the case of *The People of the State of New York against Sheryl Sohn and Belton Brims*, the defendants, especially Brims, vigorously pursued each and every one of those protections, and rightly so.

Consequently, the nine months preceeding the actual opening of the trial had been busy ones for me and my staff.

Thirty-five days after the murders, on the first of February, a cold gray day, Cliff Tallman returned to the shopping center on Rose Avenue where Willie Brims had said his cousin had disposed of several items linked to the case. A blanket of snow had prevented Cliff from searching for everything Brims might have thrown away at that spot, but temperatures had been above freezing for several days and the snow was gone as Cliff left his car behind the shopping center, entered a wooded area, and began looking—for what, exactly, he was not certain. His intuition had told him the weapon used to bludgeon Arnold Sohn was a .32-caliber gun, based on the finding of an intact bullet beside the body, an indication at the time that during the beating with the gun a bullet had dislodged. Subsequently Willie Brims stated that a gun had been used and John Riegel's statement detailing Panama Brims' jailhouse admissions made the same assertion.

A few minutes after beginning his search in the brush and brambles and over a wide area of thawing earth that was turning to mud in many spots, in an area of high grass but hard ground, Cliff found what he'd been looking for—a slightly rusty, heavy black steel semi-automatic, clip-loaded .32-caliber pistol.

A "smoking gun" is very rarely part of a criminal prosecution, but guns like the one Cliff located in the winter grass can be just as damning. Convinced that he had found the murder weapon, he understood that the determination of whether this really was the weapon that killed Arnold Sohn would be a finding for others to make. Ballistics experts would compare the gun and the bullet found in the bedroom; the medical examiner would render an opinion as to whether this particular gun could inflict wounds like those to Sohn's skull; serology laboratory technicians would look for traces of blood on the gun to see if they matched Sohn's blood type; and the fingerprint experts who could state with certainty if prints that might be found on the gun matched those of Belton Brims and/or those of James Sheffield would do so.

A nationwide alarm regarding Sheffield had been circulated widely since he had been indicted in the case; raids had been staged at several locations in Rockland where it was believed he might be in hiding; and in May there was a flurry of press speculation and accusations regarding the arrest on a robbery charge of an individual in Toronto under the name David Williams. Deported back to the United States as an unwanted alien, he was released in Detroit. (Later it was learned through an FBI fingerprint analysis that "Williams" was James Sheffield.)

This appeared to some a gross error by the authorities. Actually, they shouldn't have been blamed because in this vast country of ours it is quite easy for a person using a fake identity to slip through the system. This is a nightmare of every DA, but the cold hard fact is that the system is not foolproof and criminals such as Sheffield can be quite sophisticated in their understanding of how to use the system to elude capture.

Meanwhile, all the rights guaranteed by the Constitution to the two suspects we had in custody were being fastidiously observed.

Sheryl Sohn was being represented by Patrick T. Burke, a thirty-nine-year-old Rockland attorney who had studied the classics at Fordham and had gotten his law degree there in 1966. After a stint in the marines he joined the U.S. Justice Department's Organized Crime Task Force in 1969; he went into private law practice in Suffern in 1975. Between conferences with him, Sheryl was said to have been taking psychology and sociology courses from a Rockland Community College professor, but in the spring we filed additional charges against her alleging that she had stolen money from a prison file cabinet and mailed the cash to friends asking them to send her drugs, but those letters were intercepted. There were reports, too, that Sheryl was being advised to do something about improving her appearance. The trained beautician, it was suggested, ought to do something about getting a new hairstyle and more attractive clothing to wear during court appearances.

When it came to taking advantage of the possibilities for creating delays inherent in the exercise of his Sixth Amendment right to the "assistance of counsel" for his defense, Panama Brims proved highly resourceful. Given the representation of prominent civil rights attorney Conrad J. Lynn of Pomona, Brims refused to accept the court's choice. "He ain't going to be my attorney," Brims asserted at his arraignment, and, turning menacingly to Lynn: "Don't come over to the jail."

A distinguished lawyer with a practice in Manhattan, the seventy-two-year-old Lynn said, "The question is whether a man accused of murder has the constitutional right to have a lawyer of his choice. I don't want to be in a case where the client rejects me. That is an untenable situation."

The deputy administrative judge for the Ninth Judicial District, Isaac Rubin, replied that Brims had no right to choose his own lawyer. "He's entitled to adequate counsel," he said, "and the *court* makes that determination."

Nonetheless, always a scrupulously fair jurist, Judge Rubin located other lawyers who agreed to meet with Brims. Still unsatisfied, Brims excoriated the judge: "I don't appreciate your sending these rinky-dinky Rockland attorneys to represent me," he exclaimed angrily. "They don't have the background. They can't even represent people in jail on burglary charges!"

Exasperated, Judge Rubin sighed, "Mr. Brims, you even requested Clarence Darrow, who's now been dead for fifty years!"

Brims warned, "Judge, you'd better start setting cameras up in the jail because I'm going to be watching my trial from the jail."

"He's not going to be happy with any attorney," I argued, "and justice can't stand still. We have a right to proceed."

Then, on June 6, Brims pulled out of his hat the ultimate stalling trick—a delaying tactic not anticipated in the Sixth Amendment.

Located directly behind the courthouse, the Rockland County Jail was a red-brick relic and had had its share of troubles in its history, including a riot a few years earlier. Like a lot of jails and prisons, it was being stretched to the limits of its capacity and there was a lamentable shortage of correctional personnel. However, it appeared that Brims had had more than inadequacies within the facility itself to aid him in effecting his plan. With a hacksaw, apparently smuggled to him, he cut the bars of his cell while inmates created a noisy disturbance by rattling their cell doors and banging objects to distract guards and mask the rasping of Brims' saw. Dashing to an unlocked fire escape on the third floor, he scampered up one flight, climbed a ladder to a skylight, broke its lock, leaped from the roof, and took off.

His absence went unnoticed until eight o'clock the next morning, when a guard found Brims' bed stuffed with newspapers and lumped sheets.

My immediate reaction was shock, surprise, and anger. Instantly I decided to launch a grand jury investigation into how it was possible for there to have been an escape by one of the defendants in one of the most hideous crimes in Rockland's history.

On the loose was one of the most dangerous criminals in my memory and experience.

Deeply worried and concerned about the safety of our witnesses, especially that of Willie Brims, I called in the chief of my detective staff, Eddie McElroy, and orders were issued to protect Willie, a task assigned to Jim Stewart.

The next question was what effect there might be on the trial if Brims were not recaptured. Profoundly understating the situation, I told a reporter, "Trying Sheryl Sohn separately would be extremely detrimental to the prosecution's case."

Without Brims, the actual murderer, we would have had only Sheryl in the courtroom—a pathetic and sympathetic figure in front of the jury. Without his hulking presence we would have a far more difficult task recreating for the jury the horror of what had happened to the Sohns. Also on my mind was the unpleasant possibility of having a second trial for Brims and putting key witnesses through the ordeal of testifying more than once.

While keeping in close touch with those on my staff and the police who were conducting the manhunt for Brims, I proceeded to the pretrial aspects of the case. Hearings on the admissibility of evidence were held, especially the statement that had been given by Sheryl to Cliff Tallman and Eddie O'Neill at the state police barracks in Middletown following the polygraph examination by Jerry O'Leary.

Her attorney contended that she hadn't been properly advised of her rights and that she'd been misled by those men into believing she would not be prosecuted.

The hearing lasted three and a half days before Judge John A. Gallucci. A highly respected jurist and lifelong resident of the county, the judge was the embodiment of "old Rockland" and had a reputation as solid as the cliffs of the Hudson. Leaving his court when the hearing ended on July 27, I was confident that I'd shown Judge Gallucci that all of Sheryl Sohn's rights had been scrupulously observed and that he would rule in our favor, but I didn't let my confidence carry me away. The case had a long way to go before I'd rise and state "The People rest," and there was, after all, a serious obstacle standing in the way of a successful conclusion: the absence of Brims.

Early the next day, Rockland Sheriff's Detective Clark Hill got a phone call from Alabama. "We've got some sweet news for you," said the caller. "We've got Belton Brims for you down here in Selma." He had apparently fled to his hometown directly after his escape and linked up with a friend, Robert Lewis Williams, who was known in Rockland and had been regarded as a person with whom Brims might try to be in contact. (Most people think that criminals on the lam would not flee to their homes. In fact, most do; at home a fugitive is most likely to find help in the form of money or food, so he goes back to his old haunts.)

Based on "wanted" alarms sent to Selma, authorities had been on the lookout for both Brims and Williams when, around ten in the morning on Tuesday, July 28, police officers spotted a burly black man wearing a tight-fitting stocking cap, dark trousers, and a tee shirt and believed the man to be Brims. That suspicion was heightened when he bolted. The footrace ended in a semiwooded area with

Brims surrounded by ten Selma police officers wielding shotguns. Trapped, he yelled, "Why the hell don't you shoot me?"

That afternoon I contacted the office of New York Governor Hugh Carey and requested that he file a request with Alabama's Governor Fob James for extradition of Brims, a process I expected would take a few weeks because Alabama authorities had a charge of their own to bring against him. This made it quite possible that the extradition could be dragged out so long and to such a point that the opening of the Sohn murder trial would be delayed.

Any prolonged delay would be vigorously resisted, warned Sheryl's attorney.

Suddenly, a week after he'd been caught, Brims stunned all of us by announcing that he would not fight being returned to Rockland. "He doesn't like it down here," said Dallas County Assistant DA James Standbridge. "He was very unhappy in our jail." He was being kept alone in a cell separated from other prisoners and was denied visits by members of his family. "Whatever reasons he has for agreeing to come back, they're all right with me," I told Standbridge.

We were a month away from the date the court had set for the beginning of the process of selecting a jury for the trial.

"This is not Perry Mason." Almost always, it seems, at some point at the beginning, during, or at the end of a trial, a judge, a prosecutor or a defense lawyer voices that admonition to a jury.

Expect no sudden twists and turns! No surprise witnesses! No finger-wagging under a witness's nose as the witness is asked "Isn't it true that you are the murderer?" No confession blurted out by the guilty party squirming on the stand. Not because real lawyers and prosecutors aren't as crafty and able as Erle Stanley Gardner's fictional lawyer played so long and so well on television by Raymond Burr but because our criminal justice system doesn't work that way. Under trial rules and the law there are strict procedures that must be followed, most of them designed to guarantee that all the rights of the person on trial are observed.

Before the case ever reaches the stage at which a jury is brought in, prosecution and defense already have held numerous hearings, meetings, and conferences at which the rules to be followed in that particular case are argued by the attorneys and ruled upon by the judge.

As a result of these pretrial activities, it often turns out that some of the evidence in a case will be deemed inadmissible by the judge. He may cite many reasons for ruling against pieces of evidence or types of testimony or even on whether certain witnesses may be heard. These reasons may be rooted in precedent (findings by courts in previous cases) or he may simply accept arguments from the defense that evidence has been tainted, is highly questionable on technical or other grounds or so provocative or inflammatory that it would not permit the jury to reach a reasoned and unprejudiced verdict.

All of this is part of a delicate balancing act between the rights of the accused and the right of society at large to be protected against crime and criminals. This is the heart of the arguments about "law and order" that have characterized America's political debates over the past three decades. It is a debate that in many ways is unique to the United States. The result so far has been to create a system of safeguards for the accused that relegates the determination of guilt or innocence to a secondary consideration. First comes the consideration of the rights of the accused. Then comes the question of guilt or innocence. As a result, many criminals go free to commit new crimes.

In pretrial hearings concerning the Sohn case the defense attorneys for Sohn and Brims presented objections to evidence and testimony that, I argued, were vital to the prosecution. This material included the statements made by Sheryl Sohn during the polygraph interview and to Detectives Tallman and O'Neill, the gruesome color photographs of the bodies of the Sohns taken at the scene of the crime, and the items of clothing taken from Brims at the time of his arrest that in my view established a direct link between Belton Brims and the Sohn murders.

By this time Belton Brims had given up on his tactic of trying to delay the trial by refusing to accept legal representation and was being defended by attorney Bennett L. Gershman, a law professor at Pace University. Immediately, Gershman raised the question of whether Brims would be brought to court in jail garb and handcuffed. He won a judgment that as long as Brims acted properly he would be permitted to appear in the court in civilian clothing—paid for by the county of Rockland—and unshackled, a rule that was accepted with a shudder and grave misgivings by those who would have to escort Brims to and from court every day.

The judge was forty-four-year-old Howard Miller, whose manner on the bench was calm but effective, making it clear from the outset that in his courtroom he was in charge. He also had a sense of humor, turning after one of the heated debates that took place during the trial and saying to the jury "And you think being a judge is easy!"

Difficult, too, is being a juror. In fact, the juror's is the toughest task in any trial, especially when the charge is murder.

Despite the feeling of a judge, a prosecutor, or a defense lawyer that jurors must be warned against expecting to see a Perry Mason drama acted out before their eyes, I have discovered that jurors do not look for a show or want one. I've found that what a jury looks for is not a prosecutor's ability as a performer but the conviction and sincerity he brings with him into the court and to the case. Under our system of justice, it is up to the prosecutor to prove his case. Counsel for the defense doesn't have to prove anything. Innocence is presumed. Jurors know this.

The key to prosecution is preparation. A case is not won by a district attorney engaging in histrionics in a courtroom but by doing his homework: the painstaking, time-consuming, detail-minding, and foundation-laying work that goes into building a case that will demonstrate to jurors that—solely on the basis of evidence—they have no alternative but to bring in a verdict of guilty.

What I cannot prepare for and control is the selection of a jury consisting of twelve persons and alternates from a panel of potential jurors delivered to me and to the defense lawyers at random from the county's jury pool. Comes the day to begin selecting the people who will decide the case and before me in the courtroom is a sea of strangers out of which I in association with the defense and the judge must pick a dozen who will be fair.

Fairness is what is sought. Open minds. Of course, none of us is a mind reader. So the process is a little risky. You really don't know them or what to expect. It's a lesson that was driven home to me when I was an assistant prosecutor in New York City learning the ropes of real-life trial procedures.

The case involved Leon Campo, a con man of extraordinary daring who specialized in bilking Jewish merchants of the Manhattan diamond district. A South American Jew, he had developed a scheme tailored to those he set out to swindle, enacting an especially cruel fraud in which he would pose as a dealer in gems while passing himself off as a survivor of the Holocaust. Like all confidence men, he was glib and convincing, worming his way into the trust of the sympathetic jewelers, almost all of whom had suffered as a result of the Nazis. Having gained their confidence, Campo waited for an opportune moment to switch rhinestones for the diamonds the trusting dealers were showing him. Eventually his luck ran out and he was arrested.

During jury selection, I was questioning a prospective juror whom my gut instincts warned me not to choose. To this day, I cannot explain what it was about the man that I didn't like or why I set aside my misgivings and picked him for the jury. But I will never forget the sinking feeling of impending disaster when I stepped before the jurors to begin my summation and that particular juror calmly took an Oh Henry! candy bar from his pocket, unwrapped it, and with a look of utter disdain for what I might say slowly devoured it as I spoke. That his mind had been made up to vote for acquittal was confirmed when the jury came in hung eleven to one for conviction.

Although Campo subsequently pleaded guilty and received a three-year prison term, from that moment to this I have taken a moment at the outset of jury selection to whisper to myself "Remember Oh Henry!"

There is a recent trend for jury selection to be put into the hands of "experts" and "consultants" who devise means for evaluating the potential jurors based on all sorts of studies rooted in psychology, sociology, economics, geography, and demographics. Techniques that have been used in marketing, opinion polling, advertising, and even in the TV ratings systems are now being dragged into jury selection. I don't like it and am not comfortable with it, but I don't approach the selection of jurors entirely on my own. I have people on my staff from whom I draw advice and counsel in sizing up the choices available to us but as helpful as these trusted aides are, I go on my Oh Henry! instincts.

The twelve jurors for the Sohn case, nine men and three women, were chosen during a long and arduous selection process. At 9:55 in the morning on Monday, September 28, 1981, they took seats in the jury box of a small but architecturally splendid courtroom and from that moment on everything that was said and done in the courtroom would be directed at them.

Before them sat Belton Brims, clean-shaven, in a brand-new three-piece brown suit and brown shoes.

Before them sat Sheryl Sohn, wearing glasses, with her makeup and hair expertly done, dressed in an orange-and-brown outfit.

Before them sat the lawyers for Sohn and Brims.

Before them I sat.

Before us all sat Judge Miller who—after speaking to the jury in general terms concerning the process that was about to begin and brief conversations with the lawyers involved—peered down from the bench at me and said "The court recognizes Mr. Gribetz at this time."

It was time for me to make an opening statement.

The purpose was to outline the case being brought by the people—the charges on which the defendants had been indicted, in this case twelve counts ranging from second-degree murder to burglary and larceny; the nature of the crimes alleged and how they were carried out by Brims; the role of Sheryl Sohn; the evidence to be introduced and the witnesses to be called upon to testify to prove all of the accusations in the indictments. "I say to you, ladies and gentlemen, we *will* prove each and every allegation, *each and every allegation*, in the twelve-count indictment that was presented and handed up by the grand jury of the County of Rockland," I concluded. "And after all the evidence has been presented to you, after you have heard the testimony of all the witnesses in the case, I will ask you on behalf of the People of the State of New York to find the defendant, Sheryl Sohn, as well as defendant, Belton Lee Brims, guilty of all the counts that are contained in this indictment."

Although I don't recall anyone actually saying to the jury "This is not Perry Mason," there were over the next six weeks dramatic moments that rivaled any scenes of fiction, beginning on the second day of trial when Judge Miller let the jury see the ghastly color photos of the victims that had been taken at the scene. Suddenly, the daughter who hadn't shed any tears that I knew of in the nine months since her parents' brutal deaths began sobbing and moaning and finally had to be taken from the courtroom.

The hush of the courtroom was shattered by gasps from the shocked spectators on the fifth of October as Jody Stich testified "She said, 'I'm going to kill her' and 'I have somebody doing something for me.'"

With Cliff Tallman on the stand the atmosphere tingled as Gershman attempted to create a picture of a cop with personal motives driving him to crack the Sohn case—promotion, hatred of Belton Brims, and even of having a supposedly romantic relationship with Jody Stich. "Isn't it fair to say," Gershman asked, "that all of the evidence in this case you single-handedly were the mastermind of?"

"Absolutely not," Cliff responded calmly.

BRIMS' ATTORNEY GRILLS DETECTIVE headlined *The Journal-News* the next day. The trial had become, in the words of the Sunday edition of that newspaper, "an SRO attraction," with every seat filled and sheriff's deputies "forced to set up barricades to control the crowds."

Indeed, the courthouse had become a "hot ticket" by the

time Jackie Shoulders came up from Virginia to tell about the jewelry Panama had given to her.

Then came Willis Brims to the stand in a corduroy suit and yellow shirt open at the neck to testify under oath about his cousin Belton, stunning the court into silence with "Panama told me that he had done the murders." Then, with every ear in the courtroom straining to hear, softly he added, "He said that he made Sheffield beat the guy with the butt of a gun. . . ."

Robert C. Shaler was an important witness. He was the director of serology in the office of New York City's chief medical examiner and later would become a pioneer in experiments with the genetic building blocks known as DNA leading to the development of a system of identifying individuals that could surpass fingerprinting and blood-typing in its impact on the criminal justice system. But DNA identification was still in the future as Dr. Shaler took the stand and stated that the blood on the sneaker taken from Belton Brims could have been Arnold Sohn's, that Sohn's blood was a very rare type, and that he had found specks of tissue on the trigger of the gun in evidence.

That gun, Detective Tallman testified, had misfired in an attempt by Brims and Sheffield to kill Arnold Sohn and so had been used to beat him to death. A bullet had fallen from the gun and that bullet was consistent with ammunition for the gun located where, according to Willie Brims' testimony, his cousin had thrown away something connected with the "serious business" Brims and James Sheffield had done at 38 Jill Lane early in the morning of December 28, 1980, and which Panama, according to the testimony of John Riegel, had talked openly about in idle conversation between two men sharing the same jail.

Medical Examiner Dr. Frederick Zugibe's testimony was vitally important. In 1969, Dr. Zugibe had transformed the county's old coroner system into a medical-examiner system in keeping with the enormously expanded needs of the criminal justice system. A fellow of the American Academy of Forensic Sciences and a host of other distinguished organizations in the field of pathology, he is an internationally recognized expert. In his judgment, he testified, the blunt instrument used to inflict the injuries on Arnold Sohn was the same, or an identical type, handgun as that recovered by Tallman.

When he was given the gun, Dr. Zugibe explained, he looked for pattern injuries consistent with the weapon. "Pattern injuries are like a fingerprint of that particular weapon," he pointed out. As a result of his examination of the gun and the photographs of the wounds, he said, he was able to identify five specific pattern injuries, thereby leading him to conclude that the handgun in question, or one exactly like it, caused Arnold Sohn's injuries.

After all of that, I rose before the jury and stated "The People rest."

Could the lawyers for the defendants show that the case I'd presented had been wrong? That Sheryl Sohn deserved to be found not guilty? And Belton Brims? Had I not proved "beyond a reasonable doubt" a case of cold-blooded double homicide?

"I was never there," asserted Belton Brims from the witness chair. "I never killed Sheryl Sohn's people."

In his new suit, chewing gum, gripping the courtroom microphone, he took the stand and, sometimes in a quiet tone, at times shouting, now and then jovially, denied it all.

What about the things Sheryl and Jody had told the police? What about those girls?

"They hung together like rock-and-roll."

During testimony about the business of dealing drugs, when asked by the judge and about the cost of dope

Panama, the wheeler-dealer who "ran the store" in prison and dope on the Hill, said with a smile, "Oh, your honor, the more you go, the less you pay."

In his questioning of Brims, Sheryl's lawyer attempted to separate his client from Brims and portray Sheryl as a victim by showing that Brims had forced Sheryl into setting up the robbery of her parents because she owed him money for drugs. "She never owed me," Brims replied, almost with affectionate pride. "Sheryl Sohn always took care of business. That's why I took to Sheryl Sohn. She never gave me no excuses. She always brought the money."

"If somebody doesn't pay, isn't it a fact that you have to force them to pay?" Patrick Burke challenged.

"That ain't my way of doing things."

Incredulous, Burke asked Belton Brims, "So if somebody didn't pay you, you, out of the goodness of your heart, would forgive them?"

Brims grinned. "I'm a nice guy."

Nice guy?

Could the jury believe that? Would they?

"A trial is nothing more than a search for the truth," I said as I stood before that jury on November 4 after almost six weeks of laying out for them what I believed—and what I believed the evidence proved—was the truth, rising to deliver my summation of the people's case against Sheryl Sohn and Belton Brims. It was a lengthy discussion of all that had been presented to the jury.

Could they disregard the gun, the ski mask, the bloody sneaker, the heart-shaped diamond necklace?

Could these decent people of Rockland County ignore all they had heard and seen? The testimony of Willie Brims? Jody Stich? John Riegel? Jerry O'Leary? Eddie O'Neill? Cliff Tallman? The statement of Sheryl Sohn herself?

Were these people liars?

Or was Belton Brims the liar?

"Ladies and gentlemen, I submit to you that the defendants have been caught in the web of truth," I said, "because today is the day of justice and justice has arrived and the day of judgment is upon us."

Actually, the day of judgment did not come until two days later when, just before 5:00 P.M. on Friday, November 6, the jury returned with its verdicts and its foreman, Kenneth Donoghue, a news producer for NBC, said "Guilty."

Belton Brims—guilty of two counts of intentional murder.

Sheryl Sohn—guilty of felony murder (a felony crime that ends in a killing).

With that verdict, the jury had rendered its judgment that Sheryl Sohn in arranging the robbery of her parents had not deliberately arranged for their deaths.

Both she and Brims were found guilty on the lesser charges also, and when they came before the court for sentencing each got the maximum for the murder convictions. Because there was no death penalty in New York State, Brims received twenty-five years to life on each count of murder and Sheryl received a sentence of twenty-five years to life.

Additional time was levied for the other charges.

The day of judgment for James Sheffield was longer in coming, but on July 10, 1982, based on a tip from the Spring Valley police, FBI agents arrested him on Skid Row in Los Angeles. In a trial prosecuted by Assistant District Attorney Alan Friedberg, who had assisted me in the first trial, he was convicted of murder—but not intentional murder. In the second trial, the jury had not been allowed to see the photos of Arnold Sohn.

His sentence for the crimes was consecutive twenty-five-years-to-life terms and additional time for robbery, burglary, and larceny.

Except for Arnold and Elaine Sohn, there was one person in the case who suffered more than anyone—Mark Sohn, the loving, quiet, and sincere son and brother of that tragic family who not only had to endure the loss of his parents but also had to cope with the sickening reality that his sister had caused it. Asked for a comment at the end of the ordeal, he said bitterly of Sheryl, "She should rot in hell."

There was one other tragic note regarding Mark that took place in the aftermath of the loss of his parents. Under the terms of their joint will, an estate valued at $150,000 had been placed in trust for their children by the Sohns. The trustees and executors were father-and-son attorneys Jacob and David Pesner, lawyers who had been longtime friends and confidants of the Sohns. They also were the attorneys to whom Arnold and Elaine had turned when they were desperately seeking help in dealing with Sheryl's drug problems. It was at their suggestion that Arnold had come to my office to seek my advice and assistance regarding her addiction. Unfortunately, after the deaths of the Sohns these lawyers took advantage of their positions as executors to pillage what the Sohns had bequeathed, a deed for which I prosecuted them vigorously.

I was outraged at the conduct of members of my profession and because I felt an obligation to Mark, I wanted to be of help to him. I started by obtaining free legal assistance for him through the Rockland County Bar Association and then directing him to a system that had been established in New York by which a person victimized financially by a lawyer could seek redress from the state. In New York the system is known as the Client Security Fund. It is a pool of funds formed by fees paid by attorneys; but, to my dismay, I discovered that the New York fund was structured in a way that would not fully compensate the victim's loss.

Believing that the fund ought to be bolstered, I called State Senator Eugene Levy, an old friend who was a Republican leader with the ability to correct the system's failings. The result is that today the Client Security Fund is amply financed and victims of legal chicanery like Mark Sohn are protected.

Because I live in Monsey, right next to Spring Valley, in the course of county or personal business I sometimes have to drive by 38 Jill Lane because it is today, as it was on that bright Sunday morning in December 1980, on the way. Each time I go by I think about the Sohns, not just because it was an important case, but because I still have a difficult time believing that those fine and decent people met their awful deaths in Rockland County. At the same time, however, I also take a moment to consider the fact that it was also in Rockland that through the prosecution of their killers the Sohns received justice.

6 | THE BRIDGE OF SIGHS

THE MURDER OF the Sohns was a wrenching experience for the residents of Rockland County. Because the Sohns had so much in common with so many people, their brutal deaths struck home. For me it was a case that underscored the difficulties and challenges of being a district attorney in the suburbs, where every case that comes along is bound to be felt in a deeply personal way by many. Each case is more than a file folder stuffed with legal papers because it often bears the names of people I know personally.

The outcomes of cases are often taken personally, too. One such instance involved the son of an Orthodox Jewish family I had known for many years and whom I saw weekly in synagogue and during holiday services. A troubled youth, he became deeply involved with drugs, which led him to commit a burglary to support his habit. During the burglary, as he was fleeing from the police, he dropped his yarmulke, but when he bent down to retrieve the black skullcap, it appeared to one of the police officers that the boy had a gun. Believing he was defending himself, the police officer shot and killed the youth. It was my duty to convene a grand jury to investigate the circumstances. The panel exonerated the policeman and the boy's parents held me responsible—as if I'd killed their son—and never spoke to me again.

Their reaction is typical of how the district attorney can be associated in a direct way with cases that are the DA's duty to prosecute. It demonstrates how the DA can be held personally accountable for the outcome and suddenly be shunned by former close friends and associates or receive harassing phone calls in the dead of night, some of them death threats.

That these would become factors in my life had never occurred to me when I chose to study law; the farthest thing from my mind was that I might become a district attorney. But, during my third year at New York University Law School, while serving an internship with the city's Department of Investigation I was told by lawyers working there that an especially auspicious way to begin a law career was to be an assistant DA in the office of Frank S. Hogan, the legendary district attorney of New York.

From his eighth-floor office, Hogan had presided over the criminal justice system in Manhattan for three decades. Under him, the Manhattan DA's operation had become a model for others and Frank Smithwick Hogan himself had become famous as "the conscience of the city," regarded by all as nonpartisan and scrupulously honest, personally and professionally.

As a result, Hogan was free to hire young assistants unfettered by political considerations or patronage, a system that brought in young legal minds eager to learn from a man who'd attained the stature of a living monument and dean of public prosecutors, the person everyone assumed you meant if you said "Mr. District Attorney."

Indeed, Frank Hogan was reported to have been the inspiration for the popular and long-running Phillips H. Lord radio program of that title that was on the air in the golden age of radio and that began with Jay Jostyn as the fictional DA affirming "It shall be my duty as District

Attorney not only to prosecute to the limit of the law all persons accused of crimes perpetrated within this county but to defend with equal vigor the rights and privileges of all its citizens," a rather fine and succinct statement of what a DA is supposed to do.

In 1968, having recently married and nearing the end of my final year of law school, I applied for and was granted an interview with Mr. Hogan.

Arriving much too early, I paused a moment to gaze up at an enclosed passageway that spanned the narrow gap between the high, forbidding, slate-gray walls of New York City's men's jail known as the Tombs and the equally daunting and towering Criminal Courts Building located at 100 Centre Street in lower Manhattan, where Hogan had his office. The passageway halfway up the clifflike sides of the buildings provided an easy access between the cells and holding pens of the Tombs and courtrooms and so had been named after a similar bridge between a grim prison and the palace of the Doges in Venice, Italy—the Bridge of Sighs.

In an endless stream from their cells to the courtrooms, across the bridge flowed the losers, the luckless, the lawless, and the hapless; waiting for them in the crowded courthouse corridors were their worried, bewildered friends, relatives, and loved ones huddling in hurried conferences with lawyers or searching through the thick dockets of cases tacked to the bulletin boards or taped to the walls, babbling in multilingual confusion their fears and hopes in the courthouse's vast, bleak, echoing lobby.

Gazing at the Bridge of Sighs, I asked myself if I wanted to plunge into that maelstrom, if I had it in me to become a prosecutor, if the logical beginning of my career as a lawyer would be found in the domain of the district attorney of New York County, the busiest prosecutor in the nation.

Erect and proper in a large swivel chair behind a desk

used by his predecessor, the gang-busting Thomas E. Dewey, Mr. District Attorney in the flesh lived up to the legend. Pin-stripe suit. Vest. Gold watchchain. Stickpin in a flawless conservative necktie. Breast-pocket handkerchief. Gleamingly shined shoes. Manicure. Snow-white hair.

To my great delight, he offered me a position and I agreed to serve on his staff for at least four years beginning July 18, 1968.

That spring marked the beginning of what would become the zenith of the rebellious 1960s, a decade when antiestablishmentarianism was flaunted in the streets and on campuses.

A Columbia University alumnus and trustee and holder of that university's prestigious Alexander Hamilton Medal for distinguished service and accomplishment, Hogan had been vilified and burned in effigy by Columbia students during an uprising incited by the radical Students for a Democratic Society (SDS) led by a firebrand named Mark Rudd.

Columbia's troubles sprang out of a dispute over a proposal by the university to build a new gymnasium in Morningside Park. For the gym to be erected on city property, the university had to agree that the facility would be made available to neighboring residents of Harlem. Accordingly, an entrance in the rear of the building providing easy access from Harlem was designed, an arrangement soon construed by some blacks and the white radicals within SDS as Jim Crow racism and an affront to the people of Harlem who were, the protesters claimed, being forced to use "the back door." To show their displeasure, 150 members of SDS marched into the office of Columbia's president, Grayson Kirk, and briefly took it over.

Eventually, the blacks and Columbia officials reached an accommodation, but the SDS persisted in protests and in adding other grievances as justification for sit-ins and occupation of other buildings. When arrests were made in what turned into a pitched battle between the police and the occupiers and the cases were brought to court, some 600 people faced misdemeanor charges that ranged from disorderly conduct to criminal trespass. Among the names on the docket were some of the stellar personalities of the movement—Dr. Benjamin Spock, the elder guru of the period; Abbie Hoffman of the Yippies; Bernadette Dohrn, a Chicago lawyer who had forsaken law books and rushed to the barricades of "the revolution"; Kathy Boudin, the daughter of one of the country's most famous lawyers; and the campus leader of SDS, Mark Rudd.

Rudd's first notable act as a revolutionary had been in March 1968, when he threw a lemon meringue pie in the face of a military recruiter. Joining SDS at Columbia in his sophomore year, Rudd was an athletic-looking youth with hypnotic blue-gray eyes and a self-described "man of action."

In the midst of the occupations of campus facilities the leaders of SDS began looking ahead to the inevitable end of their protest and demanded amnesty. "We didn't think we were wrong in doing what we had to do," said Rudd, "and we didn't think that any changes would come about within the university until the administration and the trustees realized that what they had been doing was wrong. Why should we be punished for doing what was right?"

Insisted Mr. District Attorney, "Somebody has got to stand up for the rule of law."

At this time I was one of many young assistant DAs handling arraignments. The first court appearances by a few Columbia rebels were in my hands, but these were not arraignments at which the weighty issues at the heart of the cases were about to be settled, so I handled them in the same manner as the dozens of others in my daily pile of cases.

Abbie Hoffman, the flamboyant founder and leader of the notorious Yippies, was pragmatic. Charged with obstructing governmental administration by having caused a contusion of the left testicle of a New York police officer, Hoffman recognized that his case was being heard by a judge who would be more likely to impose a fine than a jail sentence and chose not to make a mockery of the proceeding and a circus of the court. Respectful and humble, he pleaded guilty and was fined $1050. He got no jail time, leaving him free to orchestrate later mayhem at the Democratic Party National Convention in Chicago and the "Days of Rage" surrounding the trial of the "Chicago Eight."

Rudd, the "man of action," skipped, jumping bail, not to be heard from again until 1977 when he, Abbie Hoffman, and several others suddenly began surfacing after years on the lam, choosing to turn themselves in when the nation was in the mood to forgive and forget transgressions of the sixties.

"Homeward bound," in the words of Simon and Garfunkel, the aging sixties radicals were washing up like beached whales on the shores of the America of the seventies, but still among the missing as Hoffman, Dohrn, and Rudd came in from the cold was Kathy Boudin. Last seen naked and fleeing in terror after a bomb factory exploded and reduced a swank Greenwich Village townhouse to ruins in March 1970, Boudin reappeared with a vengeance in 1980 at a shopping mall in Rockland County.

That Abbie Hoffman surrendered was no surprise. In my view, he was still trying to get the best deal, still looking out for himself.

Rudd was fined $2000, given two years' probation, and

went off to teach at a technical school in Albuquerque, New Mexico.

As colorful and headline-making as the radical cases were, they were an almost infinitesimal part of my years in Hogan's office. Mostly I was trying run-of-the-mill robbery cases and an increasing load of narcotics arrests in which the defendants were those who had waited for days, weeks, and months in the Tombs before tramping across the Bridge of Sighs.

A more spectacular case was that of Frank Peterson, who was accused of a terror spree of seven rapes on Manhattan's Upper East Side. The victims were primarily women with the beauty of fashion models. Convicted for six of the seven, he got thirty years and the women of the silk-stocking district breathed a little easier.

During four years with Hogan I had spent several months in the Complaint Bureau, three or four months in Fraud, a year and a half in the Criminal Court, and two years in the Supreme Court Bureau. I had reached a point where I felt I had to make up my mind as to what to do next, a decision I was mulling over in the spring of 1972 when into my lap was plunked the thorny problem of the brothers Pyles—Timbuk and Sonni.

In some ways a slapstick comedy worthy of the old Keystone Kops films, the Three Stooges, or Abbott and Costello, the Pyles case turned out to be an education in the pitfalls of law enforcement in the 1970s, when a DA was likely to find himself between the rock of civil-rights-minded liberals and the hard place of law-and-order conservatives. It was also a graduate course in law from the vantage point of prisoners caught up in a corrections system becoming swamped by sheer numbers and a lesson in how the criminal justice system is vulnerable to political opportunists and partisan rivalry.

In terms of the pressures being put on the penal system, the Tombs was both an example of its failings and short-comings and an exaggeration of them, as New York City is an exaggeration of almost everything. Dating back to 1938, the jail had been hailed as the epitome of modern and enlightened penology and a far cry from the prison that had stood on that ground a century before (its exterior design, inspired by an Egyptian mausoleum, led to the name "the Tombs"). In the intervening century, other prisons took the place of the original until the present Art Deco jail was built as the companion to the Criminal Courts with the conve-niently connecting Bridge of Sighs that made it so easy to transfer the prisoners from their cells to courtrooms. By March 1972 the explosive increase in crime and the arrests that resulted had strained the Tombs to the limit (a condition that finally got so bad that a federal court in the 1980s ordered the Tombs closed for a total renovation).

In the overcrowded Tombs on the morning of March 9, 1972, and scheduled for a court appearance were the Pyles, a pair of street-wise, daring, and fearless but bottom-of-the-heap stickup men and muggers who were successful enough to live in relatively high style in a penthouse of the fading Hotel Webster on West Forty-fifth Street. Proudly black, they wore custom-designed Afro hats made of leopardskin. This outlandish attire, plus their muscular builds and braggadoccio and the fact that they were twins, made the black duo from Mississippi Delta country readily identifi-able, but that didn't seem to bother the brothers who twice held up the Hotel Seymour, next door to the Webster. Their yellow sheet (the police department's record of their crim-inal careers) recorded their climb from a pair of street muggers to bold, shotgun-toting holdup men whose crimi-nality had culminated in their robbing a merchant as he attempted to night-deposit the day's earnings of $1100 on the fifth of March 1971. The merchant had no problem identifying the gaudily outfitted twins, but now, a year later, they had yet to go on trial for the alleged crime.

This prolongation of their pretrial incarceration in the Tombs was the result of their own efforts at stalling the legal system with a bewildering, frustrating, and bizarre array of delaying tactics that had made the Pyles unique in the files of Hogan's office. The folder was crammed with their outraged demands for a speedy trial. Yet, accompanying the blizzard of paper fomented by their jailhouse-lawyer expertise was an almost ludicrous history of delays and postponements they and their numerous lawyers had wangled, including dismissing eight court-appointed attorneys on allegations of incompetence. Of course, there was method in this madness. Their hope was that the longer they stalled the less likely it was they would be convicted. Savvy to the frailties of the justice system—witnesses no longer available or too scared to testify, errors in procedure, or just plain weariness of harried DAs and courts—they knew there was a strong chance they'd get off easily or altogether and, when they did wind up before a judge, they carried on filibusters that consisted of hours of legalistic doubletalk and mumbo jumbo that created nothing but confusion.

As the prosecutor, I shared in this frustration and the chaos—and laughed a good deal, although often bitterly—as the Pyles' antics unfolded. Each day brought a new wrinkle.

Although black, they never made an issue of race and often excoriated Black Power advocates. Rather than express unhappiness with the American system, they extolled the virtues of the nation and constantly recited the Pledge of Allegiance. Nor did they rail against the legal system in general or the judge in particular. Instead, they drowned the court in pronouncements of their respect and admiration.

Ultimately Judge Myles J. Lane agreed to allow the trial to proceed with the defendants confined to an adjoining room where they would hear the court's proceedings piped to them through loudspeakers.

When the system was in place Judge Lane decreed that the brothers be brought over from the Tombs.

What he did not know was that two days previously, when the brothers had refused to leave their cell, to avoid any possible disturbance Tombs officials assuaged them by allowing them to see their lawyer. Instead, they requested a meeting with William vanden Heuvel, chairman of the Board of Corrections, a watchdog group within the prison system. When he was told by Corrections Captain Constantine Mellon that in the interest of avoiding a riot the brothers had not been coerced into obeying the court's order to present themselves for trial, William vanden Heuvel exclaimed, "Well, it's about time you people started to defy the court."

Less than forty-eight hours later, at 8:25 on the morning set for their next court appearance, the Pyles again defied the Corrections guards who came to F cellblock to escort the reluctant pair of twenty-six-year-olds to stand before the judge at nine o'clock.

"The only way we leavin' is if you kill us first" was Timbuk's defiant response to orders to step out of the cell.

Immediately other inmates burst into a raucous chorus of support.

Instantly Tombs officials sniffed the sickening smell of incipient riot.

Especially cautious and alert to trouble because of a Tombs disturbance less than two years earlier, the officers sent out an alarm for assistance. Moments later a seven-man guard with bulletproof vests and helmets poured onto the sixth floor.

Warden Albert Glick arrived to confer with Captain Mellon, then tried to read Judge Lane's order, only to be drowned out by the screaming inmates.

Turning to one of the guards, Mellon ordered the use of the irritant CN tear gas. In a canister resembling insecticide, it could be sprayed directly into a cantankerous prisoner's face, but when Mellon himself stepped into the cell and pressed the button, he found out the nozzle was pointed backward—but too late to keep from gassing himself and filling the cell with the nauseating mist.

As Mellon stumbled gasping out of the cell, a guard managed to retrieve the canister and succeeded in squirting both of the Pyles brothers, but the twins still managed to resist until they were finally wrestled to the floor, handcuffed, trussed, and dragged bleary-eyed, vomiting, and kicking to the elevators.

Coincidentally arriving on the sixth floor was the current lawyer for the Pyles brothers, Daniel Sheehan. He gaped in amazement as the guards wrestled with the two prisoners who, though gassed and hog-tied, were shouting that they had suffered painful injuries and demanding that they receive prompt medical attention.

The jittery Tombs officials called in a doctor. That ended the likelihood of any court appearances by the Pyles for that day. Informed of this, Judge Lane, barely containing his consternation, ordered me to go over to the Tombs to take depositions from everyone involved.

During that process, guards reported to me the curious and upsetting events of the previous Tuesday, including William vanden Heuvel's startling statement encouraging disobeying the courts.

With the depositions taken, I reported the entire episode to Frank Hogan, who listened impassively to the familiar record of the Pyles and without comment on that day's riotous events in the Tombs, but when I quoted from the guards' depositions relating to vanden Heuvel, Hogan looked up, startled. "What was that again?"

" 'It's about time you people started to defy the court.' "

The unflappable Frank Hogan was flabbergasted. "You mean he was ordering them to disobey the courts? Disgraceful! I want this brought to Judge Lane's attention immediately. He may want to start contempt proceedings or order a grand jury. What did the guards say about this?"

I read from Captain Mellon's affidavit. "We just looked at Mr. vanden Heuvel with blank expressions," it stated. "We were stunned. We didn't feel we were trying to defy the court. As a matter of fact, we were trying to con the Pyles into going to court. We didn't want a riot on our hands."

By using the Board of Corrections as a political platform, vanden Heuvel had been lambasting the New York City criminal justice system in general and Frank S. Hogan in particular amid the widespread speculation that vanden Heuvel was planning to run for district attorney in the Democratic primary the next year.

It was the first time in thirty-two years that someone had challenged Hogan, and many of his supporters regarded that as more than an affront. It was a humiliation.

Sitting there in Hogan's office, I was deeply upset that the Pyles case might easily became ensnared in bitter political maneuvering by vanden Heuvel that would range far beyond their particular case and that in all likelihood the brothers would become the latest cause célèbre in a raging public debate over law enforcement, the criminal justice system, prisons, rights of prisoners, and a host of other issues that not only had split Democrats but was also threatening to undermine the cause of justice itself.

A proud man who was aristocratic in bearing, Hogan did

not believe that the position of district attorney belonged in the rough and tumble of politics. Years of being re-elected with no opposition had cemented the notion. Now, suddenly, he discovered that he was under attack. And not only was he under fire, so was the office he had created. It was, the opposition said, an ivory tower in which Hogan had become "out of touch with the times" and, in the words of William vanden Heuvel, "We are left to view the ruins of a criminal justice system when it is administered by those who have lost their sense of balance, of equity, and of justice itself."

I believed that was nonsense and was delighted when the New York Bar Association described Hogan as "highly qualified and approved" while it dismissed his challenger as "not approved."

In the campaign Hogan made a campaign issue of the prison disturbances and vanden Heuvel's statement in the Pyles case. "A great many members of my staff have a different philosophy than Mr. vanden Heuvel," he asserted proudly. "They don't approve of a man who urges prison guards to defy the courts."

Hogan beat vanden Heuvel handily in the Democratic primary, but prior to the November elections he suffered a stroke the seriousness of which was not made public until it was too late for Hogan's name to be withdrawn and for a new candidate to be chosen, so, even though he was still seriously ill, he began his ninth term.

On April 4, 1974, at the age of seventy-two, overtaken by cancer, he died in his sleep.

Timbuk and Sonni Pyles finally got their day in court and a sentence of fifteen years in prison.

Among those who crossed the Bridge of Sighs to face the music at the bar with me appearing for the people, the Pyles remain a vivid memory, but what I will always carry with me from that extraordinary episode is not just its humor and its pathos. What sticks with me is how the case was used by William vanden Heuvel for his partisan purposes and how easy it is for our legal system to be exploited for the sake of goals that sometimes have nothing to do with justice.

7 | CROSSROADS

AFTER FOUR YEARS in Hogan's office, an immense organization grappling daily with the enormous caseload that grew larger and larger and more and more complex, I decided it was time to make a move—homeward.

I was born in the Bronx, but when I was eight years old my family moved to Rockland County, geographically the smallest of the Empire State's counties outside the five that constitute New York City. With a population of about a quarter-million, it was at that time a picturesque stretch of scenic settlements on the cliffs of the Hudson between the city and West Point and an assortment of small towns nestled in the farmlands on the way to the Catskill Mountain resorts catering to a primarily Jewish clientele (and known as the Borscht Belt), where entertainers and comedians filled cool summer evenings with laughter.

While Rockland had changed considerably by the time I had earned my law degree and concluded my tenure with Frank Hogan, it still was made up of small, tightly knit communities that held out for me the promise of a more intimate relationship with the populace than I'd known as an assistant DA in New York City. So, when I became aware near the end of my four-year commitment to Hogan that there was a position open as the senior trial assistant to Robert Meehan, also a progressive and respected district attorney, I applied for it and was hired. The assignment began in 1972 and my admiration for Bob Meehan continues to this day on a personal as well as a professional basis.

There is a passage in the Sherlock Holmes story "The Copper Beeches" in which the sleuth of Baker Street is on his way to an investigation in the English hinterlands. After gazing thoughtfully through the train window, Holmes turns to his trusted companion Dr. Watson to say, "It is my belief, Watson, founded upon my experience, that the lowest and vilest alleys in London do not present a more dreadful record of sin than does the smiling and beautiful countryside. . . . But look at these lonely houses . . . Think of the deeds of hellish cruelty, the hidden wickedness which may go on, year out, year in, and none the wiser."

It certainly was a grim view of life in the suburbs of the Victorian Age, but unfortunately it turned out to be a fairly accurate prediction of the situation that began to grip many American suburban communities in the years following the second world war. Rockland County was no exception, but my first major case turned out to be one that did not fit the usual description of crime.

The case involved a tragedy for the community.

Soon after I joined the Rockland DA's office, Joseph Larkin, a fireman in New York City who was a resident of Stony Point and a part-time bus driver for Nyack schools, was charged with criminally negligent homicide in the crash of his bus and a train in which five high school students had been killed and many injured. It was a widely held belief that Larkin had been rushing to finish his morning route in order to comply with a New York City Fire Department regulation regarding the number of hours a New York City fireman could work on a second job before reporting for duty at a firehouse.

Because of the age of the victims and because the case

involved a New York City fireman, a great deal of media attention surrounded the case from the start, and when it came to trial the press of Rockland, adjoining counties, and New York City descended on the staid old courthouse in New City expecting to hear heartbreaking testimony by survivors of the crash. They weren't disappointed. "I yelled very loudly for Mr. Larkin to stop," sobbed fifteen-year-old Paul Pilgrim, who had been seated at the front of the bus that morning as Larkin allegedly raced to get through a crossing in advance of a very long freight train that would have taken a great deal of time passing.

" 'Please don't let me die,' " screamed Kathy Hart as she'd seen the train bearing down on the bus, according to her tearful testimony in the witness chair. A fourth-grader, John Fitzgerald, who was not on the bus but lived near the crossing, saw the collision from his bedroom. "I heard the train whistle and went to the window," the ten-year-old testified, "and I saw the bus at the top of the hill. It didn't stop. It looked like it went faster," he told the hushed courtroom. "Then the train hit the bus."

Two shaken Penn Central crewmen took the stand. Helpless to avoid the crash, said engineer Charles Carpenter, his freight train ran "right into the bus, right into dead center." Brakeman John S. Cary testified that after the train slammed into the bus and cut it in two, "The children were getting up out of their seats and screaming. They were throwing their hands up and trying to get away from the bus."

Larkin denied that he had not stopped the bus at the rail crossing and insisted that he hadn't been speeding. "Are you saying all the witnesses were mistaken?" I asked.

"Yes," he replied.

Thirty hours after beginning deliberations, the jury had

found the witnesses had told the truth and declared Larkin guilty.

"This is not a day of joy on the part of the District Attorney's office, not a time for happiness," I said. "Five children have died. Five children have been plucked away in the prime of their lives. Five families are still in mourning. Other children were maimed and are still injured. Society has been served. Justice has been done."

As senior trial assistant to District Attorney Meehan I handled many cases in the first months on the job: drug violations, fraud, escape from jail, gambling, the numbers racket, child molestation, drunken driving, negligent homicide as a result of drunk driving, and the deaths of two young Orangetown police officers—Michael Kennedy and Thomas Reedy—victims of a drunken hit-and-run accident. All of these were during my first year on the job, between the fall of 1972 and October 31, 1973, when District Attorney Meehan named me chief assistant district attorney.

This promotion added to my responsibilities the task of administration of the district attorney's office but left in my hands the duties I had been discharging as senior trial assistant. At the top of my pile of pending cases at that time was the murder of Byron Stout, which would lead me into Rockland's closeted and secretive world of homosexuality and deep into the heart of a most bizarre, sinister, and dangerous clan of criminals—the Zada family.

8 | THE FAMILY THAT PREYS TOGETHER

MRS. GWENNE HARD was worried. For four days she had not heard from her half-brother, Byron Stout, whom everyone called Jerry. She'd last been in touch with him on July 24, 1973, and he had never before let so much time go by without contacting her, usually by phone because she lived in Tomkins Cove and he had an apartment in the Regency Village complex in Monsey. His was quite a nice apartment decorated sumptuously and sprinkled with the antiques Jerry adored and knew so much about. If he had been planning to go away, he would have told her that the apartment would be unoccupied. Prompted by her concern, she telephoned but got a constant busy signal. Asking the telephone company to check the line, she was informed that no one was talking on the line. Turning to her son, Michael, she said, "I think we'd better go down to Monsey and check Jerry's apartment."

When Jerry didn't answer the door, Mrs. Hard's worry became apprehension and she urgently sought the help of the superintendent of the apartments. Using his passkey and opening the door, the super felt a rush of hot stale air, smelled a sickening odor that could only be rotting flesh, and heard the buzzing of hundreds of swarming flies coming from the bedroom.

One glance at the bloated and maggot-infested corpse

inside the reeking and putrescent room on that sweltering July afternoon sent the nauseated super rushing to call the police.

At the time I also lived at the Regency Village Apartments, a development of garden-style apartments occupied mostly by middle-class families, so when I was contacted by the police who'd been called to Stout's apartment, I was able to walk to the scene of the crime. By contrast to the other apartments in the complex, his was lavishly and opulently furnished. I was astonished at the difference between his style of living and that of his neighbors.

Entering the bedroom I found splayed on the floor at the foot of the bed the grotesque remains of a man who appeared to be in his late forties with a neatly trimmed beard, attired in a red terrycloth robe, blue socks, and black shoes and with a towel draped around his neck.

The first person from the medical examiner's office at the scene was the assistant ME, Dr. Burton Allyn, but it was the ME himself, Dr. Frederick Zugibe, who performed the autopsy and determined that Stout had been shot three times in the head and had been dead for four days.

There was no evidence of forced entry, indicating that Stout probably knew and had admitted his killer. It was obvious that the lushly and expensively furnished apartment had been thoroughly ransacked, but the only item his devastated sister could say with certainty was missing was a large and rather gaudy ring that looked like "a diamond in the middle of a bowl of fruit salad." Jerry was never without it, she said.

A dance instructor who had made no attempt to hide his homosexuality, Stout had been a flashy person who frequented gay bars and exhibited little concern about the character of the young men who attracted him or showed an interest in him.

The names of many of those men were listed in a small telephone book found in the bedroom, and police investigators led by Detective Eddie O'Neill began checking them out.

Listed, too, and checked were bars Stout frequented, some of them known to be gay hangouts.

A straight bar he patronized was Chic-N-Charlie's, an establishment with a primarily black clientele on Franklin Street in Nyack, an area that had fallen on hard times and stood in sharp contrast to the rest of the village.

Nyack was one of several old communities that form a necklace connected by US Route 9W on the west side of the Hudson, one of the most scenic and historic rivers in the United States, along which plaques and markers note where General George Washington headquartered and Benedict Arnold plotted the surrender of West Point to Major John André and where the British agent had been tried and hanged. Grand, elegant, vintage houses perched on the brims of steep hills and offered breathtaking river panoramas to which the West Shore Division of the New York Central Railroad's trains had once whisked well-heeled passengers from the heat, crowding, and noise of the city to Nyack's palaces overlooking the water.

Elaborately Victorian, built in an age of low taxes and conspicuous consumption, many remain, including one belonging to Helen Hayes, the First Lady of the American Theater, who came to settle in Nyack in its halcyon days when she was the young belle of Broadway married to the playwright Charles MacArthur. The lively couple held open house for theatrical and literary members of the "Smart Set" who were apt to exclaim "Let's get away from it all," although perhaps not, as the pop song of that title suggested, by taking a kayak to Nyack when Route 9W was available . . . and the New York Central!

Because of his interest in antiques, Nyack with its old things and shops that sold them was one of Jerry Stout's favorite places. For the companionship of gay bars he visited the Come-back in nearby Piermont and Mr. G's in Rockland Lake, where two friends of Jerry's were employed—Francis Finnerty as manager and George Bickman as a bartender.

At Mr. G's on July first, Jerry was introduced to a smoky-eyed and swarthily handsome youth. Radiating a subtle air of danger with looks that evoked images of exotic foreign places, the boy, like a character in an old Bogart film, appealed to Jerry's sense of theater and adventure. His name was Samir Zada; Jerry wrote it down along with a phone number and gave Samir his address and number in return.

"Watch out for Zada," whispered Dennis Lyons, a twenty-one-year-old friend of Jerry's who sported unisex outfits. Lyons had known Samir Zada as long as he'd known Jerry—about two years. "Zada's a troublemaker," he warned. "Stay away from that guy. He's bad news."

With a wave of the hand wearing the ring, Jerry dismissed the advice.

A few weeks later he was dead.

What did we know? Not a lot. Robbery seemed to have been the motive, but there was no break-in. All the signs were that Stout admitted whoever killed him to his apartment. It seemed to me that the solution to this killing was going to come from someone who was a familiar face in the gay community.

So far, Detective Eddie O'Neill was not having much success checking the names in Jerry Stout's phone book, although it was possible that because of extensive coverage of the murder in the press and the vicious nature of the crime friends of the victim who otherwise might have stepped forward to assist in the investigation had been frightened into silence. Consequently, it was going to require old-fashioned legwork to interview those listed in Stout's book and visiting bars to talk to customers who might have known him and to the employees of those establishments.

At Mr. G's, Francis Finnerty said, yes, Jerry Stout had been a frequent customer. They were friends. Had he ever been concerned about some of those Jerry socialized with at the bar?

"Yes."

A fellow named Zada seemed a little unsavory, Finnerty said. In fact, there had been a genuine fear of trouble the first time Zada had come into Mr. G's. It was the first of July and Zada had come in with a few other young men who immediately spread out through the establishment rather than staying together as a group. The bartender, George Bickman, became so concerned he'd alerted Finnerty; however, there had been no trouble. That was the night Jerry first met Zada, Finnerty said, and he'd seen them together one other time—mid-July, he believed.

On that first occasion when Zada came in and the bartender had become apprehensive, how many others came with him?

Three, said Finnerty.

Did he know them?

No.

Was there anyone else in Mr. G's that night who might have seen Stout and Zada together?

"Yes."

"Who?"

"Kissy."

"Kissy?"

"Thomas Nicoll. Everyone calls him Kissy."

A resident of Orangeburg, thirty years old and employed as a medical secretary at Rockland State Hospital, Nicoll was not surprised at being interviewed about the murder of Jerry Stout. He and Jerry were very close friends, he said, and had been together very often.

"Do you also know Samir Zada?"

"Yes, I do."

"How long have you known him?"

"About two years. I met him at the Page 7 bar in Sparkill."

"Do you know Zada well?"

"I know Sammy very well."

"Sammy?"

"Samir Zada. Sometimes he's called Sammy. The fact is, I have been to bed with him."

"Did Stout and Zada know each other?"

"Of course. I introduced them. They exchanged numbers."

The obvious question was "Is Samir Zada's name in Jerry Stout's book?"

"It might have been," said Eddie disgustedly as he tossed the book onto my desk, "only we'll never know."

Picking up the book and opening it, I saw that the pages X through Z had been ripped out.

In my files, however, there was plenty of information in folders labeled *Z for Zada*.

When Samir Zada moved into South Nyack in the 1960s with his father, Baker, of Turkish birth, and Baker's Jordanian wife Bahrieh, their daughter Samira, and their two other sons Nazar and Amer, I was still in law school and the youngest of the sons, Amer, was five years old.

Over the next decade, Amer was to witness not his

immigrant family's realization of the American Dream but a nightmare of burglary, robbery, sexual abuse, and assault.

First to stray beyond the limits of the law was the father himself. On March 13, 1967, Baker took a Marlin .30–30 rifle, loaded it, and shot it at George S. Writer, Jr., a lawyer and the justice of the peace in the town of Orangetown, who had gone to Zada's house with clients regarding a boundary dispute. In an outburst of anger, Zada fired on them and wounded Writer. When police officer Harry Nolan heard the shots and rushed to investigate, he was also shot at and wounded. For these attacks Zada was arrested, tried, and sentenced to a year in jail.

On December 11, 1969, the father was arrested again, this time for assaulting New York State parole officer Joseph Barnwell when Barnwell sought to inquire about an allegation of sexual molestation. Angered by the direction the interview was taking, Baker grabbed a pancake skillet and started flailing it at Barnwell and the Nyack police officer who'd accompanied him, Timothy O'Shea. For this, the Zada patriarch received a sentence of ten months in the county jail.

Now, in July 1973, our investigation into the Stout murder had dredged up Baker's second son, Samir.

"The family that preys together," I thought as Detective O'Neill headed out on his way to Nyack to look into who, outside his charming family, Samir Zada spent time with.

Three names surfaced quickly:

Frederick Gensel, Jr., an eighteen-year-old white resident of South Nyack who was hooked on heroin and had a reputation for doing strange things such as eating a combination of spaghetti and cantaloupe, devouring meatball and banana sandwiches, chewing glass, eating worms, and carrying around snakes and lizards. Perhaps his most bizarre behavior was his cruel habit of catching cats, tying their tails together, and tossing them onto the wires of telephone poles and then watching them claw at each other. It was also rumored on the streets that he'd once beaten up a mentally retarded gay man.

Raphael (Ralph) Cortez, a close friend of Gensel, a known druggie and all-around miscreant and ex-convict who hadn't been seen by his friends lately and who seemed to have skipped town since the Stout murder hit the papers.

Chet Swann, twenty-six, a black resident of South Nyack who cruised around Rockland County in his prized green convertible '65 Pontiac.

On August 2 William Chester Swann was very close to coming unglued. He knew Samir Zada from way back—some ten years since Samir had moved to South Nyack with his family.

Theirs was a street friendship cemented by mutual interests in cars and drugs.

Cortez he had known since high school.

He'd known Fred Gensel only a few months.

Now he wished he'd never met any of them.

Playing over and over in his head like a stuck record as he tooled around town in his treasured Pontiac was what they'd done eight days before.

He'd left his job at Rockland State Hospital at a quarter before midnight on July 24 and driven the Pontiac to Franklin and Depew, parked, and gone into Chic-N-Charlie's.

Inside he found his buddies; Samir asked him to give them a ride to Spring Valley to the apartment of a man named Jerry because he wanted to get a diamond ring.

"I'll cut off the mother-fucking faggot's fingers to get it," Samir vowed.

• • •

In bits and pieces that night came back to Chet. Flashes of tormented memory. The Regency Apartments. Samir saying that he and Ralph would go upstairs and for him and Freddy to wait in the car. They'd waited. Fifteen minutes, maybe. Then Samir came back and Samir was waving his hand in glory. On it sparkled a ring with a big diamond in it. Samir laughed, "I told you I would cut off the mother-fucking faggot's finger, didn't I?" Then he laughed louder, draped an arm around Chet's shoulder and said, "I'm just kidding. Come up to this guy's apartment and look around."

Fabulous, Chet thought as he went in. The living room was pink and it had a fireplace—a false fireplace—with golden seahorses on it. The room was full of antiques. There were two love seats with a coffee table between and on the table was a pile of homosexual books.

"Let's take the stereo," Samir said.

"Not in my car," Chet said nervously.

They'd argued but the stereo stayed.

The bedroom was a mess, torn up and ransacked.

A man in a red terrycloth robe was lying on the floor and mumbling something about paying two hundred dollars for his life.

Silly thing to say, Chet thought, since no one was going to kill him!

Turning to leave the bedroom, he saw a closet crammed with beautiful shirts and grabbed one, green and gold, then went out to the living room again and waited with Freddy. Then out of the bedroom came Ralph and the three of them stood shooting the breeze and eyeballing the room for things to steal until Samir came out with a notebook in his hand. In it was a page that had Samir's name and number on it. "I found it," Samir said triumphantly as he ripped out the page and turned to go back to the bedroom.

Ralph whispered, "He's going to ice the mother-fucking faggot."

Samir closed the bedroom door.

Bang . . . bang-bang.

The bedroom door opened.

Samir stepped out. "I killed that mother-fucker."

On August 2, with the memory of the murder eating at him, Chet looked into the rear-view mirror of his Pontiac and saw cops. Plainclothes in an unmarked car. Right behind him. Eight of them, at least.

They signaled him to stop.

Pulling over and waiting for them, he knew he was going to spill everything.

I asked Samir, "Did you really kill that guy?" and he said, "I killed the mother-fucker." On the way down the Thruway I looked in the back seat of the car and I saw a gun that was down in Samir's belt. Back at Chic-N-Charlie's Samir handed us six dollars apiece and said, "All that the little faggot had was twenty-six dollars." But Samir had the ring and said he was going to sell it at Barrett's Antique Store in Nyack and would let us know how much he got for it.

The following Saturday on the corner in front of Perry's newsstand in Nyack, Ralph and myself we met a Jamaican guy and sold the gun from the Stout thing to him for forty bucks.

But there was more to tell.

A second murder, but this was one he'd only heard about. He hadn't been involved in this murder, only heard about it from the ones who did it—Samir Zada, Ralph Cortez, and Fred Gensel.

This was several days before Jerry Stout was killed. The man they killed was Christian Gunther, who was a plumber in Congers, New York. They went to his house around ten o'clock on a Saturday night to rob him and Samir lured him out of the house by telling Gunther he had a leaky faucet that he wanted Gunther to fix. When they got him outside they forced him into the trunk of their car and took him up into the mountains, but when they stopped, somehow Gunther got of the trunk and he ran away. Samir went after him. Gunther had a hammer or something in his hand and there was a struggle. Samir got hit on the head and that's when they shot him. Samir and Ralph were there when he got shot. Fred Gensel wasn't there. They'd sent Fred to turn the car around. They ditched the car near Sparkill and called somebody to come and pick them up. They got about ninety dollars from Gunther. Later, Fred was worried because his father had worked for Gunther and after Gunther had been found the police were bothering him.

That same day Richard Ovens, a state police investigator, questioned Fred Gensel and in that process Gensel admitted his involvement in the events surrounding Gunther's murder. That afternoon he sat down with Ovens again, this time in the presence of Assistant DA Patrick Campbell.

They had been at Samir's house and decided to go to Gunther's to steal property. They hitchhiked to Congers and got a ride in a blue Ford truck from a short, skinny guy with a Russian name. While Samir and Ralph went to the house, he had waited near the garage. They were gone about fifteen minutes and then came out with Gunther. Ralph had a revolver with a short wooden handle that he'd gotten in a burglary the week before. They put Gunther in the trunk of Gunther's car and drove off. When they stopped in the mountains, Gunther got out of the trunk. Samir and Ralph ran after him. When they came back, Samir was holding his head. They left and got rid of the car and called for someone to come and get them in Sparkill. Mrs. Zada came and got them at the Comeback, a queer bar. A little later at the Tappan Zee Bar, Ralph said that they had shot Gunther.

A week later, Gensel said, he was troubled by the idea that Gunther's body had been left where he had been killed. That was not right, he believed. Someone ought to be told where the body was, so from a phone booth in New York he had phoned the police in Nyack and informed them where the body was.

On July 24 it was found lying face-up in a clump of bushes and tress along a narrow rock-strewn trail in the mountainous Blauvelt State Park. He had been shot to death.

Charles Purcell, who'd been with the New York State Police for twenty-two years and was now senior investigator based at the Stony Point Barracks, had been working on the Gunther "missing person" case. In the course of that investigation he had learned that Frederick Gensel, Sr., had been an employee of Gunther's. Aware that Fred Gensel, Jr., had been the object of police attention in the past, it seemed a good idea to interview the son concerning the murder of his father's former employer. To inquire as to where might Fred be found, he sought out a known friend of the son—a young man named Samir Zada.

Samir told Purcell that on the evening of July 14 Fred Gensel had come over to his house around seven-thirty and they'd been together until around three in the morning, mostly out on a drinking spree, but they'd never left Nyack.

Now, on August 2, Purcell knew that had been a lie.

Questioned about the Stout and Gunther homicides, Zada

vehemently denied being involved in them. Nevertheless, he was arrested and charged.

Housed together in the Rockland County Jail, Samir and Gensel talked, but what Samir was saying wasn't sitting well with Freddy. He was so upset he asked to talk to the police.

Samir asked me if I had said anything to the police and I said, "No," and he said that he had. He said that he told them that I came in the bar that night and told him to give me a cover by saying that I was with him. He said that if worse comes to worse I'm going to say that Chet was a junkie and came to me and sold me the ring and that I in turn sold it to the jewelry store and that if I did say anything I would end up like Stout.

Because of Chet Swann's pangs of conscience in the Stout murder and Gensel's admissions in both the Stout and Gunther killings we suddenly had obtained compelling cases against Samir Zada and the expressed willingness of Swann and Gensel to cooperate with us in the prosecution of Zada and Cortez.

We did not have the murder weapon in either case, but a stroke of luck dropped the Stout gun into our laps. On August 3, in the village of Nyack, Patrolman Barry Edward Shanahan responded to a report of a fight at Franklin and Depew and arrested Horace Lloyd Allen for possession of a loaded .22-caliber Rohm revolver, model RG-14. Ballistics examination and the test firing of the weapon determined that it had been used to kill Jerry Stout. While at first claiming that the gun had been given to him by a boy who'd said he'd found it, Allen later admitted that he'd bought the gun from Ralph Cortez.

The next piece of evidence in the growing case against

Zada surfaced on August 10 at Barrett Antiques in Nyack when the store manager, Burton Stern, was asked by police about a ring Stern had bought on July 27. It had been a rather flashy ring, Stern remembered. Virtually worthless, it had been broken up and no longer existed, except as separate parts, its only value being in the small amount of gold in its setting. The centerpiece of the ring, which looked like an valuable diamond, was really a fake. Total value of the ring? Twenty dollars. Locating the fragments, Stern handed them over to the police.

With the ring, the gun, and witnesses, we convened a grand jury and sought the indictments of Zada and Cortez.

A month later, Cortez was spotted in a telephone booth in Virginia Beach, Virginia.

Arrested by the FBI on warrants charging him with murder, kidnapping, and robbery, he soon made statements to detectives from the New York State Police, a deputy sheriff of Rockland County, and Assistant District Attorney Patrick Campbell in which he confessed to his involvement in the murders of Stout and Gunther but insisted that Samir Zada had been the triggerman both times. Zada killed them, he said, because he was afraid they would identify him as one of those who'd robbed him.

The two murders had gotten enormous attention in the press and the sensational nature of the impending trials was already being trumpeted, so much so that the question was raised by the defendants as to whether they could get a fair trial in Rockland. Eventually the decision was made by the appellate court to hold the first of the trials, the Stout homicide, in Putnam County.

The old wooden courthouse in picturesque Carmel, New York, faced a beautiful lake and presented a serene and tranquil contrast to the dark and horrible case of murder that was about to be tried within its walls. Going into the courthouse, I believed I had as strong a case as possible— the incriminating physical evidence and the corroborative testimony of witnesses who had participated in the crimes, that of Swann and Gensel.

As the trial opened, a guilty plea was made by one of the two people named in the Stout indictment—Ralph Cortez, who vowed he would testify that Zada pulled the trigger. In a green jacket and blue dungarees, Cortez stood before Putnam County Judge Frederick Dickinson and pleaded guilty to two counts of manslaughter, carrying a maximum of twenty-five years on each count, and was remanded to the Rockland County Jail to await sentencing, but at that point Cortez reneged on his word to become a witness against Zada. Claiming mental illness, he managed to avoid testifying and was sent for observation and evaluation to a state mental institution.

An indirect confirmation of Zada's guilt came our way as the trial was beginning. On Friday, May 3, with a pair of detectives I rushed over to the County Jail to talk to a convicted burglar, forger, and larcenist by the name of Terry Thompson, who'd had a conversation back in November with Samir Zada. "I said, 'Did you really kill the faggot in Spring Valley?'" said Thompson, "and he told me that he had knocked off a guy in Spring Valley but they didn't have proof. "All that they had was what Chet Swann had told them and he was a rat anyway and he wasn't in the same room at the time, anyway."

Ample proof we had, even without Cortez and Thompson, who I considered a highly impeachable witness, although Thompson's statement added one more brick to the structure of evidence that amounted to a sturdy edifice that neither the defense presented by Zada's attorney, Harry

Edelstein, nor denials of guilt spoken from the witness stand by Zada himself could shake.

The Putnam County jurors agreed and found Zada guilty.

Ahead of us now loomed the trial of Samir Zada for the murder of Christian Gunther, a crime for which Zada was bound to be convicted, I was sure, because the physical evidence and the testimony of Fred Gensel amounted to as overwhelmingly a convincing case as in the Stout trial.

That summer and fall of 1974 was also election time, and I was running for district attorney for the first time. This opportunity had been opened for me when Robert Meehan made a decision to seek the Democratic Party nomination for attorney general but lost his bid at the state convention to Robert Abrams, who went on to be elected in November.

In deciding to run for DA I appreciated that I was seeking to follow a man who had made significant contributions to the office of district attorney. In this, Bob had built on the work of his immediate predecessor, Morton Silberman, a highly respected attorney who later served as a revered justice of the state supreme court. Silberman had begun the process of modernization of the DA's office, which in the late 1960s was witnessing only the beginning of the complex law-and-order issues that would come to the fore in the years when Bob Meehan was DA and that would grow even more difficult in the latter years of the 1970s and into the 1980s.

In their years, Mort Silberman and Bob Meehan had seen a dramatic change in Rockland—from a quiet, out-of-the-way and rural area to a rapidly growing suburb of New York City. This transformation was given considerable impetus by the building of the Tappan Zee Bridge across the Hudson and the opening of the New York State Thruway, both of which made Rockland easily accessible at exactly the moment when the rush to suburbia was at its peak.

My decision to run for District Attorney was resisted by some Rockland Democrats who preferred another candidate, many of them apparently regarding me as too young or a carpetbagger from New York City despite that fact that I had grown up in Rockland and had lived there since I was eight years old, even while I had been working for Frank Hogan.

Other Democrats, led by Vincent Monte, the Democratic chairman in the town of Stony Point, and Ramapo Town Chairman Paul Traub, strongly encouraged my candidacy. They let it be known in no uncertain terms that we were prepared to go into a primary if necessary, a strategy that succeeded in my being nominated at the party's county convention.

My opponent was Frank Barone, the county's public defender. Running on the Republican and Conservative tickets in a county that then was usually in the GOP column on election day, he made an issue of my age, pointing out that I was thirty years old while he was a mature fifty-one, offering an "a few gray hairs" platform. What I offered the voters, despite my youth, was my years of experience with Hogan and Meehan.

When you run for elective office for the first time and are not known, the matter of fund-raising is much like the situation of a man who decides to go into the business of selling insurance—you start with the people who know you: family and friends. To organize fund-raising I was fortunate in having the enthusiasm and energy of a friend and fellow lawyer who'd been a classmate at NYU Law School, Joseph Deutsch.

A low-budget operation, the campaign was largely a matter of traveling around the county to greet potential voters in the parking lot of supermarkets and shopping centers and handing out leaflets. In today's high-pressure politics it's called boosting name recognition. An important aspect of that, given our budget, was the use of 50,000 bumper stickers and the posting of signs. In the course of a few days, it seemed to me, the entire county and much of New York City was papered with my name on placards and automobile bumpers.

In addition to awaiting the decision of the electorate, I was awaiting the birth of our third child. Judy and I had decided to follow the Lamaze system for natural childbirth, but as the election campaign intensified I began missing classes and falling woefully behind in lessons. At last I was deemed a failure by the instructor. Possibly the only prospective father in the system to flunk the course, I was nevertheless allowed to be present for the birth of our daughter on October 25, ten days before the election, although I was helpless to assist.

When the votes were counted, I had won 60 percent of them and meant every word of it when I told my supporters at the victory celebration on election night, "It's the culmination of a dream, to be District Attorney of Rockland County. I am tremendously elated."

Neither all that publicity nor being elected District Attorney completely erased my youthful image, however, as I learned shortly after taking office. While attending a conference of DAs, I was approached beside the hotel swimming pool by the wife of a DA from a neighboring county who asked me to assist her in moving her lounge chair. I did so gladly. "Thank you so much," she said with a smile as she pressed a dollar into my palm. It was a tip! She thought I was the pool boy.

With the election over, I now faced the second trial of Samir Zada. Because I was assuming my new responsibilities, I assigned its prosecution to my able executive assistant district attorney, Peter Branti. As in the first trial, the appellate division transferred the venue of the second trial, this time to the court in Goshen in Orange County because publicity surrounding the first case had made it impossible to assure a fair trial at the site of the first trial, Putnam County.

A crucial and chilling moment of testimony came from Fred Gensel when he related the cold-blooded antics of Zada and Cortez after the three had returned to Zada's house following the Gunther murder. "I asked Raphael what had happened and he stood up and pointed his finger at Samir and went like this," Gensel testified, simulating a gun with his finger, "and Raphael said 'bang.' And Samir was standing up, too, and Samir grabbed his chest and was turning around like James Cagney in the movie. He fell on the ground and Raphael went up to him and put his foot on his chest and Samir whistled. Then we all started laughing."

After only forty-five minutes of deliberations, jurors returned a guilty verdict. It set Zada off into a raging tantrum that took three deputies to quell. At the same time his mother, sister, and younger brother, Amer, broke into sobs and wailing.

Only brother Nazar remained stoic and silent as Samir was dragged kicking and screaming from the courtroom to face sentences in the slaying of Jerry Stout and Christopher Gunther that promised to keep him behind bars until he was an old man.

The course of justice, however, is often full of twists and turns and downright bumpy, especially when the Zada family was involved.

Unexpectedly, nearly four years after the murders of Stout and Gunther and almost two years after Zada's conviction for the Gunther killing, a notice was filed with the County Clerk that a hearing would be sought to have Samir Zada's conviction overturned.

The basis for this action was an affidavit by Fred Gensel alleging that he had been pressured by the DA's office to lie in court. The lawyer taking this action on behalf of the Zadas was the controversial legal activist William Kunstler.

By June 1977 Kunstler had become world-famous for rallying to the defense of civil rights activists, antiwar radicals, and a mind-boggling assortment of convicts. Tall and lanky, with an ambling stride, he wore his graying hair long and bushy in the 1960s style but with his eyeglasses propped atop the mane as if stemming a tide. His clothing appeared, always, to be a carefully cultivated rumple.

Making no bones about what he was up to in the Zada case, he said, "I feel prosecutorial misconduct is rampant. It comes from an urge to triumph, personal ambition, or the power of being Mr. DA."

"One of Mr. Kunstler's biggest problems is that he stereotypes people all the time," I replied. "None of the DAs I know has any desire to put innocent people behind bars. Statements like that fit into his ludicrous quest for fanfare. If he had his way, nobody goes to jail and we have anarchy."

So what was going on?

The Zada family was at work in the form of brother Nazar making threats against Freddy Gensel in an attempt to spring Samir. In short, he was tampering with a witness, but the ploy of strong-arming ultimately failed. When an emboldened Freddy Gensel met with him at Rockland State Park to discuss Nazar's threatening demand that Gensel recant his testimony, Gensel was fitted with a concealed tape recorder provided by my office, and on the strength of that evidence Nazar Zada was arrested at his home in New York City for obstructing justice.

In the hearing in Orange County Court that Kunstler had

demanded in his attempt to overturn the case, Gensel defiantly stood by his previous testimony and swore that the only reason he had changed his story was out of fear of the Zada family.

Kunstler howled, "This is a Nyack Watergate!"

Meanwhile, Nazar Zada was up to new tricks— promotion of prostitution of teenage Rockland girls in a Queens prostitution operation. On information from our office, the Queens authorities sought Nazar's indictment and also charged him with weapons possession. Informed of Nazar's troubles, Kunstler reared back his leonine head to snort, "The whole thing is retaliation." The skirmishing ended in August 1978 when J. Irwin Shapiro, associate justice of the appellate division of the state supreme court, denied Kunstler's appeal, which had been based on a ludicrous charge of prosecutorial misconduct.

Ironically, in June 1980, there would be a reversal of the verdict based upon an appeal by attorney Richard N. Gardella of Harrison, New York. The appellate division found that a technical legal error had been made by the trial judge in his charge to the jury about Zada's possession of Stout's ring. This did not affect the verdict and sentence in the Gunther case.

Since the election and while the second Zada trial was going on, I had been occupied with the administrative aspects of my new job. With the cooperation of the Rockland County legislature, I was able to expand all staff legal positions onto a full-time basis and enhance the investigative units with additional career police detectives. At the same time, I established a Youth Counsel Bureau designed to require first-time youthful offenders to provide useful community service for misdemeanor crimes, a Narcotics Task Force to tackle the growing drug problem and its associated crimes, a Crime Victims Assistance Bureau, the

Career Criminal Offense Bureau to target repeat offenders and to focus all local criminal justice forces on the individuals responsible for repeated serious crimes, and a Rape Prosecution Unit staffed by female assistant district attorneys and detectives.

Because of this streamlining of the processes within the DA's office, I was able to devote more of my time and efforts to major prosecutions, either prosecuting cases myself or being intimately involved in the cases being handled by others.

One of that caliber came my way in June 1979. This time it was Amer, the youngest of the Zada crime clan.

Jangled awake by the phone before dawn on Friday, June 15, I was informed that Amer was in custody for murder after being caught literally with his pants down in the act of sodomizing the savagely stabbed body of a girl. The normal reaction of a human being hearing such an allegation is disgust and revulsion, and I felt those emotions, but a DA must set aside such feelings and inquire about evidence, witnesses, whether the crime scene is being properly secured, and if the constitutional rights of the person in custody are being protected.

Accompanied by Bill Frank, who was then chief assistant DA, I arrived at the crime scene and found the investigation well in hand. It had begun at 4:48 A.M. when the Nyack police received information from anonymous callers reporting that they'd heard a woman screaming in the parking lot of the Windjammer restaurant overlooking the Hudson River at the foot of Main Street.

Rushing to investigate with Patrolman James Thurston, Nyack police officer John McCord found a nude black girl lying face down in the litter behind a green dumpster. Atop her with his pants down and his penis erect and trying to sodomize her was a young man. Dragged off the girl, he struggled with McCord and Thurston until they managed to handcuff him and Thurston got him into his police car.

As Thurston was about to search the youth, McCord called out for Thurston's assistance.

After the struggle with the suspect, McCord had turned to the victim. Fearing that she might be dead, he looked for her pulse. In his own winded and shaken condition that had resulted from the struggle with the suspect, he'd been unable to detect a sign of life in the girl, so he wanted Thurston to try.

Thurston found none, meaning the youth he had left in the car was likely to be charged with murder.

Removed to the Nyack police station, Amer was claiming that he had been trying to help her when he was arrested.

No weapon was found on him, but there were spots on his clothing and underwear that appeared to be blood.

Searching for the murder weapon within a wide area marked by orange road cones, teams were scouring a wooded area near the dumpster, storm sewers, and the waterfront. A knife seemed the logical thing to look for. Also at the scene were a medical examiner, Nyack police chief Thomas Coffey, Detective Art Keenan of the Nyack police, chief investigator Ed McElory, Detective Jim Stewart of my staff, and members of the Bureau of Criminal Identification. A county helicopter whirled above the scene, where floodlamps created a harsh false dawn in the litter-strewn parking lot and behind the dumpsters reeking with garbage where the victim lay.

She was Shirley Smith, seventeen years of age, who lived with her mother, Dorothy, on Remsen Street in South Nyack. Popular and fun-loving, never in any trouble, she had worked as a cleaning woman at the Windjammer.

Already a fair amount of useful evidence had been gathered. A brown work shoe without laces believed to belong to the suspect and bearing possible bloodstains. Amer's blue Chevrolet sedan parked in the northeast corner of the lot. Scuff marks and stains on the ground, possibly the result of the girl being dragged from the car to a narrow area between the dumpster and a chain-link fence that separated the lot from the woods.

At the station, Amer Zada told me and Bill Frank that a terrible mistake had been made. That night, he said, he'd had a bit of trouble with his car and had stopped to look at it. Suddenly, he heard a girl screaming for help and he'd run to assist her.

After that is when the mistake had been made, he said. It was when the police grabbed him that an erroneous assumption had been made. He'd not been doing anything to the girl except helping her. The stain on his shoe that looked like blood? It could be blood but it was his. He'd hurt his foot a while back.

No matter how often he was questioned, Amer stuck to his version of the events in that parking lot. He was trying to help that girl—pure and simple—and his being arrested and charged with killing her was a big mistake by the police.

The Zada family echoed his story. This is a good boy, they cried. Amer is not a criminal. Amer is a youth who is full of promise. "He's a lovable little boy," sobbed Amer's sister Samira. "He's a baby." A spoiled baby, though, she admitted. "He got anything he wanted from any of us."

Among the things he got was a Chevrolet Camaro and enrollment at a private military academy in Cornwall, but it didn't work out. He dropped out of school and then wrecked the Camaro. Now he was working in construction and driving a Chevy belonging to his mother.

That's where Amer had been that night, Samira said—out in the car. He'd left the house because there had been trouble in the family. There was a bad fight between him and his father, Baker Zada. "My father beat him," Samira said, weeping. "He threw a chair at him and missed and threw some other things at him and then he threw Amer out of the house and told him not to come home."

It was for that reason that Amer was out in the Chevy. When it broke down, he called a friend of his who had a tow truck in Congers and asked that friend to come help him. While waiting, he heard a girl call for help and, being a good boy, he rushed to her aid.

That was the truth, the Zada family swore.

Our version differed. There may have been fighting. There was some driving around in the car, but when it broke down, Amer didn't hear a cry for help and rush to Shirley's aid. He'd heard no such outcry. He saw Shirley. He knew her and asked her if she wanted to smoke some pot. He wanted sex with her and to get it he attacked her. She ran and he chased her, plunging a knife into her again and again. Even after she fell with stab wounds all over her body, even in her vagina, he still craved sex with her.

Publicly rallying to the defense of the baby of their family, the Zadas announced that they would pay a reward of $1000 to whoever stepped forward to back up their claim that someone else had killed the girl. "He's believed to be Haitian," Samira told the press, "and he's believed to be from around the area. He was seen near the dumpster and he was seen leaving. He was seen riding around with a young lady."

As we prepared to take the case before a grand jury, an exhaustive search of the crime scene including the use of metal detectors on land and scuba divers in the river still had not produced the murder weapon. But the case that we were preparing to take to a grand jury on Monday, June 18, was so strong and compelling that the knife would have been just a bonus.

On Friday came a call from the police.

The knife had been found.

Bill asked, "Where?"

"In the car."

"In Zada's car?"

"No. In the police car. It was under the seat."

It had been there since that brief moment when Patrolman Thurston had gone to assist Patrolman McCord in trying to find Shirley Smith's pulse and had been located in a stroke of luck by Sergeant Douglas MacDonnell. While suddenly applying brakes on a steep hill to avoid a collision, MacDonnell heard something slide from under the seat. Looking, he'd found a folded knife and what he surmised were bloodstains on it.

The car had been searched but the knife had been jammed deep beneath a seat. Only the jolt of MacDonnell's sudden stop dislodged it. How did it get there? "The theory is," said Bill, "that Zada had had the knife in the pocket of his dungarees and that somehow he managed, even in handcuffs, to get the knife out of the jeans and under the seat."

To further Amer's defense, the Zadas now turned to an old ally and, like the shaggy-maned lion he resembled, up from Manhattan stormed William Kunstler screaming "Frame-up!"

Questions were raised by him as to whether Zada, a Muslim, could get a fair trial from a Jewish prosecutor.

Because his parents were Jordanian and Turkish, Kunstler alleged, Amer had become the target of discrimination and he and his family "reflect all the tensions of the Third World people in America."

Astonished, I asked Bill Frank, "Is this case about the tensions of the Third World people in America?" Then, unsmiling and barely containing my outrage at Kunstler's patent nonsense, I said, "I was under the impression that this was a case of murder. The murder of a teenage *black* girl."

While the knife was important, the most telling evidence was in the fact that he'd been caught virtually naked with an erection on top of the dead naked girl. Bloodstains on Zada's clothing matched her blood type. Combined with his own implausible explanation, that evidence was more than sufficient to me and I sought his indictment on charges of murder, attempted sodomy, and sexual abuse.

On the day Shirley Smith was buried, Amer Zada was arraigned, pleading not guilty, and held without bail pending trail.

Two members of the Zada family would not be attending the proceedings. Samir was doing time for the Jerry Stout and Chris Gunther murders and Nazar had been found guilty in a federal court in Manhattan of selling heroin valued at $115,000 to federal undercover agents, for which he received fifteen years.

As we expected, William Kunstler's opening blast on behalf of his client was aimed at the knife. During a pretrial hearing he had argued, "There was some suspicious circumstances with this knife. It wasn't found for more than forty-eight hours and was eventually found in a police car, which really raises eyebrows with the people I talk to."

What's more, he stated, it was improper for Ken Gribetz or any member of his staff to prosecute Amer Zada while under investigation of charges of wrongdoing in the case of Samir Zada. "We have indisputable evidence that it happened," he said, adding that the proof soon would be sent to the office of Governor Hugh Carey.

In addition, he insisted as he addressed the judge, Amer

Zada could not get a fair trial in Rockland—a change of venue was in order.

Also, he said, because Amer Zada was a Muslim, there should not be any trial sessions on a Friday because that was the Muslim Sabbath.

There would be no objection from the people concerning not having Friday proceedings, said Bill Frank, but, "It's ironic that the death of Shirley Smith, that horrible, horrible stabbing, was committed on a Friday morning."

Although he was granted his request to have no sessions on Fridays, Kunstler failed in his bid to win a change of venue.

He also failed to have me or anyone else from my office disqualified but when Richard A. Brown, special counsel to Governor Carey declared that Carey would not interfere, Kunstler asserted that Carey was acting to protect me because the Governor was a Democrat and because my cousin, Judah Gribetz, had once been Carey's counsel. "The Brown thing wasn't completely unexpected," he said, "but I would think they would be a little more careful after Watergate."

This attempt by Kunstler to use his familiar confrontational tactic of "the best defense is a good offense" had again failed. His demagogic rhetoric convinced no one. Nor was anyone intimidated by his bluster. Unimpeded, the case moved to trial.

For technical reasons, the judge appointed to the case was Albert Rosenblatt of Putnam County, a brilliant jurist.

Immediately Kunstler took off after the knife, attacking the credibility of Joseph Lenti, a South Nyack grocer who testified that he'd sold the same kind of knife that was found in the police car to Amer Zada less than eight hours before Shirley Smith was stabbed to death. Lenti was a tainted witness, Kunstler suggested, alleging Lenti cut a deal to become a witness for the prosecution so he would get a lighter sentence on a federal narcotics charge. "You know as you sit here under oath that you have committed crimes for which you have not been prosecuted," Kunstler asserted.

Questioning Detective Art Keenan about testimony regarding bloodstains on the knife, he asked what would prevent Keenan from planting the evidence?

Keenan answered, "My conscience."

As to the story of how the knife was found? Unbelievable, Kunstler scoffed. It was impossible, he said, for any person with his hands cuffed behind his back in a police car to fish a knife from the pocket of his jeans and hide it under a seat.

Taking a deep breath and a brave risk, Bill Frank replied that it was not an impossible feat and that if the conditions were properly simulated the prosecution would demonstrate to the jury that it could be done. Officer Thurston would do it in the same car, dressed as Zada had been dressed, handcuffed and using the same knife—if Judge Rosenblatt would allow it.

The judge would, he declared.

The next day, with the jury gathered around the patrol car in the parking lot of the courthouse, Patrolman Thurston, barechested and shackled and with the murder weapon in his pocket, slid into the rear of the car.

It was a tense moment. If Thurston failed, the case would certainly be severely undermined and possibly lost.

In silence, the judge, jury, Zada, Kunstler, and Bill Frank waited and watched as Thurston twisted and writhed in the back of the car. Stretching his arms, he pushed grasping fingers into the pocket. Touching metal, he clasped the knife and wrenched it out. Flipping it to the floor, he gave it a solid kick and sent it under the seat. It took just twenty seconds, far less time than Zada had had to do it as Thurston and McCord were searching in vain for a spark of life in Shirley Smith.

Gone was William Kunstler's hope of deflecting the real evidence in the case by creating a scenario for a "frame-up." In the end, the jury did not believe Amer Zada's contention that he had only been trying to help the girl, not kill and rape her. Neither that disingenuous cry of innocence nor the attempts by Kunstler to instill ideas that a murder weapon had been contrived and planted, that the witnesses against Amer had been corrupted, that the cops were racists and that the entire case was nothing but a frame-up—none of it—washed.

The jury of eight women and four men believed in the knife and the witnesses and the testimony of McCord and Thurston that they'd apprehended Amer Zada with his pants down and his penis erect in the act of sodomizing the dead body of Shirley Smith and that Zada had murdered her.

In the courtroom as the jury rendered its verdict were Amer's girl friend, Bonnie Sue Salter, a teenage runaway who had been living with the Zadas since December 1978, and Amer's mother and sister.

"He grew up with the law," Samira sobbed, but what she was saying was not that Amer reached the age of eighteen as a respecter of the law. What she was saying was that when her brother was five years old his father was taken away to jail for shooting people. What she was saying was that Amer's brother Nazar had been in and out of jails all his life. What she was saying was that at the age of twelve Amer had seen his brother Samir sentenced to prison for two murders.

As Amer was being led out of court to await sentencing that would put him away for at least twenty-five years,

Samira raised her head and wailed, "They took Samir. They took Nazar. They took Amer. Who's next in line? The granddaughters?"

In the nighttime on March 1, 1980, amid tight security in the Rockland County Jail, Amer Zada donned a rented tuxedo and took a wife.

The brief civil ceremony was performed by county judge Harry Edelstein, who as a lawyer had defended Samir Zada.

The best man was William Kunstler.

The bride was Bonnie Sue Salter. "I love Amer," she said, "and I'll move close to him and visit him in prison wherever he goes."

Similar adoring statements about a man in prison had been expressed several months earlier by Maria Theresa Jerez.

She died regretting them.

9 | "SNAPPED"

"Car 538?"

"Car 538."

"Report of a possible assault, possible family dispute in progress at 88 Railroad Avenue."

"On my way," responded Officer John McCann of the Haverstraw Town Police.

Then the radio called another car and ordered Officer Paul Garrison to assist.

A third call went out to Sergeant Charles Ferris. McCann glanced at his watch and noted the time—10:48 P.M.

Moments later he thought there'd been a mistake. The white frame building was the Second Christian Church of the Good Shepherd; its windows were dark and the street in front was quiet. Then he saw a light in a window in the rear of the building at the end of an alley. Approaching it, he found a door open. Peering in, he saw a bloody living room. Drawing his service revolver, he waited for assistance and when Paul Garrison arrived they cautiously entered the small apartment.

To their right in a bedroom lay a woman writhing on the bed and moaning, drenched in blood from what appeared to be numerous stab wounds. Lying next to her was a man bleeding profusely from a deep gash in his right arm at the elbow. He appeared to be conscious.

While Garrison checked the rest of the apartment for other occupants, McCann turned to the woman but as he bent over her, she stopped breathing.

"Possible assault, possible family dispute" had now become "probable homicide."

Quickly to the apartment behind the church came all those whose business was murder—the Haverstraw police chief, William Ecroyd, the medical examiner, an ambulance crew, Thomas Brown and Ed Starkey of the Bureau of Criminal Identification, Haverstraw Detective Robert Freeman, and me.

Murders most often take place between people who know one another. It is usually unexpected, the result of circumstances, the violent culmination of a dispute, an outburst of pent-up anger or resentment or jealously or aggravation, the last straw.

The pattern had been set in the Bible when Cain slew his brother Abel and it has come down to modern times in the form of the domestic violence of child and spouse abuse that often crosses the line from battering and assault to homicide.

In this case, Moses Rodriguez slew Maria Theresa Jerez. Of that there was never any doubt, because Moses confessed.

They'd argued about a lot of things that irritated Moses and ones that irritated her. That day they'd had a battle over a letter he'd gotten and which he refused to let her see. That night they'd argued again after they'd attended services at the New Jerusalem Church in Haverstraw. They'd gone to church with Theresa's girlhood friend and next-door neighbor, Migdalia Oquendo. On their way home, Moses got out to cool down, buying himself some pineapple ice cream.

When he returned to Theresa's house he found Migdalia

there. Her presence upset him, but what also irritated him was Theresa's again insisting on knowing what was in the letter that he had refused to let her see and had angrily ripped up.

If they could be alone, he thought, they'd settle all this. If they could be by themselves, the trouble would disappear as it always did. They'd kiss and make up, as always, but when he demanded that Migdalia and her daughter Amy leave the house, Theresa turned angry and refused to send them away, refused to be alone with him, refused to go out with him, and refused to do what he wanted.

"She said that she wasn't going and I would have to kill her," he said. "She is always doing that to me."

"She was always saying things like that?" I asked.

"She was standing with her hands on her hips and she would spread her legs and tell me that I would have to kill her. I guess she said it one time too many."

A devout Christian, forty-seven-year-old Maria Theresa Jerez had been employed as an attendant at the Letchworth Village Department Center in nearby Theills and had volunteered to bring to the inmates of prisons the story of Jesus and the New Testament promise of salvation.

Ironically, it was a man I prosecuted for the murder of his lover who brought Theresa and Moses together. In 1973, Raphael Amengual, a former Haverstraw police officer, beat and choked his mistress, Linda Aragon, to death on Cheesecote Mountain in Haverstraw and got fifteen to life. Amengual turned to religion in prison and became a born-again Christian. He and Theresa had been childhood friends and now they shared an interest in religion. In the course of his religious activities in prison Ray Amengual introduced her to Rodriguez.

Theresa fell for him—hard. If she was not about to visit him, she wrote to him, telling him of her love, and that when he was released on September 19 she'd welcome him with open arms.

They were going to get married on December 29.

She was not the first woman to be in love with him. In 1969 in the Bronx, he'd been involved with another woman also named Maria—Maria Acevedo— and in the midst of an argument he had thrown the woman's two-year-old son, Wilson, out a fourth-floor window. Maria also went out the window, although whether she fell by accident, jumped, or was pushed out by Rodriguez hadn't been ascertained. For the death of the boy, he was arrested and charged with murder, but he did not stand trial. Instead, he was committed to Mattewan, a state institution for the criminally insane, because he'd been declared incompetent to stand trail at that time, meaning in the language of the law that the defendant lacks a capacity to understand the proceedings or assist in the defense.

After confinements in other state mental institutions, in 1976 he was ruled fit and pleaded guilty to manslaughter. Given a sentence of five to fifteen years in prison but with the 2361 days he'd spent in various mental institutions credited to the term, he began serving in the maximum security Clinton Prison at Dannemora.

In the course of his incarceration he was twice denied parole, but under New York law a convict could obtain a conditional release after he had served two-thirds of his sentence while maintaining a good record. Because he had spent more than ten years in mental institutions and prisons, he had put in the required time; when he applied for a conditional release he got it and was freed under a program designed for persons convicted of violent crimes.

Seventy-three days later he stabbed Theresa forty-one times.

Indicted and held on $150,000 bail, he was to be defended at trial by John F. McAlevey of New City.

The plea would be not guilty by virtue of mental disease or defect under the law, meaning that at the time of the crime the defendant as a result of mental disease or defect lacked substantial capacity to know or appreciate either the nature and consequences of such conduct or that such conduct was wrong. In ordinary language that is known as the insanity defense.

Rodriguez's use of it was neither the first nor the last time it would be invoked in a trial. Over the next two years it was to become a subject of controversy and heated debate in a pair of trials that were to receive far more attention than the Rodriguez case—Mark David Chapman's murder of the rock-and-roll star and former Beatle John Lennon in 1980 and the next year's attempted assassination of President Ronald Reagan by John W. Hinckley, Jr.

Probably the most controversial area of criminal law is the insanity defense, yet it is well rooted in Anglo-American jurisprudence. Although the law presumes that someone charged with a crime is sane, if it is shown that, as a result of mental disease or defect, he lacked substantial capacity to know or appreciate the nature of the consequences of his conduct or that such conduct was wrong, the law won't hold him accountable.

The insanity defense clearly has a place in the law but in my judgment the insanity defense is often abused and taken advantage of by individuals who earn a living from it. "Forensic psychiatrists and psychologists" are frequently no more than "hired guns" who produce testimony to fit almost any set of facts. Others offer opinions founded not upon what the law is but what they believe the law should be.

Nevertheless, such "expert testimony" is extremely influential when placed before juries and can readily produce not only an unjust conclusion to the case being tried but may well also result in the early release of an admitted killer. Thus it is a field that is clearly more art than science, and in light of the burgeoning number of alleged psychiatric disorders offered to explain criminal conduct, the courts must be very vigilant. And, in cases in which there is a finding of not guilty by reason of insanity, the individual must be confined to a secure facility for as long as it takes to ensure that the mental disease or defect will not surface in the same manner in the future. If it means that the individual must be confined for a period equivalent to the jail term he would have served had he been convicted, so be it. Our paramount concern should be the welfare and protection of society as a whole.

Was Rodriguez legally insane at the time he killed Maria Theresa Jerez? I did not believe so and I felt the evidence supported me. Migdalia Oquendo, Detective Freeman, Sergeant Ferris, and Officer McCann had stressed that they had observed nothing erratic or irrational in the behavior of the defendant after the murder of Theresa and that Moses Rodriguez appeared to understand what he had done and had appreciated the consequences of his act. He knew that what he'd done was wrong. He'd expressed sorrow and had attempted suicide.

If all that was true, why did Moses Rodriguez kill?

To answer that question I turned to a psychiatrist I had come to trust and admire, Dr. John Baer Train of New York City. A lifetime Fellow of the American Psychiatric Association and a member of the Board of Directors of the American Association of Psychoanalytic Physicians, his medical career had begun in 1938 and his private psychiatric practice had been established in 1945. Since 1962 he'd been active in the area of forensic psychiatry and had appeared many times in trials for the defense and for the prosecution.

In general, forensic psychiatry deals with questions of legal competence and responsibility. It includes the determination of whether the mental faculties of an individual were disturbed by mental illness to the degree that he would lack substantial capacity to know or appreciate the nature and consequences of his act or that it was wrong.

Seeking the answer to Moses Rodriguez's mental state, Dr. Train examined him on May 13, 1980. The interview lasted more than five hours and was conducted in the presence of Rodriguez's attorney, detectives from my office, and myself. In his report on the results of the interview and a review of Moses Rodriguez's medical and psychiatric report, it was Dr. Train's view that he met standards for culpability laid down in the law and had not been affected by mental disease or defect during the murder or thereafter.

"What is his state of mind?" I asked.

"He is unstable," said Dr. Train. "He has a poor frustration tolerance. He deals very poorly with aggression and he can be explosive."

There was much more about the dark and troubled recesses of Moses Rodriguez's mind, most of it rooted in a lack of a sufficient sense of self, the classic identity crisis.

"To overcome the insecurity and the anxieties that identity crisis can cause," explained Train, "he attempts to control everything in the environment to prove his macho, his masculinity. Deep down, he has a deep sense of masculinity or of individuality."

Driven by this underlying crisis of self, Moses Rodriguez was a man who was desperately attempting to better himself, Dr. Train went on. He was attending Brooklyn Community College in his efforts to improve himself. It was a hectic program and he was under great stress, wanting to do well and needing to do well. "At the same time he was very active in the church in this area and he would commute between Brooklyn and Rockland County and take an active part in the church. At this time he made a very close and important relationship with Mrs. Jerez. It was with her help that he was restoring some of his confidence. He recognized his need for her."

"If he needed her, why did he kill her?"

"The relationship with her was really a power struggle. She was an individual who had a mind. She was confident. She was an individual who did things and the power struggle was his wish to control, to dominate her for his own emotional needs."

That power struggle had reached a critical stage in their argument earlier in the day over the letter that Moses would not let Theresa see. That night there came a further test of wills over whether Oquendo would leave Theresa's apartment or stay and whether Theresa would go with him to his apartment.

"This was the ultimate challenge of his masculinity."

When she refused, he killed her.

"He knew what he was doing when he took the knife and stabbed her repeatedly?"

"He knew it was a knife and he knew he was using it against her and he knew that that was a human being and he was taking out his feelings on the very person whom he felt frustrated him. He wasn't taking it out on somebody else or some devil or some fantasy person. It was on his girlfriend Jerez herself."

This was not a case of blind and uncontrolled rage, Dr. Train said. "In this case, in the middle of the attack on Jerez, he stopped to warn Mrs. Oquendo not to interfere. He stops the attack, warns her, and then turns back to the attack."

In presenting his defense, John McAlevey describes Maria Theresa Jerez as a crutch. She broke that crutch over Moses Rodriguez's head, he said, "and he snapped, he flipped." To support that defense, McAlevey also presented psychiatric testimony. His psychiatrist, Dr. Gurston S. Goldin, stated that the primary issue confronting Rodriguez was "basically who's in control and who's not in control," a psychiatric profile of Rodriguez similar to that painted by Dr. Train but leading Dr. Goldin to a dramatically dissimilar conclusion.

It quickly became apparent that the differences between them went beyond their interpretation of the psychiatric record and the evidence in the case. As I listened to Dr. Goldin I suspected that he was not fully acquainted with all the facts concerning Rodriguez's behavior during the attack and after he had killed Theresa. And I had come to learn that in preparing a case that would focus almost exclusively on the mental state of the offender, every detail of his commission of the crime, every action taken by him before, during, and after the event were matters of enormous consequence because they permitted the observer almost to peer into his mind.

Thus, in cross-examining Dr. Goldin, I sought to explore in detail his knowledge of the facts, to demonstrate to the jury that his opinion was not based on all of the facts. Methodically I reviewed with Goldin testimony of the other witnesses concerning their contact with Rodriguez before, during, and after the crime—Moses' interrupting the act of stabbing to make a threat against Oquendo, his admissions to three police officers and Assistant DA Frank, his expressions of regret, his attempt at suicide, and his telling the police about the knife he had used. "This defendant knew this was a knife?" I asked.

"Yes."

"He knew that Maria Theresa Jerez was a human being?"

"Yes."

"And it is your testimony also that the defendant did not lack substantial capacity to know or appreciate the nature and the consequences of his conduct?"

"Yes."

All in all, the defense's expert had been helpful to my case, I believed, as he left the witness stand.

Experts in the witness chair can be very useful in discussing a defendant's mental state, but a jury being told the clinical facts is not the same as the jury seeing and hearing for themselves. I regarded it as extremely important for this jury to see and hear Rodriguez himself and was pleased that his lawyer put him on the stand because it allowed me to cross-examine.

Well-dressed to the point of being dapper, well-spoken and demonstrably intelligent, Rodriguez certainly did not look or sound like a crazy man as he answered my question concerning the contents of the letter he had refused to let Theresa see and that had caused them to argue. "I will not tell you, Mr. Gribetz, what was in the letter," he said. "It's a personal matter."

All through the cross-examination Rodriguez exhibited an ability to spar and fence in his answers to my questions. He was, I believed, engaging in the game of power and manipulation Dr. Train had described. "You have an excellent memory," I said to him. "What do you mean by excellent?" he replied. "And you're a bright, intelligent person?" I asked. "If you say so, thank you," he responded.

When I asked him if he knew what he was on trial for, he replied, "Second-degree murder and in this particular instance, the murder of my fiancée."

"There is nobody else that you know that killed Theresa Jerez, is there?"

"Not to the best of my knowledge, no."

Was it true that in the middle of stabbing Theresa he turned to Migdalia Oquendo and said, "You better get out or you'll get it, too?"

"I don't believe that she would say that I did if I didn't."

All of what he remembered about what happened, he said, was as if it were a dream or fog.

"You remember picking up the knife in a kitchen?"

"Yes, I testified to that."

"Now isn't it correct, sir, that you lost your temper in that apartment? You got angry and stabbed her?"

"That is not true," he replied. "If I ever lost my temper and I did so, it would be in a way that was outside my awareness because no matter how much I may fly off the handle and I may make a lot of noise verbally, I know that I am not capable of hurting anyone in my proper frame of mind and certainly not the thing I loved the most."

"Isn't it a fact that when you don't get your way that you lose your temper and people have to follow what you have to say?"

On that day when Theresa died he'd been angry, right? "Weren't you upset?"

"I was upset and angry and you're trying to make me angry and it's worked in part and I am upset today and people in the past and people will in the future upset me under different circumstances. I might take a nice poke at you."

"What about stabbing?"

"I would not stab you or anyone else, Mr. Gribetz."

Wasn't it a fact that Theresa had said to her friend Migdalia Oquendo and her daughter Amy that he had threatened to kill them and her?

"I did use that threat to manipulate Theresa."

"Aren't you trying to manipulate this jury at this very moment?"

"That's what you're trying to do. I'm trying to find the truth."

"Isn't it true, Moses, that this nonsensical defense of insanity is your only way of escaping?"

"It's not true, sir."

Insanity? Mental disease or defect? Had it been proved? No, I told the jury. What had been proved in this case was that Moses Rodriguez knew exactly what he was doing.

Was Rodriguez a well man? "Crime by nature involves deviant behavior. Obviously, anyone who stabs a woman forty-one times has committed an abnormal and bizarre act," I said to the five men and seven women who would decide Rodriguez's fate. "What we are concerned with is simply whether the defendant lacked as a result of mental disease or defect substantial capacity to know or appreciate either the nature or the consequences of his conduct or that such conduct was wrong."

On June 10 the jury returned a verdict of guilty of murder, a crime carrying a penalty of twenty-five years to life.

Judge William Zeck, a distinguished jurist who had been a prosecutor in the Nuremberg war crimes trials, set August 13 as the date for sentencing.

Early that morning in his jail cell, using his bedsheet to fashion a noose, Rodriguez hanged himself.

He left no note, so it was for others to explain why.

John McAlevey said, "He wanted to believe that he wasn't criminally responsible. He wanted that confirmed by a dispassionate group of people, and it crushed him when they didn't. You could come to the conclusion that rather than subject himself to the ordeal of standing before a judge and being reminded of a problem he couldn't face any more, he beat the system and took his own life."

Dr. Train differed. "I think it was purely an act of hostility toward the system."

When Moses Rodriguez murdered his fiancée he added his name to a long roster of tragic persons for whom love turned to criminality. For years, cases of murders in families had been crossing my desk with terrible regularity.

Tragically, many victims of violence in the home are reluctant to seek help through the criminal justice system. Most of the victims are women who, studies show, are often afraid to press charges against their husbands. Many blame themselves. Many are economically dependent on those who are abusing them and so they fear the consequences to themselves if they come forward seeking help. They are caught in a terrible dilemma that is a mixture of love and hate, a need for help and the fear of reaching out for it.

Illustrative was the case of Melanie Scandell.

The records of her tragedy show that, the third of four children, she began life in December 1961 in a broken home and grew up to find herself in similar circumstances— married and with two children but separated from her husband. Feeling overwhelmed and afraid of becoming an abusive mother, she sought psychiatric help but continued to struggle.

In September 1985, when she was a twenty-five-year-old, slightly overweight, brown-haired, green-eyed, troubled, restless, and unhappy woman with two small children and in the midst of getting a divorce, she met Herbert Scandell.

At twenty-five, Herbie was over six feet in height and heavy set with blue eyes, curly brown hair, thick brooding eyebrows, and a mustache. Born in Suffern, New York, he was the oldest of three sons. Because his mother and father each had previous marriages he had two half-brothers and a half-sister. He'd had a fairly typical childhood but had dropped out of school in the tenth grade because he was bored and preferred to work. He eventually became a truck driver making long-distance hauls for a moving company and liked the work, liked seeing the country.

A young man who got along well with her children and who said he was in love with Melanie, he moved in with her in November. Soon she was pregnant and looking forward to marrying him.

Like beauty, the cause of a troubled marriage is in the eyes of the beholder. In Herbie's, it was Melanie who was at fault. She started arguments over nothing. He chafed at her possessiveness, angry outbursts of unjustified jealousy, and accusations that he was unfaithful to her during those long trips. In arguments she would lose her temper and hit, punch, or throw things and yell and curse at him. She became a Jekyll and Hyde. When the baby came, she accused him of loving Herbie, Jr., more than her.

Melanie saw their difficulties stemming from him. He was the one who was possessive. He was always criticizing her for the way she dressed and accused her of choosing things that were immodest. He was always saying she was moody and very jealous. He was the one who got physical during fights.

Although she sought psychiatric counseling for herself and tried to get her husband to join her in seeking help, Melanie did not file complaints against him. Offered an opportunity to do so by two police officers after an incident in a West Haverstraw bar, she told the policemen she would take the option of going to family court but never did. Aware of the existence of shelters for battered wives, she chose not to turn to them for help. The police? Go to them, she believed, and Herbie would kill her.

Their families and friends knew about these marital problems but, as family and friends will, they either hoped to avoid involvement or took sides as the situation deteriorated to the point that separation and divorce seemed inevitable.

To this acrimony and strife was added another strain—an eviction from their home because the landlady decided she'd had enough trouble from her tenants, especially from Melanie, who she claimed was always screaming and yelling and using foul language.

Dispossessed temporarily until preparations were complete on another home, they moved in with Herbie's parents in West Haverstraw, where the troubles continued.

Frequently at the center of their disputes was the child of the marriage, little Herbie, only two months old. Herbie, Sr., was terribly worried about him. Recently the baby had had a bout of pneumonia for which Melanie was to blame, he believed. Then, on February 11, 1987, after one of their fights she had dashed out with the boy and sped off in a car, reaching dangerous speeds. Certain that she was trying to kill herself and Herbie, he took off after her in another car. Racing past her and swerving in front in an attempt to force her to slow down, his car went out of control and crashed. Escaping uninjured, he was taken into custody by police because he coincidentally fit the description of a wanted robber. Only by taking part in a humiliating police line-up was he cleared and released.

Two days later, early in the afternoon on Friday, February 13, he was in the living room of his parents' house and on the telephone seeking to arrange a second job so that he would not have to be away on long hauls as frequently. Hearing the front door open and seeing Melanie come in with her sister, Wendy Beam, and noticing that Melanie did not have little Herbie with her, he raced upstairs to their bedroom and demanded to know where the boy was.

"Don't worry," she retorted, "you'll never see him again."

With rising anger, he again asked, "Where's our son?"

"You're never going to see him again."

Furiously, he shouted, "Where's our son?"

"You're *never* going to see him again," she taunted.

Raging with frustration, he shoved her toward the bed.

"Never, never, never," she screamed as she fell.

Turning away as she screamed again and again that he was never going to see Herbie, he pulled open the door to a closet.

In the closet were several shotguns—some his father's, a few his own.

Grabbing one, at first he pushed her with it and she and her sister tried to wrench it from him as he was swinging it.

Flailing it, he hit her and then slammed the gun against the floor so hard that the stock broke. Pulling another from the closet, he swung it wildly but it also broke. A third came out of the closet and with it three bright red shotgun shells.

The first blast shattered the lower half of Melanie's head.

The second took away a good portion of Wendy's face.

The third shell was for himself but at that moment, up the stairs, screaming, rushed his mother. "Don't do it! Don't kill yourself," she cried, bursting into the room. "Don't!"

Shoving her aside, he dashed downstairs and outside to his car, the gun still in his hand.

Tossing it on the front seat, he got in the car and sped away.

Desk Officer Perry Masiello of the Haverstraw Police took the call from an hysterical Catherine Scandell and dispatched Detective Hector Soto to investigate her report of a shooting. Arriving at the same time was Sergeant Richard Rogers. Upstairs already were Sergeant Christopher Wohl, Sergeant Gary Myers, police officer Charles Miller, and paramedics Karen Stafford and Billy McNamara. Soon others came—familiar faces in another unfamiliar room. Among them were executive assistant district attorney John Edwards, Lieutenant Jim Stewart, and me.

Horribly wounded and unable to talk to the police in the house, Wendy Beam had been rushed to a hospital. Prospects for her survival were dim but it was hoped she would be able to make a dying declaration because she was the only person who knew precisely what had happened in that gory room—except Herbert Scandell.

He'd fled in a car, his mother told us, but she did not know if he was armed. Nor did she know where he might be going.

Nor did Scandell know where he was going in his Oldsmobile Cutlass but when he reached Western Highway in Blauvelt he noticed that the car was almost out of gas. At that moment he saw a woman getting out of a silver-gray Honda Civic. By the time he pulled into a snow-covered and icy driveway behind the car, the woman had gone into the house. What he had to do, he decided, was take the woman's car but, unfortunately, the keys were not in it. Quickly devising a plan to get the car, he went to the house, knocked on the door, and asked directions to an address he'd made up. The friendly woman complied and he thanked her, but a moment later he was back at the door telling her apologetically that now he was stuck in the snow and asking if she would be kind enough to help him by moving her car a bit so he could maneuver his. Again the woman agreed, scooping up a set of keys. Unexpectedly, she was now joined by a second woman who was just as helpful. Finally, quite politely, he said to them, "I'm afraid I'm going to have to take your car."

Indeed you will not, exclaimed the second woman.

"I've had it," he growled as he pulled the shotgun from his car. "I'm not fucking around with you any more." Brandishing the gun, he said, "I'll use this. I'm wanted."

Confronted with this obviously angry and desperate man, the women did not resist and when he was gone they promptly telephoned the police. "This is Sister Cecelia Lavin of the Church of St. Catherine," she said calmly. "Sister Alice Kirk and I have just been robbed of our car."

When he took their car, the Dominican College nuns told the police who came to investigate, he said they'd get back their car because he only needed it to get to the state line.

"In what direction did he go?"

"South on Western Highway."

Speeding down the Palisades Interstate Parkway into New Jersey, Scandell's intention was to get off before it connected with the George Washington Bridge spanning the Hudson between New Jersey and New York City but he missed the turn-off and was forced to head for the bridge and its toll gates.

It was bad luck, but even worse for him in his desperate dash to flee was the fact that in this day and age the criminal faces a sophisticated system of communication and cooperation between law enforcement agencies. In this case it required only moments for an alarm to be flashed to the police in New Jersey and to the police of the Port Authority of New York and New Jersey, including those on duty around the George Washington Bridge. Be on the lookout for a stolen silver-gray Honda, the alarm said, and be careful of the driver—wanted for murder in Rockland County and armed and dangerous.

Nobody knew the Palisades Interstate Parkway better than Robert Purrelli. A police officer for twenty-three years, he was assigned to the area around Alpine, New Jersey, and was just beginning the second eight hours of his double shift. As he heard the alarm on the radio, the Honda went whizzing past. Flooring the accelerator and flashing the lights of his patrol car, he took off in pursuit.

A quarter-mile from the bridge, Angel Mendez, who'd been with the Port Authority police for fifteen years, also heard the radio alarm and as he swung his patrol car to face north, the direction the Honda would be coming from if it were on the Palisades Parkway, he spotted Purrelli's flashing lights.

Also seeing the Honda with Purrelli in hot pursuit was police officer Michael Barry in his car near Mendez. Converged, they blocked the road, forcing Scandell to stop. Confronted by their drawn guns, he surrendered. Sobbing he said, "I killed her because she was taking my baby. She was taking my kid."

In the following days, as we interviewed the people who had known Melanie and Herbie Scandell, we began to get the chilling picture of their tormented domestic life—jealousies, anger, possessiveness, violence. Herbie didn't want her nursing the baby because he didn't want anyone but himself touching her. He didn't want her to lose weight. He was constantly nagging her about her clothing and accused her of trying to attract other men by wearing shorts—and making her get rid of them. She hid money at work because he didn't want her to have any. He had beaten her so bad during the summer that a friend had to take her to Good Samaritan Hospital for treatment. One day she had come to work with a split lip. She explained it away as an accident although her friends suspected otherwise. Herbie even bit her feet. So violent was his temper that she once sent the two boys from her first marriage to stay with their father because she didn't want them to witness Herbie's outbursts against her.

Not once, so far as her friends knew, had Melanie ever gone to family court, to the police, or to anyone else to find a way to halt the violence as her friends and family urged her to do.

What also developed as we probed the nature of the Scandells was a portrait of a husband also feeling the stress and strain of the relationship. There was plenty of evidence that he had been provoked frequently by his troubled wife's jealousy and by her violence against him.

As difficult as their marriage was, his troubles did not give him the right to kill his wife and certainly none of these domestic difficulties justified his shooting his wife's sister Wendy who, after being sustained on life-support systems, died on March 8.

Why had Scandell committed these crimes?

It was his contention that he had been under such duress that he had "snapped."

To find my own answer, I turned once more to Dr. John Baer Train. What he found was a man who was anxious, depressed, and frightened. When told of reports that he had been abusive to his wife, Scandell denied it and called himself the abusee rather than the abuser. He was simultaneously denying his act and acknowledging it. "I'm not the kind of person who could do something like that," he said. "I don't think I killed her but I'm angry at myself for doing it—I did it."

When Scandell took out the shotgun, concluded Dr. Train, he had passed his breaking point. For a long time he had been under great stress but he had repressed it and pent it up in his subconscious. Suddenly, in their bedroom in his parents' house, the chief cause of all that stress—his wife—was denying him his son. At that moment the rage that had been simmering within him exploded. At that point he entered into a altered state of consciousness—blind, uncontrollable, impulsive, irrational, violent, homicidal.

Two psychiatrists examining Scandell for the defense came to the same conclusion as Dr. Train.

The legal term for the condition is extreme emotional disturbance and, if proved beyond a reasonable doubt, it reduces the crime from murder to manslaughter.

Offering it, Scandell's counsel proposed a plea of guilty to two counts of manslaughter in the first degree. Because our expert, Dr. Train, essentially agreed in his analysis with the defense psychiatrist, there was no alternative but to accept manslaughter in the first degree.

Scandell was sentenced to sixteen and two-thirds to fifty years.

Expert testimony from Dr. Train would also be crucial in the 1985 case of John Bruetsch, a thirty-nine-year-old policeman with New York City's transit department whose twenty-two-year-old wife, Milta, was a rookie police officer with the New York City Police Department.

It was a marital relationship that turned sour almost immediately, fueled by Bruetsch's jealousies and suspicions that Milta was cheating on him and his conviction that she was excessively attentive to another New York police officer.

The whole thing came to a head on October 29, 1985, when Bruetsch arrived at the home of his wife's relatives in the quiet neighborhood of Piermont Place in the village of Piermont, a hilly and wooded community on the banks of the Hudson. Across the street from the home of Mr. and Mrs. Rodolfo Rosado, her brother's in-laws, lived Fred Sheffold, a lieutenant with the New York City Fire Department, and on that bright and crisp fall morning he was raking leaves when, suddenly, he heard what he thought were gunshots. Striding to the end of his driveway to investigate, he saw Mr. Rosado waving his arms frantically and shouting "He's got a gun!"

Dashing across the street, Sheffold discovered Milta sprawled on the ground bleeding profusely from what looked like gunshot wounds.

Another neighbor arrived. Tom Chapin, brother of the late singing star Harry Chapin and a popular performer himself, lived next door to the Rosado family. Checking Milta's pulse while Sheffold administered cardiopulmonary resuscitation, Chapin grimly shook his head, fearful that even with the arrival of paramedics and an ambulance she would not survive.

First on the scene from the Piermont police was Chief Thomas Gaynor and Officer Joseph Airtrip, quickly followed by Orangetown police. Soon joining the investigation would be Orangetown Police Chief William Crable, DA detectives chief Peter Modaferri, and DA detectives William Michella, John Gould, Ron Taggart, and Chris Goldrick.

Standing beside Milta's body, Rosado was shouting, "He shot her. Her husband shot her."

Chief Gaynor asked, "Where is he now?"

"He ran," exclaimed Rosado, pointing toward the woods.

Calling for assistance from the Haverstraw, Orangetown, and State Police and for a helicopter from the county sheriff's department, Gaynor organized a manhunt—twenty-five police officers and dogs—to scout the neighborhood and scour thirty acres between the Rosado house and the Hudson and a team of divers from the Piermont Fire

Department to search a nearby pond for the gun and the man accused of using it to kill his wife.

While these efforts were underway to locate and arrest John Bruetsch, my office and the police were already concerned with determining the circumstances that had led to the killing and assembling evidence. From the Rosado family we learned of the stormy relationship between John and Milta, that she had taken up residence with relatives and that Bruetsch had been persistently seeking a reconciliation she was not interested in.

That morning there had been several phone calls from him but she had rebuffed him. Then he suddenly appeared at the house and dragged Milta from the house and into the front seat of his car.

"He was holding her with a bear hug inside the car," Rosado asserted. "Milta was saying, 'Let me go. Let me go!' "

Worried, Rosado turned to his fretful wife and shouted "Call the police."

Seconds later, coming out of the house Mrs. Rosado yelled, "The police are coming."

"You called the police. I'm finished," shouted Bruetsch as he drew a revolver from an ankle holster.

Milta tried to scramble from the car and Bruetsch fired. Bleeding, she rolled from the car on the passenger side and collapsed onto the driveway.

Stepping from the driver's side, Bruetsch hurried around the front of the car, leaped onto the rising lawn, pointed the gun down at his wife, and fired again and again until the gun jammed.

Aware of an approaching police car, he turned and ran.

On the basis of Rosado's account it was obvious to me that Bruetsch knew what he was doing and that any defense he might employ based on "insanity" could be challenged on the fact that after his first shot he went after his wife again and methodically shot her several more times but had not attempted to harm anyone else. Furthermore, the fact that he had fled the scene was evidence he had understood the wrongfulness of his act.

Spotted by police as he walked along a Piermont street days later, he surrendered without resistance.

As I anticipated, the insanity defense was offered by Bruetsch's attorney, Jacob Everoff, and at trial there was presented a portrait of a man bedeviled by jealousy and goaded into irrationality by the circumstances of his marriage.

What was the state of Bruetsch's mind?

According to Dr. Train, our psychiatric expert, testifying at the trial, Bruetsch was not suffering from extreme emotional disturbance. "It was not a wild, uncontrolled outburst," he said. "He had a conscious objective and he acted only in responding to that conscious objective. He resisted attempts to restrain him. He walked around the car to get better aim. He knew what he was doing. And when the police arrived, he ran away. That is not what I believe to be extreme emotional disturbance. My opinion is that at the time he shot his wife he did not lack because of mental disease or defect substantial knowledge of the nature and consequence of his act or that it was wrong."

Of course, the defense offered psychiatric testimony to the contrary, but it is juries, not psychiatrists, who decide such questions and—persuaded by our arguments—the jury convicted Bruetsch of second-degree murder. He was sentenced by Judge Harry Edelstein to life imprisonment.

While the cases of Bruetsch, Moses Rodriguez, and Herbert Scandell differ in many ways, they nevertheless illustrate the potential for violence and even death between people who shared love at some point.

Unfortunately, not until recently has the law permitted the effective prosecution of domestic violence. What went on within the home had been considered no one's business except the parties involved, and certainly not a police matter. That attitude had changed, however, resulting in changes in law and in public opinion concerning the manner in which law enforcement agencies treat cases of domestic violence. In Rockland County local police departments operate under strict guidelines which draw no distinction between a case of spouse abuse and other forms of assault. My office works hand-in-hand with the Rockland County Family Shelter, the Volunteer Counseling Service, and the Batterer's Rehabilitation Program to help curb spouse abuse. Assistant DAs and detectives of my staff work with the representatives of the various support agencies to ensure their familiarity with the range of services offered to help spread the message that we will not judge whether a crime had been committed by reference to the relationship between the victim and the accused; that a marriage license is not a license to assault or kill.

Success in these efforts depends in the first instance on the victim. Unless they seek the help that is available, women like Theresa, Melanie, and Milta will continue to be the victims of abuse and murder.

As there is help for those who are being abused, there is help available to those who abuse . . . if they will only accept it.

To those who find themselves trapped in a vicious cycle of abuse, I offer these words, which are not mine but those of Herbert Scandell spoken from the depths of the tragedy that had overtaken him and his wife: "There isn't enough reason in the world to kill somebody. I should have gotten myself a lawyer to fight for my son. I should have walked out and settled things the right way."

The home of Elaine and Arnold Sohn at 38 Jill Lane in the comfortably middle-class neighborhood of Blueberry Hill in Spring Valley, New York.

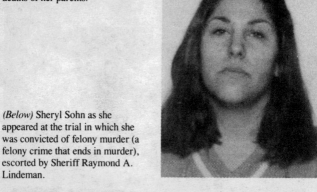

(Right) Sheryl Sohn at the time of her arrest in connection with the deaths of her parents.

(Below) Sheryl Sohn as she appeared at the trial in which she was convicted of felony murder (a felony crime that ends in murder), escorted by Sheriff Raymond A. Lindeman.

(Above) Belton Brims, clean-shaven, dressed in the new three-piece brown suit he wore at the trial.

(Right) Belton Brims, a.k.a. Panama, at the time of his arrest.

(Above) Jody Stich, with Detective Clifford Tallman, after testifying she heard Sheryl Sohn say, "I'm going to kill her," and "I have someone doing something for me."

(Left) James Sheffield, indicted along with Brims and Sheryl Sohn, eluded capture until eight months after the other two were tried and convicted.

(Above) John Bruetsch, a thirty-nine-year-old policeman with New York City's transit department, at the time of his arrest in the shooting death of his wife, Mitla. *(Below)* John Bruetsch at the Rockland County Court House where he was convicted of second-degree murder in the death of his wife.

(Left) Patrolman Waverly Brown was one of the Nyack police officers killed by the gunmen who leaped out of the back of the U-Haul truck that he and other officers had stopped on the Thruway ramp.

(Top left) A scene at the manhunt—twenty-five police officers with dogs—that was organized to find John Bruetsch, who fled into adjacent woods after shooting his wife.

(Below) The body of Peter Paige, the Brink's guard killed in the shootout at the Nanuet Mall.

(Right) From left to right, Kathy Boudin, David Gilbert, and Judith Clark in custody at the Nyack police headquarters.

(Below) The money that was recovered after the Brink's robbery is loaded back into a Brink's truck after it was counted at the Clarkstown police department in New City, New York.

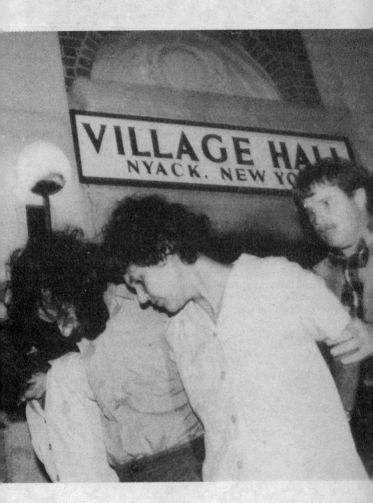

(*Above*) Kathy Boudin as she appeared at the time of trial. (*Below*) Jean and Leonard Boudin, the parents of Kathy Boudin; Leonard Boudin, a well-respected attorney, had represented many controversial people including Paul Robeson and Julius and Ethel Rosenberg.

(Above) Part of the legal team in the Brink's robbery trial, from left to right,: Susan Tipograph (for Judith Clark), Judith Holmes (for Donald Weems), Lynne Stewart (for David Gilbert), and Kathy Boudin's courtroom team, Leonard Weinglass and Martin Garbus.

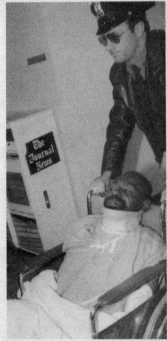

(Right) Because of injuries sustained in the crash of the Honda in Nyack, Samuel Brown, one of the defendants in the Brink's robbery, was arraigned at Nyack Hospital.

Local residents, holding placards proclaiming, "Oust the BLA from the USA," exchange shouts with the radicals supporting the defendants in the Brink's trial.

Red-shirted supporters of the defendants at the Brink's trial wave fists and shout, "The BLA is alive and well; the FBI can go to hell."

MISSING!
Foul Play Suspected

EYES · BLUE
HAIR · BLOND
HEIGHT · 5'11"
WEIGHT · 135 lb
AGE · 26

EIGIL VESTI
Norwegian F.I.T. Student

Last seen Friday, February 22nd Midnight in CHELSEA, WEST VILLAGE area

(Above) This notice was posted all over lower Manhattan after the disappearance of Eigil Dag Vesti.

(Left) Bernard LeGeros, who worked for art dealer Andrew Crispo, was convicted of the brutal murder of Eigil Dag Vesti.

(Above) Billy Mayer (center), a pal of Bernard LeGeros from his LaSalle Academy days, was a key witness in the LeGeros trial.

(Right) Andrew Crispo was the owner of a prestigious gallery on the most expensive stretch of real estate in the world—Manhattan's East Fifty-Seventh Street.
(AP Photo)

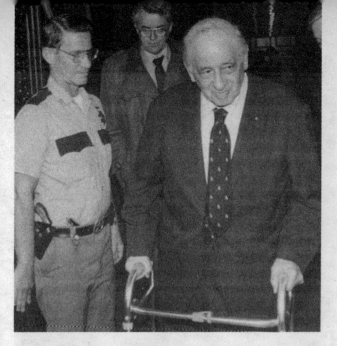

(Above) Eighty-two years old and severely hampered by arthritis, Murray Sprung was surprised to be chosen by John and Racquel LeGeros to defend their son. *(Below)* Eigil Dag Vesti's sister (left), who came from Norway for the LeGeros trial, talks with District Attorney Kenneth Gribetz.

Ruth and Donald Mason at their wedding in July 1983.

10 | MURDER AT RANDOM

PAULA BOHOVESKY LONGED to become an actress. She was pretty, pleasant, bright, hard-working, and ambitious, so hers was not an impossible dream. And she had time to pursue it: she was only sixteen. Three nights a week she worked at the Pearl River public library, a modern red-brick building with floor-to-roof windows that provided a view from the outside of row upon row of neatly arranged books—a splash of light and color in the seven-o'clock dark of a crisp night three days before Halloween 1980.

To guard her from the chill as she left the library, Paula wore a brown tweed jacket over a blue pullover sweater, jeans, and brown moccasins. A junior at Pearl River High School, she was tall for her age. Everyone said she appeared two or three years older and a few people even said she looked like a fashion model with her nice figure, good looks, long blond hair, and blue eyes.

She certainly impressed Kenneth Gordon, who owned a delicatessen and grocery, the Pilgrim Market, on Franklin Avenue near the library. When Paula came in and bought a soda, giving him two quarters and he gave her a nickel change, he thought she was a very striking person, very beautiful and very poised.

Moments after she left the market, Paula crossed Central Avenue onto North Main Street, not her usual route home.

147

She'd gone out of her way to get the soda, but not by much. At the corner watching her as she passed was Craig Entwistle, who knew Paula from school and from her working at the library.

Just hanging around with Craig in front of Bertussi's plumbing store were John Crowe and David Wallace. Always a kidder, John nodded in Paula's direction and said "Look at that guy following Paula."

Craig and David looked, saw the man and, because John was always such a kidder, chuckled at the crazy idea that the man was following Paula.

Like many American towns, Pearl River has a central square. Bounding it on the south side is the post office; business blocks housing stores, restaurants, and a few bars overlook its greenery from the three other sides. The principal streets are Main Street and Central Avenue.

Dominating the northeast corner is a wood-and-brick building, Post One of the Orangetown Police, which has jurisdiction in Pearl River. On duty on the night of October 28, 1980, working the four-to-midnight shift of foot and motor patrol duty was Edward Cordock, an Orangetown police officer for more than five years.

At 7:30 P.M., sweating and out of breath from running, a young man pulled open the door to the police booth. Cordock recognized him as Richard LaBarbera. Barely able to get out words, he gasped, "There's a guy beating up a girl up the street."

"Calm down," said Cordock. "Take your time and tell me about it."

Grasping Cordock's shirt and tie, LaBarbera yelled, "C'mon, for crissakes!"

Wrenching loose, Cordock said, "Okay. Tell me where.

Get your breath and tell me . . . calmly. Which direction? North Main?"

"Yes."

"How far up North Main?"

"Near Washington."

"Okay," said Cordock, picking up the phone. "I'm calling for assistance. Then you can show me where."

A few moments later, as a pair of patrol cars screeched to a stop in front of a large old, dark and vacant house surrounded by lawns shrouded in shadows, LaBarbera stood in the middle of the dirt and gravel driveway of the house. Between a pair of tall stone posts, he said, "It was right here."

Studying the ground in the light of his flashlight, Cordock asked, "Did you recognize the girl or the man who was beating her up?"

"No."

"And this is where it happened?"

"Right here," nodded LaBarbera.

"Well, I don't see any sign of a struggle," said Cordock, switching off his light.

Asked if they had heard anything unusual—screams, for example—neighbors told Cordock and the other police officers that they'd noticed nothing unusual.

Whatever it was, it was over.

"Can we give you a lift home?" Cordock asked LaBarbera.

"No," he said, walking away much calmer than he had been but still a little on the wobbly side.

Back at Post One, Cordock made a note of the incident in his log—there were several explanations: a lovers' spat maybe, a husband-and-wife squabble, maybe just a couple of teenagers horsing around—and put the incident out of his mind.

Suddenly, at eight o'clock LaBarbera was back at the booth and just as worked up. This time he held a flashlight in his grip and had somebody with him—a young guy Cordock also knew from having seen him around town. Robert McCain was not a native New Yorker; from the South somewhere, a drifter. Unlike LaBarbera, McCain was cool and calm.

"Somebody stole my wallet," LaBarbera was saying shrilly.

"Where was it stolen?" Cordock asked patiently.

"At the High Wheeler."

A bar just west on Central, the High Wheeler could usually be counted on for something interesting. Studying LaBarbera, he saw more obviously now than earlier that LaBarbera had been drinking a lot. "Why don't you come back and make a report tomorrow when you'll be feeling a little better," said Cordock. Turning to McCain, he asked, "Do you know he was in here a little while ago. Something about a fight. Do you know anything about that?"

"There was no fight," said McCain emphatically. "He's a little confused. The two of us have been drinking all day at the High Wheeler. He's just drunk."

That was that, Cordock hoped as LaBarbera and McCain left the booth, but half an hour later they were back with a third man who claimed McCain and LaBarbera had roughed him up after accusing him of stealing a wallet.

About an hour later he spotted LaBarbera again, this time talking in a phone booth.

"Orangetown police," said the officer answering the phones at headquarters.

"Um, yeah, listen, my name is Richard LaBarbera. I reported my wallet missing at the police booth in Pearl River. Well, it was supposedly stolen from the High Wheeler. I found it underneath a car in the front of the bar. No sense making a report."

The time was 9:44 P.M.

Twenty minutes earlier, Lois Bohovesky had pulled her car into the parking lot of the library.

Concerned that her daughter hadn't arrived home a few minutes after seven, she had first thought that it was a night when Paula worked until nine o'clock. When she did not return promptly after nine, Lois went looking for her. The library's tall windows were dark, the door locked. Thinking that Paula might be with people with whom she worked at the library, Lois drove to their homes. Told that Paula had left at seven, Mrs. Bohovesky went back to her house, telephoned the police, and reported that Paula was missing.

This was not a girl who would run away. This was a stable girl with a happy home life, seemingly countless friends and admirers. She was not a loner. There was no boy trouble. Nor were there problems at school. Artistic and creative, she had designed the cover of the 1980 yearbook and worked on sets for school plays as well as the sets, props, and puppets for her mother's company of puppeteers. A professional puppeteer, Lois Bohovesky had worked with Jim Henson and the Muppets. Basil Bohovesky was an architect, so a talent from drawing and art had been Paula's inheritance. Her dream nevertheless was to become an actress, and toward that end she had already had parts in amateur productions in the county and with her mother's Vagabond Puppet Company.

Quakers, Mr. and Mr. Bohovesky had brought their children from Manhattan and settled in Pearl River in 1968.

Now Paula was missing.

At eight-thirty the next morning, attorney Robert Clemensen of Pomona was in Pearl River on behalf of a client who owned two properties on North Main Street, numbers

48 and 40. In the back yard of number 40 was the ruin of an old barn that had burned down the previous Saturday. Clemenson was going to inspect it, but as he crossed the broad leaf-strewn lawn behind the house he saw what appeared to be someone sleeping, perhaps a drunk. Then he noticed that the figure lying facedown was naked below the waist. Suspecting that this was not someone sleeping off a drunk on his client's property, Clemensen summoned the police.

Under clear skies, the morning was crisp—49 degrees, noted by Assistant Medical Examiner Dr. Burton Allyn on arriving at the scene at 9:40 A.M. By that time the yard behind 40 North Main Street was crowded. Orangetown Police Chief William Crable was there, along with Detective Sergeant Robert Shorter and investigators Jim Searle, Vincent Winters, and Tom Sullivan of the Bureau of Criminal Identification, Supervising Detective Peter Modafferi and Detective Ron Taggart of my office, and myself.

The girl's body had not been moved from the cluster of bloodsoaked leaves where it had lain for at least fourteen hours. Lifting her sweater and jacket, Dr. Allyn discerned five stab wounds of the middle and lower back, the two lower wounds appearing to have penetrated deeply. When the body was turned, stab wounds were discovered in her chest. There was evidence of possible manual choking and it appeared that she had been hit on the head with a blunt object, possibly a stone.

The precise cause of death determined in an autopsy by Medical Examiner Dr. Frederick Zugibe was "exsanguination and mediastinal shift," which means bleeding and a shift of the heart caused by the collapse of the lungs, contributed to by compression of the neck and blunt trauma to the head. Dreadful as these wounds were, however, if

Paula had been found immediately after the attack upon her and rushed to a hospital, her life might have been saved.

Examination of her vagina and anus produced findings that, in layman's terms, were consistent with rape and sodomy, although without evidence of there having been ejaculations.

Rape, sodomy, and murder. By whom?

At about the time Dr. Allyn was arriving at 40 North Main Street, Orangetown police received a phone call. "Um, listen," said the muffled male voice, "Tommy Wilson killed a girl last night in Pearl River."

"What's your name?"

There was no reply, only a dial tone.

Spearheading the investigation was Orangetown Detective Robert Dickson. He knew Richard LaBarbera had reported an incident at the time and at the address of the Bohovesky murder. Now here was this mysterious phone call. Was it from LaBarbera?

Accompanied by his partner, Detective Edmund Conjua, Dickson drove to LaBarbera's place of employment in Nanuet and asked him to accompany them to headquarters to talk about what he'd seen the previous evening. LaBarbera agreed to go. There he blurted out, "I shouldn't've gotten involved."

"We got a phone call saying Tommy Wilson killed a girl in Pearl River last night," said Dickson. "Was it you?"

"Yes."

"Tell us what you know."

"I saw Tommy Wilson on North Main with a female. She had light-colored, frizzy shoulder-length hair. They were both on the sidewalk at the north end of Amman's Sporting Goods parking lot. I saw Tommy Wilson strike the girl about the head. I approached them and asked what was going on. Wilson pushed me and told me 'Get the fuck out of here.' "

After having LaBarbera's statement typed and signed, Dickson drove him home, but on the way he headed the car to North Main Street. "I wish I could remember more," said LaBarbera as they passed the sporting goods store, but when Dickson pulled into the driveway LaBarbera said nothing.

At ten the next morning, LaBarbera was on the phone again. "I'm sorry I got involved in this," he said. Then, after a long pause, he stated, "I don't think Tommy Wilson killed the girl."

Later in the day Dickson and Conjura confirmed that Wilson was not the killer of Paula Bohovesky because he hadn't been anywhere near 40 North Main Street and had an ironclad alibi.

"Richie, you have not been telling us the truth," said Dickson as he confronted LaBarbera at his home early the next morning. "We know Wilson didn't kill that girl. He couldn't have. It took us quite a few manhours of checking to prove that, Richie. You caused us to waste a lot of time on a wild goose chase. Now, how about telling us what really happened last night?"

It was around 7:30 Tuesday night. He'd been in a phone booth and saw the girl walking on North Main. At the same time he saw Robert McCain on the opposite side. As the girl walked north, Robert McCain crossed diagonally and followed her at a very fast pace. Wondering what was going on, he'd followed McCain and the girl and as they approached Washington Avenue, he saw Robert McCain strike the girl in the back of the head with an object. The girl stumbled and then Robert McCain dragged her to the end of the driveway. Robert McCain had made a number of punching motions at the girl's back. In a state of panic at seeing what McCain was doing, he ran down to the police booth. Then, back at the driveway as the police officer was shining his flashlight at the entrance to the driveway, he didn't tell him to have a look farther back because he was afraid and he didn't want to get involved.

"Interesting story, Richie," Dickson said, shaking his head, "but I'm afraid we don't believe you."

It didn't happen that way. Not exactly. After he saw the assault on the girl by McCain, instead of running to the police booth right away, he ran to the High Wheeler and got a flashlight and returned to North Main to see if the girl was still alive. He saw that she was not moving but he didn't touch her. Then he went to the police booth.

It still wasn't adding up, Dickson said.

After he saw Robert McCain punching the girl, he returned to the High Wheeler and got the flashlight but then he'd gone home to change clothes and then he went to North Main Street and saw that the girl wasn't moving. Then he ran down to the police booth.

"Tell us about the girl," said Dickson. "What did she look like when you saw her not moving on the ground?"

"She had on a sort of suit jacket and brownish in color. Her jeans and panties had been pulled down to her ankles. She had a large amount of blood on her left side."

"Where are the clothes that you were wearing when you first saw Robert McCain punching the girl?"

On Wednesday afternoon—that would be the twenty-ninth—he borrowed a car and threw the pants out the window on Route 304. Locating the designer jeans along the road, Dickson brought them back to the police headquarters and showed them to LaBarbera. "Are they the ones you were wearing that night and that you threw out the car window?"

"Yes."

"What else were you wearing Tuesday night?"

"Sneakers—the ones I have on now. Same jacket as I have on now. A blue shirt."

"Do you own a knife?"

"No. I never carried a knife."

Based on his false and misleading statements that Tommy Wilson had killed Paula Bohovesky, Dickson and Conjura arrested LaBarbera on a charge of hindering an investigation.

According to his story now, it had been Robert McCain who'd killed Paula. What did the Orangetown police know about McCain? And where was he at that moment? Dickson and Conjura soon had the answers.

Twenty-year-old Robert Allen McCain had been born in Los Angeles, one of five children in a Baptist family, and grew up near Monticello, Arkansas, where his parents still lived. After dropping out of school, he'd served in the army and was trained as a diesel mechanic and after his military service took jobs as a construction worker in Indiana, Texas, Utah, and Missouri before moving to Pearl River in 1980. A heavy drinker, he spent a lot of time at the High Wheeler, especially on Tuesdays. He was residing at 48 North Main but he'd been planning to return to Arkansas and, as far as those who knew him could say, he had arranged for a lift from a trucker who was heading to the south on Tuesday night, a deal he apparently had made well before the murder. Because no one had seen him since, it was assumed that he'd left town as planned.

Believing that McCain was, indeed, heading home, Dickson and Conjura notified authorities in Arkansas that they wanted to talk to McCain, but to everyone's surprise McCain phoned the Orangetown police Friday night. "One of the officers down here, a friend of mine, told me you have a warrant out for me for Murder One."

Detective Conjura was on the phone with him. "We don't have a warrant, Rob," he said, "but we do want to talk to you."

"Oh, okay," McCain said. "What's the problem? Who got killed?"

"Well, we had a young lady get killed up here and then all of a sudden, you're out of town."

"Oh, is that all it is? God, I was worried. I thought somebody said I killed her."

"Some people are on their way down there to bring you back here, so don't leave that house. You're only going to make it worse for yourself."

"Okay. I'm right here."

Rockland Chief Assistant DA James Mellion, Detective Peter Modafferi, and Orangetown Detective Roger Breshnahan traveled to Arkansas. What happened on Tuesday night in Pearl River, said McCain, was all a blur. He didn't remember anything. In exasperation, Breshnahan growled, "We've got a dead girl up there, so I'm not going to let you tell me you don't remember."

With a sob, McCain covered his face with his hands. "My God, maybe I killed the girl."

Astonished, they told McCain he would have to return to New York—voluntarily, they hoped.

McCain agreed and in a few hours was in the sergeants' room at Orangetown police headquarters but still insisting that he recalled little of that day and night. What he remembered was a fight around midday with his girlfriend, drinking all afternoon with Richie LaBarbera, and then going to his room at number 48 Main Street to get ready to leave for Arkansas.

Leaving McCain alone for a moment, Breshnahan and Detective Ray Lundy conferred in the hallway. They had been acting the roles of good cop, bad cop, a traditional means of questioning in which two police officers are alternately pleasant and unpleasant, lenient and firm, understanding and belligerent. While Lundy was a cop's cop and could be as tough as anyone, he had the aspects of a big Teddy bear, so he usually played the role of the good cop, but one of his most effective devices in questioning during "good cop, bad cop" was suddenly to cease being the nice guy and turn nasty. The time for that had come.

"I'm fed up with this crap," he yelled at a startled McCain as he went back into the room. "The games are over."

Immediately, tears welled in McCain's eyes and he leaned his head on Lundy's shoulder. "I did hit her," he cried. "I did hit her."

Moments later, along with the tears spilled a confession about what happened that crisp Tuesday evening after a day of heavy drinking at the High Wheeler.

I didn't feel so good, so I went outside to get some fresh air and take a walk. I walked down the street and fell down. So I wanted to go home, so I walked down North Main Street and my head was hurting, and I seen the girl cross the street. I picked up a rock and hit her in the head. She staggered against the column of stone and ran. I caught her and hit her many times and knocked her out. Then I raped her and after that I ran back to the bar.

Now McCain was questioned by Jim Mellion.

"Did you rape her?"

"Yes."

"After raping her, did you ejaculate?"

"No."

"What position was her body in when you left her?"

"Face up."

"Did you roll her over on her stomach and sodomize her?"

"No."

"Did you have a knife with you?"

"No."

"Did you stab her?"

"No," McCain cried, but going through it all again he was less clear in his recalling of the events and said that it was possible that when he was punching Paula he was stabbing her. It was also possible he had sodomized her.

Once Richard LaBarbera had been placed under arrest, any further questioning of him was stopped cold by his attorney, but there still was plenty of investigative work needed to pin down his role. This included searching for any witnesses who might have seen Paula Bohovesky that night.

Among those who did recall Paula was twelve-year-old Deborah Mitchell, a seventh-grader at the Pearl River Middle School who said she had been approached by a man near the Pilgrim Market around seven o'clock that evening. He had asked her if she smoked pot and when she said she didn't had walked away, passing Paula on the way. Near Main Street, Deborah recalled, the man turned to look at Paula and shouted "Wow."

Shown pictures of several men, including Richard La-Barbera, Deborah pointed to his photo as the man who'd looked at Paula and yelled "Wow."

Reaching out to everyone they could find who knew

LaBarbera, the investigators turned up Roy Spielman, a friend. He had spoken to Richie on October 30, he said, and Richie had been quite upset because he was being questioned by the police about a murder. Could he stay with Roy that night? Just to get some rest? Of course he could, Roy said, and he drove to Richie's place to pick him up.

Afraid that the police might come to search his apartment, Richie took some items, including marijuana, and they proceeded on their way toward Spielman's apartment in Stony Point. Asking Richie if he'd had anything to do with the death of the girl, Roy was assured that he had not. Having heard on the news that the girl had been stabbed and remembering that Richie used to have a knife, the kind where the blade folds into the handle, Roy asked, "Richie, where's your knife?"

"In the apartment."

Suppose the cops found it? Could they use it to try to tie him into the killing?

These questions occurred to both men and they decided to return to Richie's apartment to get it.

When he heard that Richie had been arrested, Roy told the investigators, he'd visited Richie in jail in New City. "Did you do it?" he'd asked Richie.

He'd been drinking all day, Richie said, and that night he was so ripped he didn't remember.

He was nervous, he said, because Robert McCain might try to pin the murder on him.

What had Roy done with that knife?

He'd gotten rid of it, Roy said—a lie. In fact, he'd taken it to his mother's house for safekeeping.

Leaving the jail, Roy had made up his mind that he'd better get rid of the knife and did so that Saturday, wiping it in an effort to remove fingerprints, wrapping it in a plastic bag and throwing it into a lake in Tappan.

It wasn't a lake but a manmade pond off Rockland Hill Road, but it still was a big place to look for one small knife. Nonetheless, on November 3, Orangetown Patrolman Jack Hanuick broke the ice-cold surface of six-foot-deep water in his scuba gear and soon came up with the knife in his grasp.

Comparing distinctive markings on the hilt of the knife with Paula Bohovesky's wounds, Medical Examiner Dr. Frederick Zugibe linked the weapon to the murder.

Indicted for murder, McCain and LaBarbera pleaded not guilty and went on trial in May 1981. Appearing for the prosecution was Assistant District Attorney Harvey Eilbaum, a soft-spoken and always well-organized lawyer perfectly suited for the handling of an emotionally charged case with complicated twists and turns featuring a pair of defendants who appeared determined to hang the blame on one another.

As the well-dressed pair came into court each day their movements were followed intensely by Paula's father, Basil. Because his wife Lois was to be a witness, she could not be permitted in court, but she appeared at the courthouse daily.

This vigilance by those most affected by a crime has become a hallmark of the rapidly growing victim's rights movements in the United States—a physical presence in the courtroom of the relatives, loved ones, and friends demonstrating by their attention at every stage of the proceedings that the victim is not going to become lost in a welter of legalistic arguments and motions. It is a concern for the fate of the perpetrators of crimes, especially murder, which lasts beyond the trial, extending to diligent observation of all the subsequent proceedings, such as appeals and petitions for clemency or pardon.

As a prosecutor, I enthusiastically endorse this movement, as I favor (and instituted in my county) a wide variety of aids and support services for all crime victims and their families.

While she was in the courtroom itself only for the amount of time it took for her to tell a heart-wrenching tale of her search for her daughter, Lois Bohovesky sat on the steps of the County Courthouse or waited in the corridor for the duration of the trial. "Paula died alone, and that's a terrible thing," she said early in the proceedings. "I feel I have to be here for her now because I wasn't with her that night."

What happened that night, charged Harvey Eilbaum, was this: McCain and LaBarbera attacked Paula Bohovesky. McCain had struck the first blow, chased her up the driveway of the vacant house on Main Street, beat her unconscious and attempted to rape her before LaBarbera attempted to sodomize her and then stabbed her in the back five times, leaving her in a pool of her own blood to perish amid the already dead leaves of autumn.

Unfolding in Judge Harry Edelstein's courtroom as Harvey Eilbaum developed the case against McCain and LaBarbera was, as *The Journal-News* put it, "a tangled scenario of phantom assaults, lost or stolen wallets, changes of clothes and heavy drinking" marked by attempts by the lawyers for the defendants to shift guilt from one to the other and otherwise undermine the people's case.

Late on a warm June afternoon after eleven days of testimony from forty-six witnesses, the jury came in with its verdict—guilty of murder. It was 6:00 P.M. There was no sound in the courtroom except the emphatic "Yes" from each of the jurors as they were polled to assure that the verdict was unanimous.

As each juror answered affirmatively, McCain's expression was impassive but LaBarbera appeared shaken, as if he had never believed that he would be found guilty.

For the Bohovesky family, the ordeal of the trial was over

but the agony of their loss would be everlasting. "Day after day, Lois Bohovesky's presence stood in contrast to the trial of the two men who killed her daughter," observed George M. Walsh in the *Sunday Journal-News*. "The rage, sorrow and anguish she spoke during the trial could not be spoken of in the Rockland County courtroom. Throughout the trial the jurors were isolated from the emotions and anger generated by the grisly killing of the 16-year-old girl. The horror over the beating and stabbing death of a talented and peaceful girl had to give way to the presumption of innocence and fair trial for LaBarbera and McCain."

Following the trial, Lois Bohovesky continued her interest in the issue of the rights of victims and victims' families by joining a burgeoning grass-roots movement that gained momentum throughout the 1980s and promises to continue to be a weighty counterbalance to the rights of the defendant in the scales of justice.

Historically, the criminal justice system has focused its attention and resources almost exclusively on the rights of the defendant. The Constitution guarantees the defendant an attorney in all stages of the proceedings and investigative or expert services if needed, at the public's expense. There are "speedy trial" rights that effectively only burden the prosecution. A defendant can delay things almost as will. In felony cases that defendant has a right to an array of hearings and then a trial itself, all ordinarily requiring the appearance of the victim, without regard to the financial or other cost or inconvenience imposed on the victim.

I don't suggest that these rights are inappropriate or unnecessary. Nevertheless, it is clear that for years this tendency to focus solely on the defendant has unfairly resulted in very little attention being paid to the victims of crime.

It is not right, fair, or constitutionally mandated that a

person once victimized by the commission of a crime be victimized a second time by the criminal justice system. But, until recently, the system seemed to work in just that fashion.

Over the last decade, however, the criminal justice system has become more attuned to the rights of the victim. For example, many prosecutors' offices, including my own, have established Crime Witness/Victim Aid Bureaus. Staffed by full-time professionals, these agencies keep victims and witnesses fully apprised of the status of cases and assist in processing claims for medical costs and any requests for other services, most of which are available at no cost.

Equally important, victims in many states are now being entitled, as a matter of right, to be heard prior to imposition of a sentence. Legislation creating his "victim's right" in New York State was enacted into law during the period when I was President of the New York State District Attorneys Association, and the law includes elements strongly supported by the DAs. These include the requirement that every presentence report include a crime-victim impact sentence setting forth the position of the victim with respect to the sentence. Recent legislation in New York also ensures that any financial loss suffered by a victim is not overlooked or ignored.

It had long been my position that victims should not be shut out of the system. While it is true that the criminal law exists for the benefit of society and not as an instrument by which to vindicate the rights of private litigants, the victim is nevertheless an integral, if unwilling, party to the process and certainly should not be further victimized by it.

In murder cases in which the victim cannot speak for the rights of the victim, the families and the loved ones of the victim can—and should—be heard and seen.

The fact that Paula Bohovesky had been alive and brimming with glorious potential was never forgotten as the wheels of justice turned.

Of course, her family couldn't forget Paula. The Orangetown police did not forget. Harvey Eilbaum didn't. I didn't.

Neither did Paula's classmates and teachers at Pearl River High School. Early in the trial, they put on display at the library where Paula had worked an assortment of her artwork that showed its progression of her talents from a crayon version of Jonah and the Whale done in the third grade to soft designs of mythical creatures, a bold composition of peacock feathers made out of cut paper as a design for wrapping paper, a watercolor for her younger brother, Peter, and a drawing in Magic Marker of dogwood berries outside her bedroom window—her last work.

11 | TERROR AT THE MALL

ON THE JEWISH calendar, Tuesday, October 20, 1981, was Simhath Torah—a holy day I was observing at home because religious rules prohibited travel. It was also a crucial day in the preparation for the Sohn trial. I was therefore awaiting the arrival at my home of Detectives Jim Stewart and Philip Burden, who were bringing our star witness, Willie Brims, to me to prepare for his appearance at trial.

A few miles away it was also an important date on the calendar for Joseph Trombino: he and his friend Peter Paige were making their last run together. For fourteen years they'd been sharing the tight confines of the backs of Brink's armored vans and trucks. In all that time they'd handled and rested their feet on bulging bags containing hundreds of millions of dollars on their way to and from banks. Now it was their last day as a guard team. Pete was transferring to a new route.

On the front side of the thick bulletproof glass that separated Pete and Joe from the driver's compartment, Jim Kelly held the wheel of the lumbering square-backed gray truck following a route that began at 6:30 A.M. at Brink's headquarters in Newark and proceeded stop-and-go from New Jersey into Rockland County picking up bulging bundles of cash from branch banks for removal to Federal

Reserve vaults. By midafternoon they had piled $759,000 into the back.

At ten minutes to four, Kelly wheeled off Route 59 into the sprawling Nanuet Mall and along a rising, curving driveway that took them into the rear parking lot, where there was an entrance to the upper level of the mall. Immediately inside the entrance was a branch of the Nanuet National Bank, their last pick-up of the day.

Usually Kelly would have parked their truck directly in front of the doors to the mall, but repair work was in progress on the roof of the building and scaffolding had been put up, so he had to park farther away from the door than usual and facing it instead of pulling up close.

Seated on a nearby bench next to a square-jawed, bearded black man as the truck stopped, Mrs. Barbara Patnett looked up with interest. She'd been watching the workers on the scaffolding and chatting amiably with the man about the men and about the lovely fall weather but now, like her, the man was silently observing the armored truck.

Following standard procedure, Kelly remained in the cab from which he controlled a switch that activated a lock to the rear door and allowed Trombino to use a key to open the door.

As Trombino was inserting the key and pushing the door open, Paige had his .38-caliber revolver drawn. Bounding out, he waited with his hand on the gun as his partner took a handcart from the truck, closed the door and locked it. Together they walked through outer mall doors into a vestibule. To their left was an automatic-teller machine. To their right was a row of public telephones. Using one of them was a black man who watched them as they passed through a second set of doors and turned left to enter the bank.

It took only a couple of minutes for Paige to sign a chit

for three white canvas sacks containing $839,000 and for Trompino to load them onto the cart and return to the truck. There he signaled Jim Kelly to push his button to activate the lock, inserted his key, opened the door, and began lifting the heavy bags into the truck while his partner stood guard.

Like anyone who has ever watched money being loaded into an armored truck, Mrs. Patnett on her nearby bench was wondering how much money was in the bags and was going to comment about it to the man next to her. But, when she looked into his eyes, he gave her such a chilling look that words stuck in her throat.

At that instant a small red Chevrolet van screeched to a stop alongside the Brink's truck. Mrs. Patnett noticed it right away because of its similarity to one owned by her fiancé, only his did not have rear windows covered with reflective material.

Suddenly, the van's door opened and three men jumped out, all wearing ski masks, all carrying guns.

The guns opened fire.

Shots were going off everywhere, it seemed to Mrs. Patnett as she fled in horror. Worried about the moody black man she'd been talking to, she glanced back and was surprised to see that rather than fleeing the gunfire, he was running toward it with his arm stretched out before him.

A gunman at the front of the Brink's truck leveled his weapon and fired twice; the blasts ripped open Peter Paige's chest. Crouched on the front seat of the truck, Kelly fired his pistol through a small gunport until the gunman who'd cut down Paige fired twice into the windshield, the blasts pulverizing the bullet-resistant glass and the concussion stunning Kelly.

At the back of the truck in a desperate attempt to close the door and lock it, securing the money, Trombino was hit, his left arm flung back and twisted off, it seemed. "Jim, help me," he screamed. "I don't have my arm. Where's my arm?"

Through a suddenly lowering darkness as he was fainting in pain, Trombino saw a pair of arms that also seemed to be disembodied grabbing the blood-soaked moneybags.

Pulling onto Middletown Road in his car, Glen Michel could not believe his eyes as a red van with stick-on mirrors on the back windows darted out from the Nanuet Mall and nearly ran him from the road. As if that weren't bad enough, a beige Honda car with a pair of women in it did the same thing, the van and the Honda then turning together onto Orchard Street and speeding away.

A few minutes later on Main Drive in Nanuet less than two miles from the mall, Sandra Torgersen, a student doing her homework, heard unusual noises coming from the parking lot of an abandoned Korvette shopping center and looked out the window through trees and shrubbery that separated the house from the parking area. Usually it was an uninteresting and dismal view, but now she saw a small red van skidding to a stop next to a parked silver orange-striped U-Haul truck. A second later, a beige Honda pulled up. From the van popped a man with a rifle.

The police had better hear about this, she decided.

The radios of Rockland County law enforcement organizations already were crackling with calls and orders—abrupt and no-nonsense, clipped, hard-edged, tense.

Officer Brian Lennon of the Nyack police had been taking a coffee break at the Village Donut shop. Now his portable radio was chirping an urgent "101" for him to call the office. "Get into service, Brian," said desk officer Jack McCord when Lennon called. "There's been an armed robbery at the Nanuet Mall with shots fired." Lennon dashed to his car, Number 384.

At the same time, Detective Arthur Keenan and Sergeant Edward O'Grady rushed out of police headquarters to their car. "They took off in a yellow Honda and a U-Haul truck," the radio was reporting. "They ditched the red van and now have a U-Haul. Possibly making for the Thruway on Route 59."

The Thruway was the quick way out of Rockland, a logical escape route, and the on ramp from Route 59 was a short distance westward from Main and Broadway.

The New York State Thruway crosses the Hudson River over the Tappan Zee Bridge and then swings northwesterly in a long easy arc before straightening out due west as it passes over Route 303, Mountainview Avenue, and cuts through the Strawberry Hill section of Nyack. Ramps connect Mountainview with the highway a little over four miles from the Nanuet Mall. Route 59 runs almost parallel to the Thruway and is called Old Nyack Road until it enters Nyack and becomes Main Street. The area falls within the jurisdiction of both the Clarkstown and the Nyack police.

In Car 383, Officer Waverly Brown was parked beside a phone booth in the Texaco station at Route 59 and Mountainview Avenue and also listening to the radios when he spotted a U-Haul truck coming east on 59.

Brian Lennon also saw the truck in the left-only lane with two cars in front, all in position to turn onto Mountainview toward the on ramp.

"We're going to pull over the U-Haul," O'Grady radioed to Lennon. "Brian, go up there and make sure he doesn't get on the Thruway ramp."

In the right-hand lane, Lennon kept his eyes on the U-Haul and waited anxiously until he felt the traffic light was ready to go green for the U-Haul, then shot across

Mountainview and parked his cruiser in the middle of the ramp.

A BMW ahead of the U-Haul stopped parallel to him and a woman asked, "Is the Thruway closed?"

"Move on," said Lennon curtly, his eyes on the U-Haul.

The woman obeyed and the Honda behind her BMW swung past without being told. The U-Haul was next with Keenan and O'Grady behind, the red grill lights of Car 382 flashing. Lifting a shotgun from its cradle under the dashboard, Lennon stepped out to the roadway and wiggled the gun at the U-Haul. "Out!"

A white woman wearing a brown leather coat, green pants, and cowboy boots eased from the passenger's side, her hands halfway above her head, her face ashen with fright.

A thin light-skinned figure in a dark coat and hat stepped down from the truck and around to its front with hands raised. By now Keenan, O'Grady, and Brown were out of their cars.

O'Grady had his eyes on the woman. Trembling, she fixed her wide blue eyes on Lennon's shotgun. "Please put away the gun," she begged.

For O'Grady, it was a split-second in which to make a decision. "I don't think it's them, Brian," he said. "Put the gun away."

Turning to stow the shotgun, Lennon heard Keenan asking, "What's in the truck?" Leaning into the car and snapping the gun into its holder, he did not hear the response to Keenan's question. Looking back, he saw that the woman, the driver, and O'Grady and Brown had moved onto a tree-dotted grassy patch.

Keenan was looking over the U-Haul. Opening the passenger door, he reached inside and popped open the glove compartment. Finding nothing, he checked under the seat and behind it. Moving to the rear door of the truck, he tried lifting the door but it wouldn't give. Turning away from the truck to the man and woman, he said, "I want that back door open."

At that moment he heard a thud, as if something had fallen in the U-Haul. Looking back, he saw the door open and six men vaulting from the back of the truck, all with guns, all firing.

Drawing his gun, Keenan dove to the side. Rolling, he returned fire from behind a small evergreen without realizing he had been superficially hit twice.

Chipper Brown hadn't been so lucky. Unable to get off any shots, he'd been raked with bullets and dropped to the ground with his chest torn apart.

O'Grady got off six quick rounds from his .357 service revolver and was now hunched behind the door on the passenger side of Lennon's cruiser reloading, but before he was able to finish he was hit by a volley of automatic fire from all sides.

In the car, Lennon wrenched the shotgun from its holder, spun around to the driver's side but found himself pinned inside the car by withering fire from three sides. Holding open the door of his cruiser with his foot, he pumped off two shots. A moment later the U-Haul roared forward and rammed the patrol car. Crouched on the front seat and shooting backward over his shoulder, he pumped off two more shots, tried again but found the shotgun empty, and drew his pistol, getting off two rounds.

Sliding across the front seat to try to get out on the passenger side, he discovered it was blocked, then remembered O'Grady had been on that side of the car. "Eddie," he shouted, "is that you?"

O'Grady was unconscious. So was Brown.

Walter Rooney had seen the whole thing. Driving east on Route 59, he'd noticed the police stopping all traffic on the eastbound entrance to the Thruway. A former cop, he recognized the officers on the ramp and understood immediately that they'd set up a roadblock. Curious, he pulled into an Exxon station, got out of his car, and strode toward the ramp.

Suddenly, men leaped from the back of the U-Haul and all hell broke loose as they opened fire with rifles and pistols.

Immediately, Waverly Brown went down.

Ducking for cover, Rooney saw O'Grady get off three shots and when he looked up again he saw O'Grady trying to reload as two gunmen from the U-Haul loomed over him, firing.

Then the shooting ended.

Mrs. Norma Hill had her elderly mother with her in her BMW. They'd been intending to enter the Thruway when they found the ramp blocked by a police car. "Is the Thruway closed?" she'd asked, only to be abruptly told to move on. Having driven onward and made a U-turn, she heard an outburst of shooting coming from the Thruway entrance—a tremendous blast of gunfire that seemed to go on for eternity. She saw six men with guns and rifles, three on the left-hand side of the U-Haul and three on the right, blazing away at the police. One of the policemen was a black man and when he was shot it looked as if someone had put a rope around his ankles and yanked him to the ground.

While all this was going on, she noticed a woman at the side of the road under a sign closer to the Thruway ramp, but the woman was soon forgotten as Norma Hill realized with growing terror that one of the gunmen was nearing her car.

Then he was beside the BMW, the muzzle of the gun was

pressed against her head, and he was shouting "Outta there."

When she did not react quickly enough, the gunman pulled her out of the car, shoved her to the ground, and climbed behind the wheel.

Mrs. Hill grabbed the door handle and screamed, "My mother! Please! My mother's in there!"

Ruthlessly the gunman shoved the elderly woman out as the car sped up Mountainview.

Dr. Ronald Dreyer had been on his way home. Like Mrs. Hill, he had found the Thruway entrance blocked, but before he could go past the U-Haul truck that the police had stopped he found himself the witness to an incredible gunfight. Ducking out of his Olds, he threw himself onto the roadside and when the firing stopped he was looking into the muzzle of a rifle held by a black man and being told to get out of the way.

Crawling aside, Dreyer heard his car start, and when he looked up he saw it speeding away.

The car was of little concern to the doctor, however, as he rushed to the aid of one of the policemen, but by then Waverly Brown was beyond help.

A burly bearded man passing by on the Thruway also saw it all.

A New York city corrections officer who had finished his day's work as a desk officer at Riker's Island, Michael Koch was eyeballing a bizarre scene where cops were pinned down by a gang with extraordinary firepower.

For a split second it was Vietnam all over again. After thirteen months under fire in that war, Koch knew automatic weapons and he knew the sound of an entire arsenal. This was a lot more than a couple of cops in a shootout with a bad guy. This was combat. This was 'Nam in Nyack! So what the hell was going on? How come all this shooting, this firefight, this war on the Thomas E. Dewey Thruway?

A cop is a brother, Michael Koch thought as he watched and heard the battle. Anyone with a badge is fraternal. They go to one another's assistance. Wondering how he could help, he saw out of the corner of his eye a flicker of movement—a woman on the run, dodging, weaving, scurrying madly at the side of the Thruway. She's running away from the scene, he thought. She was not fleeing out of fright. This woman was running to escape!

Jumping from his car, Koch raced after her across six lanes of Thruway traffic. She was running and he wanted to grab her. He didn't want to lose her. A lawman even off duty, he had his badge and gun with him. "Halt!"

The woman flinched at the word, stopped beneath the Mountainview Avenue overpass, and thrust her hands above her head.

Grabbing her long brown hair, he jammed the muzzle of his pistol against her neck. "Move and I'll blow out your fuckin' brains."

"I didn't shoot them," she cried. "They did."

For an instant after capturing the woman, Koch thought he might bag a second suspect—a black man who was commandeering a BMW—but as he leveled his gun to try to get off a shot in the man's direction, he saw an elderly woman in the car. Suddenly a second woman he hadn't noticed previously leaped directly into his line of fire.

In that instant, he and the black man had had eye contact and in that split second as the black man's eyes lit up, Koch was certain the black man was figuring that he'd had it, but it was not to be and he's sped away in the BMW, leaving Koch with only the woman from the Thruway.

As they reached the scene of the shooting, the air still

smelled of burnt gunpowder. For him it looked like any scene of recent battle, littered with the dead, the wounded, the stunned, and the curious.

One glance at Waverly Brown was enough for Koch's experienced eye. Massive chest wound. A lung hanging out. The only thing anyone could do for him was break the bad news as easily as possible to his kin, bury him with honors, and punish the ones who'd killed him.

Chipper Brown was, anyone in Nyack could attest, a man who regarded improving relations between the races a personal obligation. He was forty-five years old, lived in Spring Valley, had joined the Nyack Police Department thirteen years earlier, and was the only black on the force. A responsibility went with that, he believed. The way to make things better between whites and blacks was through the kids, he believed, so he'd spent his off-duty hours talking to them and telling them to stay off drugs, study hard, and make something of themselves.

He had a young son. Two daughters were in the Air Force overseas, as he had been right after the Korean War.

Now he was dead, gunned down by a black man.

Mortally wounded, Eddie O'Grady was rushed to Nyack Hospital. He was thirty-three years old and had spent a third of that life on the police force. A marine Vietnam veteran, he'd been raised in Nyack but had moved his family a year ago to a modern ranch home on a hillside on rustic Blauvelt Road in Pearl River. He'd been a sergeant for four years and was taking courses in criminal justice at St. Thomas Aquinas College. Now he was in a losing fight for his life and his partner was dead. A week ago they had assisted in delivering a premature baby; when the infant died, they cried together.

There would be mourners for him and Waverly Brown.

Cops from all over the country would come to their funerals because all lawmen are brothers.

The time was 4:05 P.M. Fifteen minutes since the Brink's truck had stopped at the Nanuet National Bank.

Mayhem and murder in a quarter of an hour.

At 4:07:49, the Rockland County police radio crackled a new message: "Orangetown car is in pursuit of a large white Buick north on Mountainview."

Richard Bartoline had seen the beginning of the getaway from the driveway of the Tappan Zee Townehouse. Having spent a day in business conferences in the hotel that overlooked the New York Thruway and Mountainview Avenue, he was leaving the hotel in a car with his boss driving and a woman fellow employee in the back seat when he heard the shooting. "Let's get the hell out of here," he said anxiously. His boss a former marine, said, "In the military, we hold."

"Hold?" Bartoline said. "Idiotic," he thought as the air around them crackled with bullets. Fifty rounds, he figured as he watched three cars speeding up Mountainview Avenue.

Moments later, Mrs. Kathleen Scott was looking out the window of her house on Mountainview to see what all the noise was. It sounded like gunfire, she'd remarked to her children. Drawing back the curtains to peek outside, she could hardly believe what was going on in her driveway and on her lawn. Three cars—a tan Honda, a BMW, and a white Olds. Six or seven black men running around. Lots of guns. One of the smaller black men was trying to squeeze into the trunk of the Honda and a bigger man was vainly trying to close it. Like some scene in a Laurel and Hardy movie or the Three Stooges, except for those guns, Mrs. Scott thought as she hurried to her telephone to call the police.

Having notified them, she peered through the window again. The BMW was still in her yard but the other cars were gone.

Not far away, Mrs. Terri Schwartz was coming from Valley Cottage toward the village of Nyack by way of Christian Herald Road. As she slowed at its intersection with Mountainview Avenue she noticed a tan Honda and a white Oldsmobile stopped on Christian Herald Road just beyond Mountainview, apparently with some mechanical problem because the Olds had its trunk open. Easing past the cars, she glanced at the occupants of the Honda and saw three people, one of them a white man with long straggly hair, a large nose, and a beard.

Moments later Mrs. Schwartz passed another car hurtling past in the opposite direction. In it was South Nyack police chief Alan Colsey. Having heard the police radios in his office, he was rushing to the scene, but suddenly, in the opposite direction on Christian Herald Road, came a couple of cars moving like bats out of hell. Wheeling around, Colsey began hot pursuit.

Nearby in their car at that moment, detectives Jim Stewart and Phil Burden of my staff found themselves on the horns of a dilemma. In their custody for safekeeping was Willie Brims, the star witness in the Sohn murder case who was due at my house at that hour to prepare for his appearance. But hearing the radio transmissions concerning the robbery, the reports of wounded police officers in the shootout at the Thruway, and Chief Colsey's radio report of his pursuit, Jim and Phil realized they were near the scene and might be able to set up a roadblock. They also realized that to do so might place Willie Brims in jeopardy. On the other hand, to do nothing might permit the escape of those who'd shot police officers they both knew and admired. Deciding to join the pursuit, they sped to the intersection of

Christian Herald Road and Route 9W. Skidding to a stop in the center of the crossroads, they warned Willie to stay down and stay put, sprang from the car, drew their guns, and took up positions on each side of the road.

Seconds too late, they heard Colsey on the radio again. "We're coming down Sixth toward Broadway." The location is in the heart of one of the village of Nyack's quaintest neighborhoods. Directly across Sixth where it deadends with Broadway, next door to the home of actress Helen Hayes, is 219 North Broadway, a century-old Victorian house with a cement wall in front.

On this gorgeous October afternoon, people were outdoors and were startled by two speeding cars coming down Sixth. The first was a large white Oldsmobile. The second was a beige Honda Accord. Veering sharply right on Broadway, the Olds got away but the Honda didn't make it, clipping a pole and slamming into the wall in front of 219.

An instant later, a third car screeched to a stop and out of this green police vehicle leapt Chief Colsey, gun in hand, yelling at the gathering crowd, "Keep back. Get away. They may be armed."

A white man lurched out with his hands up.

A woman in the car appeared to be reaching behind a seat. Warned repeatedly by Colsey to get out of the car, she finally obeyed meekly.

A black man in the rear of the car was dazed from a head injury.

Soon other police cars appeared, sirens screaming, lights flashing. Doors were flung open and grim men with guns bounded out.

Sixth and Broadway had turned into a crazy concoction of Mardi Gras and combat zone as curious residents gathered and police swarmed.

It was 4:15 P.M.

From the Honda the police took a fully loaded .380-caliber semiautomatic pistol with nine live rounds. From the woman's purse came four rounds of .380 ammunition. In an ammo clip stuffed into a sock of the black man were fourteen 9mm bullets. Also found: a brown ski glove, a ski mask, dark eyeglasses, a white bulletproof vest, and a pair of binoculars.

In the trunk was a green duffle bag and in it were two white canvas money bags containing $800,000—half the proceeds of the bank robbery at the mall.

Informed of all this in a phone call from Jim Stewart, I quelled what had been a rising anger at his not having arrived on schedule at my home with Willie Brims. I swallowed my astonishment at hearing that an important witness had been in the midst of a high-speed chase and informed Jim that I would be in Nyack right away, religious strictures regarding travel not withstanding.

When I arrived I learned that the white woman from the Honda had identified herself as Judith Clark. The white male carried identification cards in the name of James Lester Hackford. The injured black man gave his name as Solomon Bouines. The white woman nabbed by Michael Koch was insisting that her name was Barbara Edson.

What they said didn't count.

Their identities would be established through fingerprints. We all have them and there are no duplicates. How to classify them for identification purposes was the achievement of Juan Vucetitch and Sir Francis Galton in 1891. Modern technology in communicating information on prints and the use of computers and other scientific equipment has enhanced their work. If there is a file of an individual's prints, that person can be identified very quickly. In this instance, the process moved rapidly and within hours those of us who gathered at the Nyack police station knew the true identities of our guests:

JUDITH A. CLARK, thirty-one, a member of the Weather Underground who'd served a nine-month jail term in the "Days of Rage" riots in Chicago in 1969, last known to have been living and working in Manhattan, not wanted.

DAVID J. GILBERT, thirty-seven, a Weather Underground fugitive wanted in Colorado on charges of arson and assaulting a police officer, one of those involved in the Columbia University riots.

SAMUEL BROWN, forty-one, no known affiliation with radicals but a dangerous former convict with a long record of arrests and convictions for armed robbery, assault, burglary, and possession of weapons.

KATHY BOUDIN, the woman Michael Koch had apprehended, thirty-eight, a fugitive member of the Weather Underground wanted for jumping $10,000 bail in the "Days of Rage"; last seen running naked from the flaming rubble of an Eleventh Street townhouse in New York City's Greenwich Village that had been blown to bits when a bomb factory in its basement exploded in 1970.

12 | THE BIG DANCE

IN THE 1967 movie *The Graduate,* Dustin Hoffman hit it big—instant stardom as post-grad Benjamin in love with Katherine Ross while being pursued by the relentlessly seductive Anne Bancroft as Mrs. Robinson, all to the captivating music of Paul Simon and Art Garfunkel.

A contemporary observer of the music scene in America in the sixties believed Simon and Garfunkel were dealing with the meaning of life itself and not just offering a sweet collection of dream-world images and that their songs of love, loneliness, and alienation were the expression of the deepest feelings of the rock generation.

What many in that generation seemed to desire was an uprising against the old ways set to the music of Simon and Garfunkel, the Rolling Stones, the Beatles, Phil Ochs, and Bob Dylan, who'd let it be known "the times they are a-changin'" and that "you don't need a weatherman to know which way the wind blows."

By March 6, 1970, Dustin Hoffman was a major movie star and lived in a townhouse on Eleventh Street in the historic cradle of dissent and radicalism, New York's Greenwich Village. Next door to him in a nineteenth-century brownstone at No. 18 lived James Wilkerson and his family, including his attractive daughter Cathlyn, who was at home that morning as Hoffman put aside a script he'd been reading in his living room and left his house for a business appointment.

Moments later the Wilkerson house vanished in a thundering explosion. In the rubble, three bodies were identified: Tex Gold, twenty-three, a leader of the 1968 riots at Columbia University; Diana Oughton, twenty-eight, a former member of the Peace Corps, the daughter of a banker; and Terry Robbins, twenty-one, a former Kenyon College student, leader of a radical group known as the Weathermen. They died because one of them working in a basement workshop had connected one wire to a wrong one while making nail-stuffed antipersonnel bombs. There were at least sixty sticks of dynamite in the basement when the error was made.

When the house blew up, Cathlyn Wilkerson was on the second floor with another woman; both managed to scramble out as the building collapsed into a pile of wreckage within a cloud of suffocating dust and smoke. The force of the blast was so great that it ripped off their clothing. Naked and dazed, they stumbled toward Sixth Avenue. A neighbor gave them clothes and they got into a taxi and disappeared.

The second woman, according to officials who investigated the explosion, was Kathy Boudin, daughter of Leonard Boudin, a highly respected attorney. A traditional mainstream lawyer with liberal and leftist sympathies, he'd been Fidel Castro's American lawyer; an attorney for singer Paul Robeson, whose leftist leanings had led to difficulties with the government; counsel to the antiwar priest Philip Berrigan; and the famed defender of numerous other controversial people, including "atom spies" Julius and Ethel Rosenberg.

At the time of her arrest in Rockland County, Kathy was wanted in Chicago for jumping bail and not showing up to stand trial for taking part in an attack by a hundred women wearing crash helmets and swinging clubs on an armed forces recruiting center on October 9, 1969, in the "Days of Rage" surrounding the trial of the radicals who had disrupted the 1968 Democratic Party's National Convention.

Born on May 19, 1942, under the same astrological sign as two revolutionary luminaries, Malcolm X and Ho Chi Minh, she grew up surrounded by left-wing intellectuals who were friends of her parents in the 1950s. It was a time when Senator Joseph R. McCarthy was in his prime and making a political issue of Communists in the government who were being shielded by people McCarthy called "left-wing, bleeding-heart, phony liberals."

The kind of people McCarthy had in mind frequently gathered in the Greenwich Village parlor of Leonard and Jean Boudin and talked about how to attain their vision of a better world, a more caring world, a world of peace, a world no longer under threat of nuclear annihilation, a world of diversity, a world freed of the ancient curses of war, disease, and famine, a world of black and white together. A salon for thinkers and activists of the left, the Boudin home was a magnet for these people. Kathy found them enthralling and inspiring.

Boudin's legal practice enabled him to provide the best in education for his children. For Kathy, that was Bryn Mawr, where she majored in Russian literature and in her senior year made a pilgrimage to the Union of Soviet Socialist Republics, returning to graduate with honors in 1965 and setting out immediately to work as a community organizer in Cleveland, Ohio, for Students for a Democratic Society.

"We are the people of this generation, bred in at least modest comfort, housed now in universities, looking uncomfortably to the world we inherit," proclaimed SDS in their "Port Huron Statement." Written in 1962 by Tom Hayden, this description of the new SDS revolutionary certainly fit Kathy.

Disappointed by the lack of zeal of some SDS members, hard-core revolutionaries formed a faction. Taking a cue from Bob Dylan's lyric, they named themselves the Weather Organization. Their marching song was from the Beatles' *Yellow Submarine*. "We all live in the Weatherman machine, the Weatherman machine, the Weatherman machine. . . ."

If racism and the war in Vietnam were symptoms of what was wrong with America, the Weather revolutionists contended, it was necessary to go after the illness itself . . . the cancer that was the American system. One could attack the capitalist system easily, the Weathermen suggested. Shoplifting became a revolutionary act. Undermine the nation's moral structure and sense of propriety with shocking language; thus the emergence of a "free speech movement" that seemed to rest primarily on the use of one four-letter Anglo-Saxon word meaning fornication. Free love, meaning unbridled sex, was advocated and practiced. For America's "crimes," put the nation on trial. Put America in the dock for its sins against the colored peoples of the Third World. Spell it "Amerika," by the way. Haul Amerika up on a charge of racism not just at home but around the world. Unite. Link arms and take up arms in the socialist revolutions of the Viet Cong and the Fidelistas.

In 1969, Kathy was one of six SDS representatives who met in Havana with the Cubans and with North Vietnamese leaders. By now she was on the SDS national action staff. Also in the group was Bernardine Dohrn, a graduate of the University of Chicago Law School who was the mastermind of the attack on the recruiting station in Chicago in which the women dressed like men. "We are against everything that's good and decent in honky America," Dohrn proclaimed. "We will loot and burn and destroy. We are the incubation of your mothers' nightmares."

Side by side with Dohrn and Kathy marched Judith Alice Clark. All were arrested and released on bail. All skipped. All went onto "wanted" posters. All scrambled underground. "The Weather Organization is finished" some people proclaimed, and it seemed true until the Wilkerson house blew up and, in the years between 1970 and 1975, the Weathermen claimed responsibility for bombings that included explosions at police headquarters in New York City in 1970, the U.S. Capitol in 1971, and the State Department in 1975.

By the late 1970s, disillusioned, tired of being on the lam or just getting older, some of the Weatherman fugitives began giving up, including Dohrn and Wilkerson—but not Kathy Boudin. Wanted though she was and having lived underground for a decade, she had no plans for turning herself in. She now was part of a new group—the May 19th Coalition—affiliated with the Black Liberation Army. To come in, she felt, would be to concede the government's and the media's "propaganda campaign" that contended "the sixties are over" and that all the battles were finished and the "war" was over, as if the "struggle" of the 1960s could now be dismissed as if it had been a game of hide-and-seek and now it was time to come home free. She was not a child (indeed, she had a child of her own) so there would be no surrender, only action.

Thirty-eight years old, her dark hair now tinged with gray and framing wary deep-set blue eyes, with chiseled haggard features, Kathy was a typical Taurus personality—bullishly determined to tough it out, to struggle on. No giving up.

That was her resolve and her purpose on the way to Nanuet in an operation code-named The Big Dance, and it remained her purpose as she was brought handcuffed into the Nyack police station, insisting her name was Barbara Edson right up to the minute the fingerprint report came in from the FBI and erased all pretense.

Looking at her, I knew (as she did) that soon the whole world would learn that Kathy Boudin was in custody. I had decided that what the world had to see and appreciate was that she was not a romantic revolutionist being held for a dramatic revolutionary act and that she was not in jail in the name of a just cause. She was under arrest, I would make clear, for an armed robbery and three brutal and wanton murders.

From the instant I knew her identity I was determined not to prosecute an elusive radical butterfly who'd been flitting in and out of public sight and consciousness for twenty years.

I was going to prosecute her and her associates as robbers and murderers.

At 1:05 A.M. on Wednesday, October 21, Boudin, Clark, and Gilbert had been arraigned under their aliases in the Nyack justice court. Because of his injuries, Samuel Brown had been taken to Nyack Hospital and was arraigned there. All pleaded not guilty and were held without bail for a hearing on Friday.

In that interim there occurred many significant events, including their positive identification. Within hours, police in Rockland County traced the white Oldsmobile which had fled from Nyack to an East Orange, New Jersey, apartment. In association with New Jersey State Police they found materials for making bombs, a cache of weapons and ammunition, disguises, and diagrams of police stations and the Queens County DA's office. Also discovered were documents that linked the Weather Underground to the Black Liberation Army of fugitive Joanne Chesimard, who had escaped from a New Jersey prison in 1979 after her conviction for killing a New Jersey state trooper.

At midmorning on October 21, FBI agents and police swooped down on a hastily abandoned apartment in Mount Vernon, New York, where they found two safes, a ski mask, a bank-bag seal, ammunition, and bloodstained clothing. Simultaneously, raiders hit an apartment in the Bronx and found guns, ammo, and disguises.

In the afternoon, the FBI and other law enforcement organizations announced that they were investigating a possible conspiracy of violent radical groups and their involvement in a series of crimes—a Brink's truck robbery in the Bronx in June, a Purolator armored truck stick-up in April and another Purolator heist in March, an April 16 shootout with a pair of New York City policemen in Queens, and a bombing at a Schenectady, New York, rugby club that was host to a South African rugby team. It was also announced that the Oldsmobile used in the events of Tuesday in Rockland County had been traced and that authorities were looking for Marilyn Jean Buck, thirty-three, believed to have been wounded in the gun battle at the Thruway.

A thirty-four-year-old committed revolutionary, she had been described by Judge Samuel Conti in 1973 as very intelligent, very clever, and very dangerous. The only white member of the Black Liberation Army, she was its quarter-master, acquiring guns and ammunition, and had been responsible for maintaining several apartments used as hideouts and safe houses by the Brink's gang. She was believed to have accidentally shot herself in the leg while getting into the white Oldsmobile that had sped away from Nyack after the Honda crashed.

The first lawyer for a defendant to make an appearance in Rockland County was Leonard Boudin. He'd come not only as the attorney for Kathy but as a father. In his dual roles he had my sympathy and my empathy. He was a lawyer with a formidable job ahead of him and in that sense, as a lawyer myself and the one who would be prosecuting Kathy, I could appreciate the difficulties he faced legally because he had to recognize that we had a strong case against Kathy. I also saw Boudin as a father undoubtedly heartbroken over his daughter's plight. "We are going to defend her as well as we can," he told the reporters swarming outside Rockland County Jail in New City.

The *we* he referred to eventually included Manhattan civil rights lawyer Martin Garbus and Californian Leonard Weinglass, a brilliant counsel known for his defense of the "Chicago Seven" in the 1969 conspiracy trial, the focus of Kathy's actions during the "Days of Rage" that first made her a fugitive.

David Gilbert's lawyer was to be Lynne Stewart of New York City.

Samuel Brown's attorney was Evelyn Williams, also from Manhattan.

Judith Clark's representative was Susan Tipograph.

Two other defendants subsequently were added to the docket:

DONALD WEEMS, thirty-five, using the name Kuwasi Balagoon, was also a Black Panther and had been a fugitive since his 1978 escape from Rahway State Prison. His lawyer was Judith Holmes.

NATHANIEL BURNS, thirty-six, a fugitive former Black Panther who was arrested when a team of New York City detectives tracked him down in Queens two days after the Brink's robbery. In a gun battle with the police, a Burns accomplice named Samuel Smith was killed. On Smith's body was found a bulletproof vest that had a dent in it over a bruise. In his pocket was a .38-caliber slug that proved to have been fired from Sergeant Ed O'Grady's gun in the one-sided duel on the Thruway ramp. The bullet, the vest, and the bruise added up to compelling evidence that Smith had been one of the gunmen. Apparently he had kept the bullet as a souvenir.

Burns, using the name Sekou Odinga, was to be defended by a Detroit black-activist attorney, Chokwe Lumumba, who was also a dedicated radical advocating the establishment of a new nation carved from six Southern states to be known as the Republic of New Afrika, of which Chokwe Lumumba claimed to be the Minister of Justice.

Representing Judith Clark, Susan Tipograph appeared to me a political extremist herself, deeply committed to the same cause as her client and determined to use a trial to promote that cause. It was also evident to me that there was a very deep personal bond between Tipograph and her client.

I found Lynn Stewart, representing David Gilbert, equally committed to revolutionary ideas and difficult to deal with.

Different from the others was Martin Garbus, a forty-nine-year-old Madison Avenue lawyer who'd earned a reputation for defending civil rights cases in connection with the American Civil Liberties Union. Among his celebrated clients were the comedian Lenny Bruce and the farm workers' activist Cesar Chavez. While much in sympathy with the leftist causes of the 1960s, by the time he wrote his 1971 autobiography he had decided that the time had arrived to "move the battle from the street to the courtroom."

Garbus' co-counsel, Leonard Weinglass, was described in *The Journal-News* in contrast to me. "Although the most apparent conflict between the two men is a product of their adversarial roles in the courtroom, there is a deeper, fundamental conflict between Gribetz and Weinglass that flows from their personal philosophies and careers," wrote George M. Walsh.

"While both were raised in Orthodox Jewish households," he continued, "Weinglass quickly points out that he does not support 'the false Judaism of Zionism.' While he favors the existence of a Jewish homeland, he opposes an 'imperialist Israel,' which he said was formed at the expense of 'innocent Palestinians.' Gribetz on the other hand is active in organizations raising funds for Israel and takes annual trips to the Jewish state."

Being an activist in the cause of Zionism was a distinction I was proud of. In addition to numerous visits to Israel, I've also visited Jewish communities in Czechoslovakia and traveled to the Soviet Union to meet with Jews struggling against rigid restrictions that prevented them from emigrating to Israel. In support of their efforts, I have been privileged to serve as chairman of the Rockland County Committee for Soviet Jewry and as a member of the board of directors of the New York Coalition to Free Soviet Jews.

Balancing my adherence to Orthodox Judaism with the demands of being district attorney might appear to be difficult. It is not. For instance, the day of the funerals for Waverly Brown and Eddie O'Grady was a Saturday—the Jewish sabbath, a day I could not travel by car. To attend the funerals, I left my office on Friday afternoon and checked into a hotel near enough to the two churches where the services would be held for me to be able to walk to the ceremonies.

In his comparative article, Walsh also noted that I had been a prosecutor for my entire legal career and Weinglass had always been a defense attorney. "There is an itinerant quality to Weinglass' career. The unmarried lawyer has followed cases across the country, settling for years at a time and then moving on," he pointed out, while Gribetz was "firmly settled with his wife Judy and three daughters, Vicki, Tamar and Lisa, in Monsey and lived in Rockland since 1953."

Even in our physical appearance Walsh found opposites to write about. "The two men are completely different, one the model of 'eastern establishment' dress and the other California casual. Gribetz dresses impeccably in conservative suits and keeps every hair in place. Weinglass seems to dress up as a concession and, while he manages to look at home in a suit, he prefers casual dress and his reddish hair is frequently disheveled."

A turning point in my career had been my association with DA Frank Hogan. A turning point in his career, Weinglass told reporter Walsh, was when he first met Tom Hayden at the time of the 1967 riots in Newark, New Jersey, where Weinglass had been living and working in a black and Hispanic neighborhood. Becoming friends, each went his own way in the "movement," with Weinglass making a transition from a simple community legal practice to a national reputation as a defender of political radicals and Hayden going on to draft the SDS Port Huron manifesto.

In the end that manifesto was too tame for the woman

Weinglass was defending against charges of armed robbery and murder.

The code name Boudin and her co-defendants had chosen for their ill-fated robbery—The Big Dance—now seemed an appropriate description of the prosecutorial dilemma facing me and my associates as we prepared for a trial that would be conducted in the glaring lights of the world's news media.

13 | MEDIA CIRCUS

"AS AN AFRICAN Revolutionary," announced Donald Weems, "I intend to represent myself."

Judge Robert J. Stolarik peered down from his bench at a row of defendants staring back at him from a long table. At one end of it sat Kathy Boudin and her lawyers. At the opposite end were the other defendants and their attorneys.

"Mr. Weems," responded the judge, "you are aware of the nature of the charges against you? Basically, they amount to a homicide and a robbery indictment, and you feel capable of representing yourself against such charges?"

"Yes."

Was his desire to represent himself the result of his dissatisfaction with his lawyer?

"My dissatisfaction is with the government and with the legal system and this court particularly," retorted Weems.

The exchange took place in the Rockland County courthouse on Monday, September 13, 1982, almost eleven months after the explosive events at the Nanuet Mall and the Thruway on ramp. This verbal duel between the judge and Weems in the first few minutes of the hearing established the pattern that would be followed during most of the next year.

The defendants Judith Clark, David Gilbert, Nathanial Burns, and Donald Weems seemed an unlikely combination of whites who'd come from the middle-class, all-American mainstream and black men rooted in the hard times and bitterness of inner-city slums in New York and Newark. Along the way they had become allies in a mix of Weather Undergrounders, former Black Panthers, and "soldiers" in the Black Liberation Army. They all proclaimed loyalty to and citizenship in "New Afrika" and were dedicated to probing for an opening to turn the proceedings into a political forum for their radical views and a stage from which to express revolutionary condemnation of the U.S. legal system while taking advantage of it.

Kathy Boudin's courtroom team of Martin Garbus and Leonard Weinglass were attempting to build a record of pretrial error for use in any appeals that might be filed and to create a record for a change of venue to New York City and to find out more about our case.

The judge was striving to maintain decorum and propriety and to be fair to the defendants while on guard against errors that could mean reversals on appeal and to keep the process going.

The severely tested man on the bench for the hearings was Robert J. Stolarik. At fifty-two, a colonel in the Marine Corps Reserve, he was a father of six who had lived in Suffern since age thirteen and was a graduate of prestigious Xavier High School in Manhattan, St. Peter's College in New Jersey, and Fordham Law School. From being a country lawyer with a small rural practice he went on to become an assistant district attorney, a family court judge, county court judge, and finally a justice of the state supreme court. (In New York, the supreme court is not *the* supreme court—that is, the court to which ultimate appeals are made—but is a "lower" court. New York's "supreme" court is the court of appeals.)

In the tempestuous period of pretrial hearings at which

Judge Stolarik was to preside, he showed enormous patience in coping with rambunctious and often contemptuous defendants and their sympathetic lawyers even though it was obvious to observers of the process that there existed a yawning political gulf between his world and the "revolution" being espoused in his courtroom.

They were not defendants at all, said the defendants, but citizens and officials of the Republic of New Afrika, which had been proclaimed at its founding convention in Detroit in 1968. Among the demands of this "provisional" government was for the United States to give up land of former "slave states" which would become the Republic of New Afrika. These states "where black people have worked, slaved, bled and died," said Nathaniel Burns, were to be North and South Carolina, Alabama, Mississippi, Georgia, and Louisiana. "Now we understand that the United States Government is not going to give us anything," he explained from the witness chair. "They don't give nobody nothing. Oppressors do not give freedom to oppressed people. The people have to take their freedom. So we have formed the Black Liberation Army to struggle and help free the land. That's what we mean when we say 'free the land.'" Those involved in the struggle had abandoned their "slave names" for African names, he said, pointing out that his name was Sekou Odinga and no longer should he be called Nathaniel Burns.

Nothing more clearly demonstrated the chasm between the Judge and those who were on trial than the question of what names were to be used when addressing the defendants, an issue made by all the defendants and their lawyers, as this exchange between attorney Chokwe Lumumba and Judge Stolarik illustrates.

STOLARIK: I can't allow these proceedings to go on without every defendant having counsel.

LUMUMBA: Mr. Stolarik . . .

STOLARIK: So long as we are very, very technical as to how we are to address ourselves, I would suggest that you address the Court properly.

LUMUMBA: Well, the name is Stolarik, right?

STOLARIK: It is customary, at least in this jurisdiction, to address the judge by his appropriate title.

LUMUMBA: Since you are so technical, perhaps I should inform you something you may not know. Mr. Sekou Odinga is a citizen of the Republic of New Afrika. I am likewise. Mr. Sekou Odinga is a Freedom Fighter and a prisoner of war. Whenever a person claims prisoner of war status, you are required to assume that that is the case until these jokers over here prove that is not the case.

STOLARIK: Are you referring to the prosecutor?

LUMUMBA: Yes, I think that is what we call them.

We "jokers" in general and I in particular came under constant attack in these pretrial proceedings. More than once I was snippily referred to as "Gribetz" without the customary "Mr." Rebuked by the judge for this, Lumumba retorted, "I can call him 'Skip the Dog' if I want to."

Other complaints voiced by the defendants centered on the security measures that had been taken by the sheriff. The main thrust of this argument was presented by Garbus. As he came to the court the first morning, he said, "I saw thirty to forty helmeted police. We saw barricades. We saw men standing on the rooftops. When we came into the courtroom today we passed through three separate scannings. We also had a very rigid system of identification. It is a way of saying to potential jurors that these people are very, very dangerous and that these people are very, very guilty. It becomes impossible to get a fair trial."

In fact, the security that had confronted him that day was the direct result of genuine concerns growing out of the fact that no one knew what might be attempted by associates of those on trial—even accomplices to the crimes who had avoided arrest—who were perfectly capable of unleashing new terroristic attacks.

The scene outside the courthouse was a well-orchestrated event, a three-ring circus put on for the media. Fist-waving radicals exchanged shouts with local residents. While the demonstrators who supported the defendants were chanting "Gribetz, Gribetz, you can't hide; we charge you with genocide" locals were yelling "The USA is here to stay; if you don't like it, go away." The more than 100 red-shirted supporters of the defendants shouted back, "The BLA is alive and well; the FBI can go to hell." Most were in their twenties, although a few were as young as twelve. Shrill blasts from auto and truck horns answered the cry "Honk if you love the USA," and a crowd on the east side of Main Street sang, "God bless America, my home sweet home" in counterpoint to the crowd on the west side of the street chanting, "The KKK shoots to kill, the FBI foots the bill."

Inside the courtroom, full-bearded David Gilbert said in his New England accent. "The government that dropped napalm in Vietnam, that provides the cluster bombs used against civilians in Lebanon, and that trains the torturers in El Salvador calls us terrorists. We are neither terrorists nor criminals. It is precisely because of our love of life, because we revel in the human spirit, that we became freedom fighters against the racist and deadly imperialist system."

He made no mention of Chipper Brown, the black police officer assassinated almost a year ago.

Waving and smiling to supporters in the courtroom, Gilbert and Clark and Weems offered the court a choice of either allowing each personally to present a "political defense" or see them refuse to participate in the proceedings.

Another item on the agenda at the defense table was the jail in which the defendants were being held. It was unacceptable and inadequate all around, the lawyers maintained.

Then there came the day when a crowded airliner caused yet another delay. Rising before Judge Stolarik, Leonard Weinglass solemnly announced, "Your Honor, I have just been informed that Mr. Chokwe Lumumba has been bumped off a flight."

The Detroit-based lawyer had arranged to fly stand-by and when his flight to Newark was full had been left behind.

The judge turned mildly sarcastic. "How dare they bump him from that flight. He should have priority."

"Maybe they should give him a pass," said Weinglass with a bemused shrug.

In any event, the incident made it impossible to go on with the case that morning. In the afternoon, more time was consumed in a discussion of whether Kathy Boudin's father might be seated with her lawyers at the defense table, raising in my mind the prospect of all the defendants wanting additional counsel and the table being crowded with eighteen lawyers.

Reserving his decision on the issue, the judge ordered the defendants brought into court.

When they arrived, the question of how many lawyers we could fit at a table vanished in the face of a thorny problem of armbands. They were black bands and were meant to represent the "mourning" of the defendants for Palestinians "massacred" in refugee camps in Lebanon.

I had been to Lebanon twice with Jewish groups at the time of the Israeli invasion, so this demonstration appeared to me to be aimed at me. That I was not only Jewish but also pro-Zionist was known to them. They knew I had studied at the Hebrew University in Jerusalem. They knew exactly where my sentiments lay regarding Israel. Their armbands were, I was sure, their way of needling me. Aware of their goal, I refused to play into their hands and left any objections to the wearing of armbands in court strictly up to the judge.

Armbands, ruled Judge Stolarik, were not "in keeping with proper decorum in this courtroom."

Outraged, Donald Weems exclaimed, "This is consistent with the acts of the imperialists at Wounded Knee, Attica, and the South Bronx and we would like to have our armbands back."

Having caught a plane at last, Chokwe Lumumba nodded at us at the prosecution table and asserted "The fellows up at the table are dressed the way they want to dress." Lifting his eyes to Judge Stolarik, he added, "You dress the way you want to. I think your robe looks silly."

Turning to an aide, Detective James Woodward, I whispered, "It's amazing the amount of crap a judge has to put up with."

Next came a lengthy propaganda speech by Nathaniel Burns that ended with "Free the land," the slogan that was to be heard again and again in the court and outside.

"Mr. Burns," said Judge Stolarik, "I understood you wanted to make a statement concerning your legal representation."

"My name is Mr. Odinga," snapped Burns. "That is my name."

"You have been indicted as a Mr. Nathaniel Burns," said the judge.

"I don't need a lawyer before this court," said Burns. "I am not a criminal."

"Mr. Burns, are you saying that you don't want Mr. Lumumba as your lawyer?"

"I have no need at all for a lawyer."

Turning to Lumumba, Judge Stolarik asked if Lumumba understood that Burns was discharging him.

"I understand exactly what he is saying," said Lumumba. "He is a freedom fighter. He doesn't need a lawyer and he shouldn't be here. These proceedings are illegal and he is a prisoner of war. I understand that completely."

Thus unfolded the defense—disruptive tactics spiced with revolutionary rhetoric by Weems, Burns, Gilbert, and Clark with the support of and joined in by lawyers Lumumba, Lynne Stewart, Judith Holmes, and Susan Tipograph.

Among the "highlights" of the circus that they made of the pretrial phase of the proceedings:

- refusals by defendants to appear voluntarily in lineups
- an abortion for Judith Clark paid for by the taxpayers
- a demand by Burns "to be returned to the black community where I belong" rather than be held in jail; when that was refused, a demand to be put in a "prisoner of war" camp
- refusals to submit court-ordered handwriting samples
- resistance to providing hair samples, including Weems shaving his head and Clark and Gilbert finally having to be strapped in a dentist's chair so strands of hair could be cut
- Burns defying a court order to shave a beard he had grown and being wrestled to the floor and shaved by my detectives
- hours of speechmaking in court on subjects that had nothing to do with armed robbery and murder
- seemingly endless vilifications of the United States in the courtroom and outside the courthouse.

Compounding these difficulties as the case progressed was a problem that has bedeviled me for years: a chronic back ailment that in times of extreme stress causes me excruciating pain. If ever there were a situation likely to provoke a flare-up of the old problem, the Brink's case was it, and it promptly did so, to the point of requiring an interruption of one day's proceedings while I was whisked to a hospital emergency room for treatment. Thereafter, whenever there was a break in the trial routine I would stretch out on the floor of the courtroom in an effort to ease the tension and the pain and at day's end hurry for treatments from my chiropractor, Dr. Ernie Landi.

Partly because of my back ailment but primarily to maintain my physical fitness, for years I had followed a daily routine of swimming, weight-lifting, cycling, and aerobic exercises. During the course of the Brink's trial I became even more diligent in carrying out that regimen because I did not want the case jeopardized as a result of any inability on my part to continue growing out of trouble with my back.

The antics of the defendants and the whimsical condition of my back notwithstanding, the case moved forward.

Except for Kathy Boudin, of all those arrested on the day of the aborted robbery or rounded up since, Samuel Brown was the most mysterious and puzzling character in the case.

In every sense, he was an odd man out. A forty-two-year-old Staten Island resident, he had a record of robbery, larceny, and gun possession but no known political affiliations and no record of running with radicals until he was pulled from the wrecked Honda on Broadway in Nyack and gave his name as Solomon Bouines.

The FBI and federal attorneys were interested in Brown from the start, apparently recognizing in him an individual who could be "turned" and with whom a deal might be made wherein Brown would become a witness in the case of radical conspiracy the federal government was determined to build.

The discovery of the linkage between the Weather Underground and the Black Liberation Army as demonstrated in the Brink's case was the chief concern of the federal agencies; while I understood and respected their obligations and efforts, I had to be concerned with possible legal conflicts between our cases. Strains developed between us, primarily over Brown.

My interest in Brown was rooted in the testimony of Detective Art Keenan identifying Brown as one of the shooters of Waverly Brown and Eddie O'Grady. I was loath to enter into any kind of deal, even if he might be the key to an important federal conspiracy case.

Brown was in federal custody, which created serious problems because of differences in the rules under which we and the federal system operated. After state indictment, a defendant could not be interviewed by officials unless he waived his rights in the presence of his attorney, but that was not the case with the federal judicial system. A problem would therefore exist if information gathered under federal questioning reached us, raising the real possibility that our case could be legally jeopardized. I thus made it clear to all concerned that I did not want to know anything that Brown might have told the FBI in interviews conducted without my knowledge. Furthermore, I felt that the fact that he had been in federal custody and under questioning might create legal problems for us.

At some point Brown had suffered a broken neck, presumably in the crash of the Honda. Although X-rays at the time did not show such an injury, later ones did. Mr. Brown insisted that he'd been injured while in custody and was the victim of police brutality, a theme his temporary lawyer, William Kunstler, latched onto, describing Brown as a "disturbed, pained, drugged man" since his arrest. "The FBI has a man they can't rely on," he said—one of the few remarks by Kunstler that I could agree with. Public disclosure that Brown was regarded by the FBI as an important source of information, Kunstler asserted, would "ultimately redound to the defendants' advantage."

Was Brown a federal informant? Brown gave his answer to Judge Stolarik in a January 1983 hearing. "I am not an informer," he stated in an offended manner. "I haven't furnished no information to nobody."

Well, who was Samuel Brown and what was his story of how he wound up in Rockland County on that fateful day?

At a later date in the course of his own trial, Brown would give this version of what happened beginning early that morning of October 20, 1981:

Harlem acupuncturist Mutulu ("Doc") Shakur had asked Brown to accompany him. "I want you to see something," Shakur said, without being specific. For two years, Brown said, he had been living at Shakur's Black Acupuncture Association of North America in New York City, doing odd jobs and learning acupuncture as a means of treating drug addicts. "I trusted him," Brown testified. "Wherever we went before, it was never wrong."

They drove for a long time in a tan Honda and in Mount Vernon they got into a red van with other men he didn't know, Brown said. After being on the road for a time the van stopped and two white women got into the front because they were in a white neighborhood and blacks would look suspicious.

The robbery at the Nanuet Mall was a total surprise, he said. He'd shouted, "This is madness," as the action began. When someone handed him a gun, he testified, he refused to accept the weapon. He told the jury, "I said, 'This is crazy. We didn't come here for this.'"

Moments later, Brown said, the van door opened and the other men opened fire on the Brink's guards, but he'd stayed in the van during the robbery and was threatened with death as the vehicle was driven from the mall to a parking lot where it was abandoned as the gang switched to a U-Haul truck.

"Why didn't you flee at that time?" I asked him.

"I didn't know what I was doing. I was just prayin' I didn't get killed for something I didn't know anything about."

Nor did he do any of the shooting at the Thruway ramp, he insisted. Most of that was done by Cecil ("Chui") Ferguson, a thirty-seven-year-old black nationalist with an M-16 automatic rifle. "It was like the Fourth of July," Brown said. "Shooting, shooting, shooting." He said he waited until the others left the truck and then sprinted to a Honda in which Judith Clark and David Gilbert were waiting, although he did not know them at that time.

Neither did he know anything about a bulletproof vest found in the Honda, he said. What about the three layers of clothing he was wearing that day? Didn't he wear all that in order to shed it a little at a time so as to appear differently at different times to different witnesses and to confuse witnesses?

"I don't like cold weather."

I asked him if police hadn't found a .9mm ammo clip stuck in his sock.

Yes, but he'd found it on the floor of the Honda as he dove into the car during the gunfight and he'd kept it because he'd thought Gilbert might need it at some point.

"So you went basically as a consultant?" I asked incredulously.

"That's right."

In contrast to this fairy tale four prosecution witnesses,

including Art Keenan, would swear that Brown was one of the men shooting at Waverly Brown and Eddie O'Grady.

Whether Brown had or hadn't been a revolutionary when he was shooting police officers was irrelevant to the criminal case I was pursuing, but I was concerned about possible legal problems affecting our case while the federal government probed linkages between the Weather Underground, the BLA, and other terrorists.

Looking back I can see that friction was inevitable; I am amazed that there wasn't more, given the natural intensity of criminal investigations. That things moved as smoothly as they did was due in great measure to United States Attorney John Martin, a dedicated law enforcement official and highly skilled prosecutor. A good deal of credit for helping to smooth out any difficulties that did arise also goes to Robert McGuire, at the time New York City's police commissioner. I'd known Bob in my days in Frank Hogan's office and was appreciative when he stepped between my office and federal investigators to smooth feelings.

A concern raised by the defense was whether the defendants could get a fair trial in Rockland County, so a venue hearing was held in the appellate division in New York City. With me for the arguments were Harvey Eilbaum and John Edwards, who presented our side brilliantly, but when the court finally handed down its decision, it was to move the trial from Rockland to the Orange County court in Goshen, a pretty, rural community famed for its racetrack.

Named to preside over the trial was Judge David S. Ritter. At forty-eight, he had devoted much of his career to criminal law. After graduation from Cornell Law School he joined the U.S. Justice Department and did research in the federal prosecutions growing out of the quiz-show scandals of the late 1950s and then took part in the federal investigation of the Teamsters Union pension fund under Attorney

General Robert F. Kennedy. He ultimately decided to leave government for private practice and returned to Orange County in 1962. In 1970 he was an assistant DA. Appointed district attorney in 1975, he won election to the post in 1976, serving until his election to the county court in 1981.

In my first meeting with him I found him strictly professional and judicial in bearing with slightly graying hair, eyeglasses, and an accent that seemed like a cross between a Southern drawl and Western twang, a surprise coming from a man who'd lived outside New York less than three years. His manner of speaking could be quite homey, but he had a way of making it clear that his courtroom was never going to be less than a place of absolute decorum.

Nothing illustrates this better than what happened at our first appearance before him on June 2, 1983. As he entered the courtroom, a group of supporters of the defendants elected to show their contempt for the court by refusing to rise as the judge came in. Immediately there was a wrestling match between them and a handful of court officers attempting to get them to stand.

Leaping to her feet, Susan Tipograph, Judith Clark's lawyer, pointed at Judge Ritter and shouted, "This was provoked by you, Judge. You show us a law where people have to stand up in a courtroom."

Clark cried, "Fascist dogs! Fascist dogs!"

David Gilbert added loudly, "Call off the thugs."

Tipograph yelled, "What law is there that someone has to stand up in a courtroom when a goddam judge walks in?"

Donald Weems, known as Kuwasi Balagoon, joined the chorus. "If you want people to stand up, you have to have a New Afrikan flag. No supporter of ours is going to stand up to the American flag."

Judge Ritter ordered the defendants and their lawyers removed from the courtroom, and as they were being taken out the spectators who had supported them also left, shouting, "BLA freedom fighters; FBI night riders."

I welcomed Judge Ritter's firmness. He seemed to me a straight-down-the-middle jurist who was determined to keep the case moving. I saw in him a judge who would look to the law. I was proved correct in this assessment on the first day of the trial—August 9—when, rather than allowing Donald Weems to make a rambling propagandistic speech, Judge Ritter sustained my strenuous objection that Weems' speech had not a thing to do with the case or any evidence he might produce and therefore the longwinded monologue was out of order.

"In that case, I'm leaving," grumbled Weems.

What happened next was a fleeting moment of theatrics by the defendants but a major breakthrough for us. To show their disdain for Judge Ritter and the trial, all the defendants stormed out of the courtroom, vowing never to return. Shouting "All oppressors will fall" and "Death to the U.S. Imperialism," Clark and Gilbert followed Weems out, as did their small group of noisy supporters shouting "Free the land."

This tactic grabbed a few headlines for them, but it was a blunder on their part because it made it possible for the trial to proceed rapidly. Suddenly we were looking at the very real possibility that the trial would be over in a matter of days rather than months. We had been liberated from constant disruptions and harassment.

The federal case in New York in which the government was attempting to prove a conspiracy among various violent radical groups came to an end at this time, resulting in the conviction of Nathaniel Burns and others on the conspiracy charges that carried far less serious penalties than those we were seeking in the criminal proceedings.

With the federal case completed, Burns was called to the stand by the defense.

In effect, however, he became a witness for the prosecution during his hour and a half on the stand being questioned by Donald Weems (Kuwasi Balagoon) and cross-examined by me and describing the events in Nanuet and Nyack in brutally damning terms.

His direct testimony under questioning by Weems began as an exercise in propaganda as Weems asked, "Having been born in New York City, New York, doesn't that make you a citizen of the United States?"

"No. That makes me a victim of the United States."

He was, he said, a citizen of New Afrika, a nation inside the United States consisting of "the Afrikan descendants of the slaves that were brought here."

"And what does the term *freedom fighter* mean?" Weems asked.

"Freedom fighter is simply a person who fights for the freedom of their people, and I am fighting for the freedom, liberation, self-determination of the New Afrikan nation, the New Afrikan people," Burns replied.

"As a New Afrikan freedom fighter, do you belong to any group or organizations?"

"I consider myself a soldier of the Black Liberation Army."

What happened on October 20, 1981?

An "expropriation" happened, said Burns.

"What do you mean by expropriation?"

"Expropriation is when one tries to take back some of the materials, finances, whatever, that has been illegally taken from them. When I speak of expropriations such as from a bank—the banking industry in this country have historically backed, supported slavery. So when New Afrikan freedom fighters tried to take back some of that wealth that was robbed through the slave labor that was forced on them, and their ancestors, that is called expropriation."

In the course of an expropriation or other action, Burns replied as he was questioned by Weems, freedom fighters and members of the BLA would kill police officers who stood in the way of the expropriation.

Following up on that assertion, in my cross-examination I asked Burns, "It would have been justified to take the life of Sergeant Edward O'Grady if he resisted you with a weapon on October 20, 1981, at a roadblock at Mountainview Avenue in Nyack, New York?"

"If he put soldiers of the Black Liberation Army's lives in danger, it was definitely justified to put his in danger. If the soldiers were fortunate enough to beat Sergeant—who did you say?"

"O'Grady."

"If they were fortunate enough to beat him on that day, then yes, it was definitely correct and it was justified in every way."

"Would it also be justified to take the life of Officer Waverly Brown, a black police officer?"

"The color is not what we are talking about right here. We are talking about the agents of one army versus the soldiers of another."

"With regard to Peter Paige, who was a guard for the Brink's Corporation, would it be justified to take his life during an expropriation?"

"If he had a gun and he was putting soldiers of the Black Liberation Army's lives in jeopardy, yes, it would be justified."

"If a Mr. Trombino, who is also employed by the Brink's Corporation, was trying to close the door when the funds were being taken, would it be justified to then shoot him in the arm?"

"Well, if it was the arm that was trying to block the expropriation, then it was justified to shoot that arm off."

He had not shot off Joe Trombino's arm, but only good luck and expert medical care had saved it. Years would be required before he would have the full use of it again, if ever. Of all that had happened on that brutal day, I thought as I ended my questioning, what illustrated the depravity of that gang was the deliberate attempt to shoot off Joe Trombino's arm simply to keep him from closing the door of that armored truck.

What they had before them, I said to the jury in my summation, was "armed robbery committed by three criminals and the killing of three innocent people and the maiming of another." A "justification" of those acts as the legal action of an army of freedom fighters, I said, was nothing but a sham and an insult to the intelligence of Americans.

"In fact, they attempted to rationalize in the most contemptible way," I said. "The distorted rationale is totally absurd and cannot be accepted by civilized society."

The jury agreed.

On October 11, 1983, nine days short of the second anniversary of the robbery and murders, Judith Clark, David Gilbert, and Donald Weems were sentenced for what Judge Ritter described as "cold, calculated and deliberate" crimes. "They hold society in contempt," he stated, "and have no respect for human life. They anticipated resistance and went about their task armed to the teeth. I harbor no illusions. Everything that the defendants have said indicates they will repeat their lawless conduct. Each defendant represents a clear and present danger to society."

On each of the three he imposed a maximum term of life in prison for each of three second-degree murder counts and a twenty-five-year minimum, the terms to be served consecutively, meaning a total of seventy-five years each before parole could be considered.

There would be no appeals; to do so would be a recognition of the authority of the court, the judicial system, and the government they despised.

None of the defendants was in the courtroom to hear the sentences imposed, however. After one more propaganda speech, each of them lifted a clenched fist in final defiance and tramped out of the room while their diehard supporters shouted "Free the land."

Three hours after sentencing, wearing matching tee shirts bearing the initials OCCF (Orange County Correctional Facility), David Gilbert and Kathy Boudin stood before the jail chaplain and three guards and got married.

Kathy had not stood trial with Gilbert, Clark, and Weems because her case and that of Samuel Brown had been ordered severed from theirs.

The next act of her drama would unfold neither in Orange nor Rockland but across the Hudson in Westchester County.

14 | REFLECTIONS FROM UNDERGROUND

NOTHING MORE CLEARLY demonstrated what appeared to be the ludicrous hypocrisy of Kathy Boudin's self-professed "devotion" to radicalism and justice for blacks than the glaring gap that quickly materialized between her, the other defendants and Samuel Brown. Throughout all her years in SDS and the Weather Organization she and her colleagues made it clear that they'd been motivated by an outraged concern for the plight of blacks in America, but from the beginning of her troubles in Rockland County the thrust of the legal activities on her behalf was to distance her from her comrades and Brown.

As we headed into trial, she had full-time lawyers working on her case and the full support of her father's law firm; Brown was an indigent defendant with no resources beyond the court-appointed attorney. Boudin attorneys were working without let-up to have her case severed from his, a petition that was denied by the court, much to my relief. It was crucial to my case, I felt, for Kathy Boudin to be on trial with one of her companions who actually engaged in the shooting with the police on Mountainview Avenue. I wanted to be certain the jury in her trial would never forget that three people had been murdered and that the woman before them was not the sympathetic figure she appeared to be but a lifelong radical whose idealistic political views did not prevent her from participating in a carefully plotted armed holdup that ended in murder.

What also became abundantly clear at this time was the far-reaching influence of Leonard Boudin within the "establishment" his daughter was dedicated to destroying. It soon became apparent that a well-coordinated and far-ranging effort was underway by the Boudin defense, Leonard Boudin himself, to place Kathy in the most favorable light possible on the eve of her trial.

Having successfully argued that the first trial had tainted the objectivity of the people of Orange County and gotten the case transferred to Westchester County, the Boudin lawyers now wanted another venue change, this time to Brooklyn, New York (Kings County), apparently in the belief that Kathy would be more sympathetically received in an urban setting with its substantial minority population from which the jury would be chosen.

In light of that stratagem and with jury selection to begin in White Plains in Westchester, the publicity campaign on Kathy's behalf moved into high gear. From the beginning of the case in October 1981, Kathy had been the focus of media attention, but in the days immediately preceding and during jury selection there was what amounted to a media blitz whose aim was, it seemed to me, to influence prospective jurors.

It began with an eleven-page article in *The Village Voice*. Ordinarily a story in the ultraliberal weekly newspaper published in New York's Greenwich Village would have had minimal impact, but this one, "Conversations with Kathy Boudin" by Jane Lazarre, was picked up by the wire services and their newspaper clients, including some in Westchester County where the jury was being selected. The article began on page one and featured a large photo of Kathy that was an example of how to create a sympathetic atmosphere. Taking half the front page the black-and-white photo depicted a lonely-looking, somber, wistful-appearing woman in drab prison garb leaning against a bleak and bare brick wall, immediately evoking the impression that she was waiting for the firing squad.

Themes of isolation, vulnerability, and being misunderstood permeated the entire text. "Kathy was disturbed by the silence surrounding her case" and was unhappy that newspaper reports referred to her as "a terrorist and depicted her as a thug."

"It was her cry, of a woman enveloped in silence, that initially touched me," said Lazarre. After visiting her in the jail in Goshen, she described Kathy as appearing sallow with deep rings under her blue eyes. "She is 40, like me. She is very thin. She was a mother separated from her three-year-old child."

Much of the article delved into Kathy's history as a radical leading up to her being arrested "in connection with the Brink's truck robbery and related killings," a curious phraseology, leading a reader to conclude that Kathy had not been on the scene willingly and was merely "connected" to the Brink's robbery by happenstance and that somehow the killings of Brown, O'Grady, and Paige were not the direct result of the robbery but were only "related" to it.

"Kathy Boudin struck me forcefully as a woman in transition, and that engaged me," wrote Lazarre. Kathy was a person who saw herself primarily as a woman of conviction, a woman who had lived her life as a fighter. "She's been involved in all the major struggles of the American left and she believes she deserves more support from the left than she has received."

Two weeks after the Lazarre article, Kathy received an ample amount of support from columnist Sydney Schanberg in *The New York Times*. The theme is similar to Lazarre's article, that Kathy was *"associated* with people who had been convicted for attacking a Brink's truck in Rockland County and killing a Brink's guard and two police officers *in the process."* (Emphasis mine.) She had been underground as a fugitive since 1970, Schanberg wrote, *"in connection with* an explosion in a Greenwich Village town house whose basement, *the authorities said*, was a bomb factory."* (Again, emphasis mine.)

Even in the more liberal climate of the 1960s, Schanberg continued, Kathy's causes as an activist of the left did not enjoy wide public approval. "Now, in the Reagan years, the public mood marks them as anathema.

"All of this is apparently why the authorities—the prisons, the courts, the elected officials—have decided they can treat her with less than fairness and less than constitutional propriety and get away with it."

While considerably more sophisticated, Schanberg's language and that of Lazarre added up to what Clark, Gilbert, Weems, Burns, and their lawyers had maintained in court: that the people on trial were victims of oppressive and tyrannical government. A major weapon in this oppression of Kathy was, in Schanberg's view, the deplorable condition of the jail in which she was being held. But she was being held in Rockland's jail because the cost of additional security in placing her in Westchester's was unacceptable to Westchester authorities and we could no longer hold her in Orange County's jail.

Describing the jail as "terrible" during an appearance on the NBC television program *Today*, Leonard Boudin himself generated a sense of sympathy for himself and his daughter.

That Boudin was on national television was a tribute to his ability to use his very considerable fame and influence to the benefit of his daughter and a reflection of the almost insatiable appetite of the news media for stories about her.

From the outset, she had been the focus of intense news coverage, all of it stemming from her being seen as a romantic figure. As the opening of her trial neared *Newsweek* reported, "Not only is she the daughter of prominent left-wing lawyer Leonard Boudin, she also spent 11 years as a fugitive, disappearing after a 1970 explosion of a Greenwich Village town house that served as a radical bomb factory." That was her mystique—the dedicated activist on the run, and a woman, too.

Until this time, the attention paid to Kathy Boudin had been the result of the natural tendency of journalists to focus on names and personalities. Certainly, she was a better news story than any of the other defendants, but the sudden explosion of stories about her as we began jury selection in her trial went beyond normal journalism, I believed. What was going on, I felt, was part of her defense team's strategy to depict Kathy Boudin as deserving of sympathetic treatment. She hadn't been a shooter, after all, the argument went, and had done so little on that fateful day as to be almost blameless.

Indeed, jury selection for the Boudin-Brown trial was one of the most difficult I'd ever encountered. The trial was going to be long. I expected that the jurors would serve at least six months and was certain that few of the prospective jurors would be willing to make that much of a commitment of time.

While we were examining jurors, Kathy Boudin was there looking very sympathetic and very harmless—exactly the person described in the *Voice* article and in a glowing piece on her in *Mademoiselle*.

One prospective juror was not persuaded. Asked if she knew anything about Boudin, the woman—a secretary at an

IBM facility in Westchester—replied that she knew Boudin had been a member of the Weather Underground and that the group was antigovernment, terrorist, and responsible for bombings. The woman was excused from the jury, and that very night a bomb tore through the IBM plant. It was a coincidence, but the next day Leonard Weinglass took advantage of it. "All the IBM employees in this case may very well have to be excused because their employer has been the target of a bombing," he suggested. At that time twenty-five potential jurors were IBM employees.

More than any event in the long course of the Brink's case, the bombing at IBM dramatically underscored the problem of the security of all of us involved in prosecuting the gang. Tight security surrounded the defendants to guard against possible attempts by their allies to free them. Steps had been taken to secure the sites of trial—jails, courtrooms, routes taken by the defendants. Protection had been provided for the judge. And whether or not I and my family ought to be provided with bodyguards was discussed.

Initially my feelings ran strongly against doing anything that would intrude on the normal routines of my family and on the tranquility of my neighbors, but in this instance I agreed to police patrols near my home. This was as much for my neighbors' safety as for mine. Many of them were understandably on edge living near me at a time when I was prosecuting some of the most dangerous revolutionaries in the country. That their concerns were real was illustrated when a parcel delivery service left a package on the doorstep, a bundle some of the neighbors feared might have been a bomb until the police determined that it was harmless mail-order merchandise.

Always keenly aware of the effect my work might have on my family, I generally discussed that work with them, especially if a particular case was receiving extraordinary attention by the public or the news media. These glimpses at my professional life usually happened during the family sabbath dinner on Fridays. Besides making my family aware of my work, I discovered another benefit in relating cases to them. If after having laid out a case for them I discovered that they were confused or otherwise missed the thrust of the evidence, I asked myself, "If they don't get the point, how will a jury?"

Selecting Brink's jurors was a painfully slow process punctuated by attempts by the defense to delay it further. There were fresh attempts to have the trial moved to Brooklyn based on allegations by Weinglass that the jury-selection process in Westchester demonstrated a widespread prejudice against Boudin, an ironic assertion considering the blizzard of sympathetic publicity she'd received. Their objections notwithstanding, the jury screening continued and by April 12, 1984—two and a half years after the crimes were committed—we were close to the end of jury selection.

On that day, out of the blue, Weinglass approached me in court and took a step that appeared to make the entire process moot: "I'd like to talk to you about glass." Glass fragments were part of the circumstantial evidence in the case.

"If we're going to talk about evidence," I replied, "we'd better do it before Judge Ritter because you and I are going to disagree."

"No, I don't want to talk before the judge," he said.

Suspecting that glass had not been on his mind at all, I told him that if we weren't going to do our talking in front of the judge, then it would have to be with Jim Stewart present. He agreed and three of us went into a room used by court security personnel for coffee breaks.

Immediately, he said he wanted to talk about a plea

bargain and a disposition of his client's case. Kathy had changed, he said. "She's contrite."

"That is bullshit. This is more of this public relations job that you people have been doing," I said, mindful of the *Village Voice* piece, Schanberg in *The Times*, Leonard Boudin on *Today*, the *Mademoiselle* profile, and a flurry of private communications I'd been getting from prominent persons on Kathy's behalf—all of them a lesson in how a case can be fought outside the courtroom as well as inside.

Very early in the case, Martin Garbus had been sounding me out regarding a plea, but always in terms of her entering a plea of guilty only to robbery with a minimal prison sentence—which I summarily rejected. This time, suddenly, Weinglass was opening the door to a murder plea.

On a strictly personal level, I had grave philosophical problems in entertaining a plea bargain in a case involving the killing of three people, two of them cops, and I held firmly to that position. If they wanted to bargain for a plea, fine, but it had to be murder with a stiff sentence.

He'd have to get back to me, he said.

When he did come back it was to agree to my conditions of twenty-to-life without the possibility of parole before twenty years and that there would be no appeals of any kind. This total capitulation of the Boudin defense was a shock to me. Bitter disappointment was etched in Weinglass' face.

Now we took it to the judge.

Before he accepted my plea, Judge Ritter informed us, he wanted Kathy Boudin to submit to a lie-detector test to determine if she had been involved in any other robberies and to be certain that she had not fired any weapons or had done anything to facilitate the shooting of a police officer.

Because the federal government had proceeded with their investigations into the Brink's robbery from the conspiracy angle, I asked U.S. Attorney John Martin in New York if he could provide assurances based on intelligence files that in her role in the Brink's robbery and subsequent events she had not done any shooting. Those assurances were given.

On the crucial questions relating to Brink's, she passed the test. Had she carried a weapon? No, she said, the polygraph registering a truthful answer. Had she acted in accord with a plan to enable others to shoot the police? "No." Truthful. Did she ever *directly* participate in any other robbery or bombing in which someone was physically injured or shot? "No." True.

With the polygraph test completed and the judge satisfied, the way was cleared for a guilty plea.

Then there was a last-minute hitch.

On April 25 Harvey Eilbaum telephoned me and reported that it appeared the deal was falling apart.

Boudin was prepared to admit very little, Harvey reported, and what she would admit might not even constitute a crime.

"We cannot be put in a situation where all she admits to is robbery," I insisted. "Convey those sentiments to Judge Ritter and to Mr. Weinglass. We have an agreement. If Boudin doesn't like it, there won't be any plea at all. If they want a trial, we'll have a trial. It's up to them."

On Wednesday, May 2, Weinglass came to my office again, looking haggard and clearly upset, and at that instant I knew he was going to stick to my terms and therefore Kathy Boudin was going to be sentenced to a term of twenty years to life with no possibility of parole before the year 2001.

It was victory for the people, for the victims living and dead, for justice.

"It's my understanding that Miss Boudin is prepared to enter a plea of guilty to the crime of murder in the second degree and robbery in the first degree," I said for the record in court the next day. "It's my further understanding that at the appropriate time the people will recommend and that Your Honor will sentence Miss Boudin to an indeterminate term of prison with a minimum of twenty years to a maximum of life imprisonment, as a result of which the defendant Boudin will not be eligible for consideration by the Board of Parole before October 20, 2001."

Now came the time for Judge Ritter to admit into the record from her own lips that Kathy Boudin was guilty of all counts of crimes agreed to in the plea. "Please tell me what it is that you did that makes you criminally responsible for the charges contained in those counts," he asked.

Kathy replied, "On October twentieth 1981 I went to Rockland County as part of a robbery plan. That plan was to seize money from Brink's guards at the Nanuet Mall. My role, as a participant in the plan, was to wait in a parking lot behind the Korvette's store in order to help those that took the money flee from the area with the proceeds in a U-Haul truck." She knew the nature of the undertaking, she said. She had been unarmed throughout. She was not motivated by any plan to either disarm or distract the police so they could be shot. "I feel terrible about the lives that were lost," she said.

In the courtroom as she expressed her sorrow and remorse were Diane O'Grady, Sergeant O'Grady's wife, and six members of his family. Greg Brown, Officer Waverly ("Chipper") Brown's nineteen-year-old son, was there. Peter Paige's family had chosen not to face the horror of his death again, but an official of the Brink's Corporation was on hand. Art Keenan was there bearing scars. So was Brian Lennon, with his memories of the blazing duel he'd fought pinned down in his patrol car. Michael Koch was there because he'd been scheduled to testify that day, as was Norma Hill, still haunted by awful memories of her BMW being commandeered by a gunman and her mother thrown out onto the road.

The Boudin family and many of their friends and supporters were there, including William Ayers, a former Weatherman now married to Bernardine Dohrn of the "Days of Rage." The veterans from that dim and distant era were now caretakers of the son Kathy and David Gilbert had parented underground.

Members of the news media were present for one last extravaganza with Kathy. Again she would be their front-page headlines and lead stories on the evening news from coast to coast, because of all those who'd been implicated in the Brink's case she was and always had been, in the words of *Time*, "the most notorious."

A few weeks later, the scene was very different in another courtroom as the final act in the Brink's drama unfolded with the trial of Samuel Brown. For most people it was a nonevent. There was nobody in the courtroom. "What upsets me very much," I said to John Edwards, "is that nobody gives a damn any longer about the fact that two police officers and a Brink's guard have died."

The trial opened on May 21. It ended on June 12 with a verdict of guilty. On June 27 Judge Ritter sentenced Brown to three consecutive sentences of twenty-five-years-to-life.

Although I'd achieved all of my goals in our case, the saga of the Brink's gang was to continue to unfold at other places, other times contributing to the crushing of a movement that had been aimed at the destruction of the American system:

- Marilyn Jean Buck, arrested on May 11, 1985, raising a fist in court and declaring "I am an anti-imperialist freedom fighter," her conviction in federal court in New York City in May 1988, and a fifty-year sentence.
- Dr. Alan Berkman, a thirty-nine-year-old Harlem physician alleged to have sheltered Buck and treated her leg wound after she had fled from Nyack, arrested two weeks after Buck in a Philadelphia suburb; charges dismissed Oct. 7, 1987
- Judith Clark, convicted of conspiring to escape from the Bedford Hills correctional facility in September 1985
- The U.S. Supreme Court in October 1985 turning down a bid by Samuel Brown to have his trial invalidated because, he said, Judge Ritter "exploited his trial rulings in order to get elected to the New York State Supreme Court"
- The February 13, 1986, arrest, in Los Angeles of Harlem acupuncturist Mutulu Shakur, the ringleader and mastermind of the Brink's robbery, also convicted in a federal trial in New York City in May 1988 and sentenced to sixty years

The financial cost to Rockland County, when finally tallied and paid off by County Executive John T. Grant with a check for $72,200 payable to Orange County, was $5.4 million.

Ponder that figure, I say to people to whom I speak about the Brink's case, because it is a measure of the grandeur of the American system. Here was a gang whose admitted purpose was the overthrow and destruction of the American system. Yet that system spent millions of dollars and required the expenditure of thousands of hours of labor by hundreds of individuals to guarantee a fair trial to gangsters who would not stop at murder and, had the tables been turned and they had put us on trial, would have rendered no such justice.

Reflecting on the life she chose to live in the Weather Underground, Boudin said at her sentencing, "I was there out of my commitment to the Black Liberation struggle and its underground movement. I am a white woman who does not want the crimes committed against black people carried in my name. I see the black freedom movement as both a way of providing fundamental justice for black people and a key to bringing about change for the entire country. Although underground for twelve years, a step I took initially because of my opposition to the war in Vietnam and the repression of the black movement, I think I remain essentially the same person I was before. Looking back on twelve years underground and forward to at least twenty more years in jail, I cannot help but reflect on my life. Fundamental change is long and hard. Setbacks from mistakes are as much a part of that process as victories. The meaning of my life has come from being part of a worldwide tradition of fighting for a more just and humane world. My ideals give me strength today as well as yesterday and tomorrow."

My reflections upon the life of Kathy Boudin were somewhat different as I addressed that packed courtroom on judgment day. "We care not what Miss Boudin's motivations may have been, what prompted her to rebel in the manner which she did. Her motivations may have been well intended. Her concerns for the unfortunate may well have been sincere. But her methods were violent and despicable.

"Peter Paige, Edward O'Grady, and Waverly Brown were also concerned and compassionate human beings, individuals who had much to offer society, to those who knew and loved them, and to those who might have come to know and love them.

"Unlike Miss Boudin, however, they expressed their concern in a manner consistent with their feelings. They had sought to brighten, rather than destroy. In the final analysis that is the distinguishing factor—how one transforms ideals into action—that sets the civilized apart from the uncivilized."

15 | DEATH MASK

EIGIL DAG VESTI had the future on his mind. A twenty-six-year-old Norwegian, he had the looks of a male fashion model. He was a student at the Fashion Institute of Technology, but it was the designing of clothing that interested Eigil, not wearing high-style garments in the shows of other designers. The start of the future he was dreaming about was close—graduation—and he'd spent the early hours of February 22, 1985, working on his résumé in his loft apartment on West Twenty-sixth Street in Manhattan.

Getting this far toward his dream had not been easy. The son of a Norwegian seacaptain, he'd grown up with two older sisters in a large house on a quiet Oslo street. In his early teens he realized he was homosexual, had no problem accepting it, and took no steps to deny or hide the fact, although friends found him charmingly shy, naive, and easily embarrassed by the blatant exhibitionism of others who were gay. At sixteen he decided on a fashion-design career. Studying in Norway and Denmark, he soon realized he wanted to study design in America, but language difficulties were a major stumbling block. He set out to overcome this problem by shipping out for a year on Norwegian cruise ships that catered to predominantly English-speaking tourists. The result was not only a marked

229

improvement in his English but also the development of a cultivated continental charm that would become a hallmark second only to his handsomeness.

Accepted at the Fashion Institute of Technology in September 1982, he was soon the talk of the school. Slender, a shade under six feet tall and with blond hair and blue eyes, he was, said a friend, "so good-looking and so fashionable you couldn't help but notice him." Impeccably dressed in expensive clothes borrowed from designer Richard Gaines, he liked going out to trendy clubs and discotheques frequented by the powerful figures in the world of fashion and art he desperately wished to become part of.

Not far from Eigil Dag Vesti's apartment stood the most popular of these discos, the Limelight. At the corner of West Twentieth Street and Sixth Avenue, it occupied what had once been the Church of the Holy Communion. Despite outraged complaints by neighborhood residents who didn't want the noise and crowds of a disco on their doorstep and clergymen who saw sacrilege in converting a church—even an abandoned one—to such a purpose, the property was bought by a Canadian developer and renovated at a cost of nearly five million dollars. An instant hit, like other fashionable discos it lavished special attention on the celebrities and other patrons who by virtue of their style and looks had been deemed worthy of exception. A private room was set aside for these "very important people" and, not surprisingly, was called the VIP Room.

The room's manager was Fred Rothbell; his duty was to see that the favored customers were admitted promptly and catered to properly. He was so good at the job that his boss had recently rewarded him with a vacation in Puerto Rico that included the use of a villa in the exclusive resort of Palmas del Mar nestled in quiet seclusion overlooking beaches of snow-white sand and turquoise sea an hour from San Juan.

Fred had unexpectedly encountered other guests at the idyllic hideaway—a man named Edo Bertoglio, a photographer and filmmaker who was a regular at the Limelight, and his girlfriend, Lynn Smith. The situation was unpleasant and abrasive and worsened after Edo left. Fred was displeased with the manner in which Lynn was behaving. He believed she was mistreating their absent host's property and expressed that displeasure. Lynn thought he was bossy and trying to take over, and when she reported this to Edo he became furious. That resentment lingered, and Edo made no secret among his friends that he would be happy to get even with Fred for his treatment of Lynn.

Almost an obsession, how to settle the score was never far from Edo's thoughts and frequently a subject for discussion between him and his friends.

One of these was a moody young man named Bernard LeGeros. Known as BJ and sometimes as Frog, he was the twenty-three-year-old son of Racquel and John LeGeros, who, as chief of the management review and analysis section of the United Nations Development Program, administered financial aid to Third World countries. After he graduated from LaSalle Academy in 1980, Bernard had attended New York University's School of Continuing Education as a part-time student for four years and had earned an Associate of Arts degree. An amateur photographer, he enrolled as a film student at New York University in May 1984 but dropped out and worked for art dealer Andrew Crispo.

A troubled youth, he had been prevented from leaping from the roof in a suicide attempt, talked out of it by the security guards at the Waterside Plaza apartments beside the East River where he lived. Three months later he swallowed cyanide but was again saved from death. Disturbing behavior had also been noted by people who lived near the LeGeros family's small country estate on Buckberg Road in Tomkins Cove in the northernmost corner of Rockland County. One girl said she'd gotten obscene phone calls from him and had seen him "parading up and down the hill in camouflage fatigues with a rifle."

Originally a full-time home, the residence set among old trees and screened from the road by dense shrubbery, the white frame house had become primarily a summer place for the LeGeros family. Set on two and a half acres, the house had been known during the eighteenth century as Eyrie Inn because it sat like an eagle's nest high above the Hudson River in the steep and wooded hills south of West Point and Bear Mountain. In addition to the main house, there was a small cottage. In a grotto on a slope facing the river was a smokehouse, long since abandoned.

For Bernard the estate was a place to escape from the city with many of his friends. Among them were William Mayer, a pal from his LaSalle Academy days, and Edo Bertoglio.

Bernard had introduced Billy Mayer to Edo in mid-February 1985. At the same time Billy met Edo's girlfriend, Lynn Smith. The subject of their conversation soon turned to Edo's desire to wreak some kind of revenge on Fred Rothbell for the unpleasant incident in Puerto Rico. A fistfight seemed the way to do it, Edo thought. Just sock the son of a bitch in the nose.

No, said Bernard, Freddy would have to be eliminated. He would have to be killed. For two hours vengeance was discussed until, finally, Edo said he'd figure his own way of doing it, the punch to the nose being the most likely way, he figured—dismissing all the other notions, including "eliminating" Rothbell, as absurd.

For Bernard, however, the subject of revenge and punishment was not forgotten and he brought it up with Billy Mayer on February 22, an almost springlike night that began around midnight for the two school chums in a setting that set the mood for talk of dark and dangerous deeds.

Located in a basement at Ninth Avenue and Fourteenth Street was a bar catering to persons whose sexual preferences ran to sadomasochism (S&M) and bondage and discipline (B&D). Available for those activities were a pair of large rooms painted black and dimly lighted in which individuals who were either straight or gay could engage in S&M and B&D activities or watch others doing so. The place was called Hellfire.

There they encountered Bernard's boss, Andrew Crispo.

A man who moved in several worlds and was well known in all of them, Crispo never had any trouble getting into the Limelight's VIP inner sanctum watched over by Freddy Rothbell's discerning eye for celebrities in all the fields that counted—rock music, movies, the theater, the arts, and that peculiar class of people who are famous or infamous not for their work or their money but simply because they possess a flair for self-publicity or outrageous behavior.

Crispo's VIP status grew from his stellar position in the world of fine art as the owner of a prestigious gallery on the most expensive stretch of real estate in the world— Manhattan's East Fifty-Seventh Street. Anchored by the solid majesty of Tiffany & Company, along both sides of the four blocks from Fifth to Third Avenues are legendary establishments that give meaning to the quip "If you have to ask how much it costs, buddy, you can't afford to buy it."

In the heart of this mecca for the fine arts, artists, and art connoisseurs stands at Madison Avenue and Fifty-Seventh the Fuller Building, a grand example of black, white, and gray Art Deco. There in 1973, allegedly with financial backing from a very well-known and influential woman, Crispo opened his own gallery and began selling the works of such famous artists as Georgia O'Keeffe, Arthur Dove, and Robert Motherwell. At thirty he had won the patronage of Baron Hans Heinrich Thyssen-Bornemisza, heir to a German industrial fortune and one of the world's most important art collectors. With a client of that stature, Crispo had arrived.

It was an impressive achievement for a person who grew up in poverty. Abandoned by his mother at birth, Crispo was placed by Catholic Charities in St. John's Orphanage in Philadelphia. As a teenager he worked as clerk to a judge and through an employee of the courts had the opportunity to look into a sealed record that would have revealed his mother's identity; he'd declined the offer because, he said, he wasn't interested in his past, only in what the future held.

To find out, he left Philadelphia for New York determined to carve a niche in the world of art, an ambition born and nurtured during hours of exploration in the Philadelphia Museum of Art. In New York, working for an antiques dealer and dressing windows for the Georg Jensen silver-goods store, he studied art, became a courier for galleries, and eventually broke into freelance dealing. In 1970 he landed a job with the prestigious ACA Gallery, but what he wanted was a gallery of his own. With persistence and nerve, he succeeded.

With success came wealth.

Both permitted him to become a familiar and flamboyant figure not only in art circles but also in the moneyed aristocracies of celebrity in Manhattan and Southampton, Long Island.

Expensive art was prominently displayed in both his cooperative penthouse apartment at 380 West Twelfth Street in Greenwich Village and his three-story, ultramodern Mediterranean-style home on Gin Lane in the posh Fairley section of Southampton, where his neighbors were Gloria Vanderbilt, Lee Radziwill, Alan Alda, and Angier Biddle Duke.

One of the most impressive objects on display outdoors at his Southampton address was a stunning black-marble-and-bronze Oriental statue resembling an alphabet character. Inside the house were thousand-dollar ashtrays, rare rugs, paintings, and many works of sculpture—including one in the form of a bizarre mask of the kind used by adherents of S&M and B&D and sported sometimes by the denizens of the darkened S&M and B&D rooms of Hellfire.

There Crispo was as well known as in his gallery and the arty haunts of the East Side and the Hamptons.

He was also known in New York's gay community and was the subject of considerable gossip and rumors about S&M scenes enacted at Crispo's gallery. In these frightening dramas, it was said, unsuspecting young men were enticed to the gallery and then found themselves confronted by a youth dressed like a cop, "arrested," shackled, and subjected to the humiliation of vile verbal abuse and sometimes even physical assault, with Crispo and others taking turns beating, kicking, taunting, and threatening.

A person who frequently played the part of the policeman in Crispo's cruel charades was Bernard LeGeros, whose relationship with Crispo dated from Bernard's teenage years when a job as a messenger and delivery boy often brought him to the gallery. In time Bernard was hired as a gallery assistant, but his contact with his employer often extended beyond business hours and into the dark interiors of such West Side clubs as the Anvil, the Stable, the Mineshaft, and Hellfire.

On the night of February 22, Bernard's chum from

LaSalle, Billy Mayer, descended with Bernard and Crispo into Hellfire's eerie and dank underworld of dim and shadowy shapes; when his eyes adjusted to the dark, he saw men and women dressed in sleek black leather clothing crowded around a naked man and a woman in leather hitting the man with a large wooden paddle.

After about forty minutes, Billy, Bernard, and Andrew ascended into the unseasonably warm night. Talk turned to Freddy Rothbell and why he deserved to be killed. Noting the balmy weather, Crispo said, "This is a good night to kill him."

"That's a good idea," said Bernard. "We should take care of Freddy. But how?"

"Lure him from the Limelight with a story about a hot party," Crispo said, adding that one of them would invite him and then they would drive to the LeGeros house in Rockland County, where they'd shoot him in the head.

The problem was, they discovered at the Limelight, Freddy was not interested in leaving his duties in the VIP Room for any party, no matter how hot it promised to be.

Undaunted, the trio tried again to persuade Freddy, this time while they sat in a back room and passed around a spoonful of cocaine. Freddy still would not agree to leave the club for a party and soon he returned to his duties.

"I will get Freddy," said Crispo confidently. "You two leave now and meet me at Hellfire in forty-five minutes."

Leaving the Limelight, Bernard and Billy drove to Bernard's apartment, where Bernard took off the coat he'd been wearing and put on a long overcoat.

From a closet he took a knapsack and then a rifle, which he placed in the bag.

Discovering that Crispo was not waiting for them at the Hellfire club, they drove to Crispo's apartment, where

Bernard buzzed Crispo's intercom. When Crispo answered, Bernard said, "It's us."

"I have somebody here," Crispo said, but after a momentary pause, he said, "Well, why don't you come up anyway?"

The apartment was on the seventh floor and the door was partly open.

Immediately upon entering, Bernard and Billy saw Crispo in black leather shorts and a black tee shirt holding a curled black woven-leather whip. "Hey, Bernard," he said, pointing it at a young man seated in the corner of a couch, "this guy does not believe I'm a faggot."

Looking up with a smile, the boy on the couch was exceptionally handsome, with blond hair and blue eyes. Naked, he was masturbating.

Eigil Dag Vesti had had a busy day.

Completing work on his résumé, he strolled a few blocks to the McBurney YMCA and paid sixty dollars in membership fees, telling several people there that he was looking forward to going to Florida in about a week to help his roommate, photographer Stephen AuCoin, shoot a layout for a book. The year before he'd helped AuCoin produce *Man Alive* and posed for two pictures in the book.

The afternoon was spent at the Metropolitan Museum of Art, after which he met his friend Dallas Bosendahl for a leisurely dinner at Rick's Lounge, a trendy supper club in the Chelsea section of Manhattan. Around midnight, Bosendahl said goodnight to Eigil at his apartment, but Eigil was bored and went out again, wound up at Hellfire, and ran into Andrew Crispo.

"This guy doesn't believe I'm a faggot," repeated Andrew Crispo as he handed Billy Mayer the whip. "Punish him."

Billy took the whip and advanced toward the couch, where Eigil was now kneeling with his head resting on his crossed arms on the back of the couch, his buttocks upraised.

After smacking the youth once, Billy thrust the whip into Bernard's waiting hand.

Driving a knee into Eigil's back, Bernard brought the handle of the whip down hard on his head.

Peering over his shoulder, Eigil asked, "Who are you guys?"

Snapping the whip, Bernard growled, "Never mind."

Backing toward the door, Billy said to Bernard, "I'm taking off."

Discarding the whip, Bernard said, "Wait. I'll drive you."

"I'll take the subway."

"No, I'll drive you," insisted Bernard, pursuing him.

Outside in the car, noting that Billy was upset, Bernard said, "Andrew was only fooling around."

According to LeGeros, after he left Billy he returned to Crispo's apartment and joined the S&M activities again and at some point it was agreed that they leave the city and continue their diversions at the LeGeros house in Tomkins Cove.

Eigil accompanied them.

"Don't go through any tolls," said Crispo to Bernard as they crossed the George Washington Bridge into New Jersey.

"There aren't any tolls," Bernard replied.

"Good," said Crispo. "I don't want to be seen with this guy."

In Stony Point, according to LeGeros, they followed steep winding roads while in the rear seat looking through the window at the wintry landscape, Eigil said, "This is nice. I should have brought my skis. Where are we going?"

With a laugh Crispo replied, "You're going back to Norway in a fucking box."

To Eigil Vesti it probably seemed like one more taunt in another of Andrew's S&M games, thought Bernard as he turned his car onto twisting, ascending Buckberg Mountain Road, but there was an unusually hard and cold edge to Andrew's voice that sent a chill down Bernard's back.

As he turned into the driveway and the headlights flashed across the white walls of his parents' historic house, now dark and deserted, he knew that Andrew wasn't fooling around.

This was going to be for real.

16 | THE POLICEMAN

THE RUGGED TERRAIN of Buckberg Mountain has always been great hiking country. In the days of the American Revolution soldiers of the Continental Army had plodded up and down its steep hills on their way to or from West Point; since that time people with an appreciation of the outdoors and the spectacular views of the Hudson Valley had made the region a popular spot for outings. Late in the afternoon of St. Patrick's Day, Sunday, March 17, 1985, the weather was especially ideal with crisp air, warming sun, and a hint of springtime as five boys, two from Rockland and three from New York City, picked their way along a steep eastern slope until they discovered what appeared to be the remnants of a very old stone doorway leading into what might be a cave or perhaps an ancient ice- or smokehouse. Curious, one of the teenagers approached the opening, peered past a heavy tree limb that blocked the entrance, then turned away in horror.

Patrolman Patrick Brophy of the Stony Point Police Department was on the job, patrolling in his radio car on the eight-to-four shift when he got a radio call, a report of a body on the grounds of the LeGeros property at 100 Buckberg Mountain Road.

Arriving at the address, Brophy found that Sergeant Joseph Liszack of the Stony Point police was already there.

Within a few minutes, the hillside estate was swarming with other lawmen waiting for medical examiner Dr. Frederick Zugibe to finish his examination of the corpse. There was not much to work with. All of the flesh and much of the bone of what had been a human male had been either eaten by animals or consumed by what appeared to have been at least two fires. Dr. Zugibe discovered that a black leather mask of the type used in sexual bondage practices had been tightly fitted over the head and had preserved it, apparently intact.

In his subsequent autopsy Dr. Zugibe would confirm that the head had indeed been excellently preserved and that two bullets had been fired at point-blank range into the back of it.

The fires that destroyed a large portion of the rest of the body apparently had been an attempt to dispose of the remains. What flames did not devour, hungry animals had. If the hikers hadn't been curious about the smokehouse and its grisly contents hadn't been found at that time, probably not even the black leather mask could have preserved the head and facial features much longer. Because of the mask, a positive identification of the young man's face would be possible—if the police could locate someone to make that identification.

Finding out who the victim of this hideous murder was became the job of Stony Point Detective Sergeant William Franks and New York State Police Senior Investigator Santo LiDestri. Working with them were Lieutenant Frank Tinelli and Investigator David Shea of the BCI and Peter Moda- ferri, Jim Stewart, Chris Goldrick, and William Michella of my staff. Because there were no reports of recent missing persons in the county, a notification of the finding of the body and its description was sent by computer to police departments nationwide.

At 10:05 A.M. the next day, Sergeant Marcia Stanton of the Missing Persons Bureau of the New York City Police Department telephoned to ask for more information and at 12:50 she called again. "Sergeant Franks, we have reason to believe that your unidentified deceased is Eigil Dag Vesti," she said, "last seen alive by a friend shortly after midnight on February 23."

That Eigil Dag Vesti was missing had been widely known in New York City since February 25 when, on almost every lamppost all over Manhattan a small poster appeared bearing his picture and description. "Foul Play Suspected" said thousands of these flyers distributed by Dallas Bosendahl, the friend with whom Vesti had dinner on the night of his disappearance.

Before the week was out, Vesti's older sister had arrived in New York and the family had hired a private investigator, but other than unearthing details about Vesti's frequenting of clubs including the S&M places of the West Side, the family's investigation had made no progress and the flyers produced nothing.

If the body found in the LeGeros smokehouse were to be positively identified as that of Vesti, the face would have to be seen. This emotionally charged formality was accomplished by the use of television, a camera in Dr. Zugibe's laboratory focusing on the face while Vesti's sister Margrethe viewed it on a monitor in another room. She made the required visual identification. Dental records she had brought from Norway verified it.

Because the body had been found on his property, John LeGeros was interviewed. There was nothing he could tell the police that would be of any assistance, he told Detective Franks, but, he went on, perhaps his son Bernard could help. On another occasion, LeGeros related, Bernard had been helpful to the police regarding a pursesnatching and had received a letter of commendation.

Bernard could be contacted at his place of employment, Mr. LeGeros said. That would be the Andrew Crispo Gallery on Fifty-seventh Street in Manhattan.

The following day Bernard appeared at the Stony Point police station with his brother David. Assigned to talk to Bernard were Senior Investigator LiDestri and Investigator Shea. In that conversation, Bernard told them he owned a rifle—an AR-7 survival weapon—which he normally kept at the house on Buckberg Mountain Road. Perhaps whoever killed Vesti had been in the house and taken the rifle, he suggested. On the other hand, he added, he sometimes kept the rifle at his apartment in New York. Would he have a look for it there? Of course, he said with a smile. "I'm always happy to help out the police."

Maybe he'd get another letter of commendation for his help on this case, Franks suggested appreciatively. "If you can be of any help in this," he said, "I'll make you an assistant detective."

In a phone call the next day, Bernard reported that he'd not found the rifle, but "Maybe you should look in the woods."

"Why in the woods?" Franks asked.

"If the killer stole my gun," said Bernard, "maybe he threw it in the woods."

A few hours later he was on the phone again . "There's a closet in my brother David's room. Maybe my gun is there. It's very easy to get into that house without a key."

On March 19 Bernard arrived at the Stony Point police station to be interviewed again by LiDestri and Shea. Name some people who had visited the LeGeros home, he was asked—people who might know about his gun, about the smokehouse. Names that came readily to mind, Bernard replied, were a girl named Josephine whom he'd met at the Limelight and brought to the house for sex, Edo Bertoglio, and Billy Mayer. Others had been to the house, too, and he named them. He knew a person who was a member of the Moonies who'd been to the house. As far as the smokehouse was concerned, he'd once found evidence that it may have been used by a cult of some kind—melted wax, mostly.

"Do you know anybody who might be involved in S&M?"

"No," said Bernard disgustedly. "No one I know is into that stuff."

The next evening he traveled from Manhattan to Stony Point again, driven there by LiDestri and Jim Stewart of my staff, who had been in the city in connection with the case and had been asked by Franks to rendezvous with Bernard. On the way to Rockland the detectives asked Bernard to speculate about his theories concerning the murder. Whoever did it, he said, was not from upstate. Anyone familiar with the area would not have tried to burn a body because anyone who lived in the area would know that the smoke would soon attract unwanted attention. "They should have buried the body."

"Maybe the victim wasn't killed there but somewhere else."

"Perhaps this guy was killed because he was a homosexual. A person who hated gays might have done it. Maybe a chicken hawk did it. Do you know what a chicken hawk is? He's an older homosexual who enjoys sex with boys or younger-looking men. This killer may have been a psycho who hung around gay bars."

At police headquarters Bernard repeated his theories for Franks. "What do you figure was the significance of that black mask?" the detective asked.

"It could be worn by either the master or the slave. The

master is a sadist one who likes to inflict pain. There is a master-slave relationship. The mask is to take away the personal aspects. It makes that person just a sex object. You guys ought to be looking for people like that. You should be going into the gay bars and the S&M bars in the city. You should either use a homosexual cop or one who's pretending to be one. If you do, you should have a look at the movie *Cruising*, with Al Pacino. It tells the story of a police officer who goes into an investigation of a homosexual killing and takes on the role of a homosexual and becomes wrapped up in what he's doing and eventually becomes a killer himself."

"Do you have homosexual friends you might have taken up to the house?"

"I'm not homosexual, but I know some people who are. You should check out the bars like Uncle Charlie's, the Bad Lands, the Anvil, Mine Shaft. Those are all gay or S&M bars. You should check out the discos, too. Area. The Limelight. The last time I was there was February twenty-second. I stayed late to talk to a guy named Freddy who's in charge of the VIP Room and with my friend Billy Mayer. We left around three-thirty in the morning and Billy stayed at my apartment until around nine."

Curious about this detailed recitation, Franks asked, "What else did you do that weekend?"

On Saturday, he said, he'd visited his boss, Andrew Crispo, at his apartment. That evening he had dinner at the Van Dam restaurant with Edo Bertoglio. On Sunday morning he and Andrew Crispo traveled to Southampton via Black Tie Limousine Service. Later that day they went to a movie, *Witness*, and then to dinner at the Driver's Seat. On Monday they came back to the city.

"You've got a terrific memory, Bernard," said Detective

Franks jovially. "Just for the heck of it, tell me what you did on the weekend of March first. How about Friday night?"

"I think I went out with a guy who was staying with me that weekend."

"Saturday night?"

"I think we went to my Aunt Virginia's to work on some furniture, or maybe that was Friday night."

How very strange, Franks thought, that Bernard could recall so much about the weekend Vesti was murdered and so very little about the weekend of March 1. He was being very casual about all this, he thought, as if this were some kid's game of "policeman." Maybe I'd better jolt him into understanding the seriousness of this investigation, he decided as he drew from his pocket the small card he carried that contained the wording required when reading someone his constitutional rights against self-incrimination, commonly called the Miranda warning.

Finished reading the warning, Franks asked, "Do you still want to talk, Bernard?"

"Yes."

"I feel I have to ask you this, Bernard. Did you have anything to do with this homicide?"

"No, I didn't."

"Do you have any personal knowledge of the homicide, either directly or indirectly?"

"No."

Later, after having dinner and following a period of rest when he'd been left alone in a room in the police station, LeGeros said to Franks, "I haven't told you the truth." Visibly upset, he blurted, "I don't want to be a snitch."

"This isn't a case of who copied whose homework or who broke Mrs. Jones' window, Bernard," said Franks sympathetically. "You won't be a tattletale or snitch. If you know something about the homicide, tell me."

With a deep breath Bernard said, "Billy Mayer did it."

He'd gone to the Limelight with Billy Mayer. He had his father's car. At the Limelight they met Andrew Crispo. While in the club Billy talked to Andrew about Freddy Rothbell and said he wanted to kill Freddy. Billy's plan was to invite Freddy to a party upstate and then take him to Tomkins Cove and kill him. Then they got separated and Billy had disappeared. So had the car. Both were back a few hours later and Billy was seated in the front seat. "Where the fuck were you, Billy?" he'd asked."

"I just killed some fag at your place up in Rockland County," Billy said.

A few hours after relating Billy Mayer's confession to him that he'd killed Vesti, Bernard asked Franks if he could write it out in detail. Given yellow legal pads and a ballpoint pen, he sat opposite Detective Shea and began writing a new story.

When Billy Mayer was unable to get Freddy to leave the Limelight, he met Eigil Dag Vesti and invited him to go to a party upstate with the intention of killing him. Unlike Freddy, Vesti was glad to go. As soon as they crossed the George Washington Bridge, Billy Mayer began the master-slave ritual with Vesti. Billy was master and Vesti was a "Jew fag, a scum-eating Jew, and a Jew-loving cock-sucker." Somewhere along the Palisades Parkway during a pause in the ritual, Vesti had looked through the window and said, "This is nice up here. I should've brought my skis. Where are we going?"

"You're going to Norway in a fucking box," Billy laughed.

At the house, Billy and Vesti went to the basement and a few minutes later the sounds of Vesti being beaten with a strap were heard. Still later, Billy and Vesti came upstairs. Vesti was naked except for a black leather mask covering his whole head. Realizing that Billy was going to kill Vesti, he'd asked Billy not to kill Vesti in the house.

"Take your slave outside," he told Billy and Billy did as he was asked. Looking through a window he saw Vesti kneeling and performing oral sex on Billy.

Billy had the AR-7 rifle tucked under his arm.

Following Billy and Vesti to the smokehouse, he saw Billy execute Vesti by shooting him twice in the back of the head.

To get rid of the body they got gasoline and wood and started a fire.

The rifle was thrown into the Hudson somewhere along Route 9W.

Vesti's clothing was discarded in a dumpster at some construction site.

They returned to New York.

Six days later, without Billy knowing it, he went back to the smokehouse and again burned the body.

When Bernard finished writing, Franks asked, "Is that the whole truth, Bernard? We'll be talking to Billy Mayer, you know. We'll ask him about all of this—where he was on the night of February twenty-second, if he can prove he wasn't at Tomkins Cove."

Suddenly Bernard cried, "I shot him. I took my AR-7 and shot him twice in the back of the head."

It had happened exactly as he'd told it, Bernard said after again being advised of his Miranda rights, but it was not

Billy Mayer who'd been engaging in a master-slave ritual with Vesti, it had been Andrew Crispo.

"Now, Bernard," said Franks, "I want you to tell us what happened one more time, only this time I'm going to ask someone from the District Attorney's office to hear what you have to say."

As executive assistant DA Thomas Zugibe listened, a few more details were added to the narrative. In the S&M ritual there'd been other paraphernalia used, including handcuffs and a large artificial penis. The cuffs were taken off Vesti's wrists and the dildo removed from his rectum after the killing. These objects and Vesti's clothes had been thrown away during a high-speed ride back to the city. They had tried to bury the body by using a sledgehammer to collapse the smokehouse but had failed and set fire to the corpse.

The rifle had not been thrown into the river, he said, but was hidden in the air-conditioning unit on the second floor of the Crispo Gallery.

Efforts were made immediately to recover all the items he said had been disposed of on the way back to New York, because if his story were true and Andrew Crispo had been included in the murder we would need evidence beyond Bernard's confession implicating Crispo. We hoped that evidence might be found among the items that had been dumped.

To ascertain the role of Billy Mayer, if any, in the events Bernard had recounted, Mayer was questioned. He seemed astonished as he reported that Bernard had told him he had murdered a Norwegian fashion student.

"You remember that guy who was at Crispo's?" Bernard had asked. "That night, we took him up to the country and we killed him. He was on his knees. Crispo got him ready. I had my long coat on and I whipped out my AR-7 and let him have it in the back of his head." After a thoughtful pause he added, "When you kill, you can't be angry or upset. You have to kill as if you were just lighting a cigarette or driving a car. You have to do it with no emotion."

"It seemed like typical Bernard LeGeros bullshit," Billy said of the incident, but a few days later, he said, he saw a missing-persons poster bearing Eigil Dag Vesti's picture and the words *Foul Play Suspected* and the date Vesti was last seen. "It added up," he said, "but I still don't believe it."

A few days later, Bernard showed him one of the flyers and said. "That's the guy I killed," adding with a smile, "I may start a scrapbook and this will be the first thing in it. It's going to be a scrapbook with Vesti and all the others I might kill."

17 | YOU WILL REMEMBER

"IF YOU SERVE on this case," Judge Robert Meehan said as jury selection began on September 27, 1985, "when the century turns, you will remember what you were doing in the early fall of 1985."

These were meaningful words coming from Judge Meehan, a worldly man who'd seen combat with a navy destroyer squadron in Korea before earning his law degree from Rutgers in 1959. During eight years as Rockland district attorney and since becoming a county court judge in 1982 he had been familiar with homicide and every other kind of criminal behavior, but no previous case in his two decades of experience with murder came anywhere near this one. The jurors would be hearing testimony about "cocaine, deviant behavior, sadomasohism and homosexuality," warned this genteel family man and father of six.

The indictment was for second-degree murder, he explained. In New York, first-degree murder could be charged only in the death of a law enforcement or corrections official. A verdict of guilty of murder in the second degree would mean that the jury found Vesti's death intentional.

The defense counsel planned to maintain that LeGeros was not guilty by reason of mental disease or defect—the insanity defense.

Eighty-two years old and severely hampered by arthritis,

Murray Sprung admitted that he had been surprised to be chosen by John and Racquel LeGeros to defend their son and told a newspaper reporter, "My first reaction was: 'Me go to court at my age in a case like this?' But they said they would have no one else." A friend of Mr. and Mrs. LeGeros for many years, he had attended their marriage in Tokyo almost thirty years before. At that time he was serving as a prosecutor for the Department of the Army in war crimes trials in the Philippines, Racquel LeGeros' native country.

Speaking in a low, rumbling, cultivated voice, walking with the aid of a shiny metal walker and proudly displaying Asiatic-Pacific service ribbons on his lapel as he delivered an opening statement to the jury we'd selected, Sprung looked less like a lawyer than like an Old Testament prophet in a blue suit as he shook his head in dismay and grappled for words to describe what the trial was about. "We have there in clubs that exist in New York and parts of Greenwich Village," he said, "a Sodom and Gomorrah."

These were places, he went on gravely, "where people are interested in S&M and B&D, outlandish sexual activities." He warned, "We are going to take you through the sewers and mud and slush that this case has as its scenes."

The cornerstone of the defense, he told the jurors, is that "Bernard LeGeros is innocent by reason of mental defect." Their case would prove, he said, that Bernard LeGeros had become a cocaine addict because of the influence of Andrew Crispo.

"Andrew Crispo procured the cocaine," he said. "He bought it. On many occasions he had sent Bernard to the narcotic sellers with money to purchase cocaine. It was a daily ritual. That became a regular part of the days that Bernard worked for Andrew Crispo."

Besides introducing Bernard to cocaine, Sprung asserted, he had also ensnared Bernard into deviant sexual behavior, into S&M and B&D. How could Bernard have been so easily influenced? Because, said Sprung, Bernard always had been a troubled and disturbed youth; but now, in Crispo, Bernard had found a father figure. "He did anything and everything asked of him by Andrew as an employee." Then, in the fall of 1984, Sprung said, Bernard was drawn into Andrew Crispo's grim S&M activities, playing the part of a policeman. "He would go into the room occupied by Andrew Crispo and make an arrest of one of Andrew Crispo's victims." Pausing, slowly shaking his head, his brow furrowed with puzzlement, he said, "Now in S&M practices, victims for some reason enjoy baring their bottoms and being whipped. Crispo enjoyed ordering them for that purpose to assume the position and take the whipping and enjoy it. It is a species of mankind that we, you, decent people would not believe possible.

"Now, you have Andrew Crispo directing the act. He would have what he would call a bag of toys. They consisted of generally a mask, handcuffs, whips, and dildos of various kinds and sizes. Bernard followed all of Andrew Crispo's wishes. 'Go here, go there,' and he went. He went willingly and gladly. He felt in his acting as a policeman he was protecting Crispo. He took pride in such an act."

What about Bernard's "helping" the police in their investigation of the murder? Why did he make those various trips to the Stony Point police? "They were done at the direction of Andrew Crispo. Why did Bernard make certain statements to the police officers? Those statements were rehearsed by Andrew Crispo so that Bernard knew exactly what his function was, and he did it!"

Was this a true portrait of Andrew Crispo? Was he a 1980s Svengali who had Bernard LeGeros under a spell, an evil spell? Sprung believed so, telling reporters, "Bernard didn't know what he was doing. Crispo brainwashed him with dope and money."

After being retained as the attorney, Sprung had taken a number of steps in the months before he made his opening statement to the jury. The first was to change Bernard's plea from not guilty to not guilty by reason of mental disease or defect. If he achieved this goal it would mean that LeGeros would undergo a period of psychiatric evaluation and could, conceivably, go free after that.

Sprung also sought to have Bernard's written confession thrown out on the grounds that it had been made without benefit of legal counsel. And he sought a change of venue from Rockland County to Brooklyn, saying, "I want jurors who haven't heard about the mask murder."

In the spring and summer of 1985 that was a tall order. The "death-mask case" had been all over the media not only in Rockland, Brooklyn, and the rest of New York State but also across the country. It was a story with all the elements of sensation. It was a tale of murder, money, drugs, homosexuality, bizarre rituals with scenes played out in trendy New York discos, the world of fashion and fine arts, and with a mysterious central figure.

So intriguing was Andrew Crispo that a long article was devoted to him in *New York* magazine featuring a peekaboo portrait of him on the cover. Written by Anthony Haden-Guest, it contained tales of necrophilia, of S&M sessions in Crispo's art gallery, and assorted rumors about Crispo which Crispo dismissed as fabrications. It wasn't true, he said scoffingly, that he had pointed to a large Oriental outdoor sculpture at his Southampton house and said to a houseguest, "That is where I bury my enemies." Nor was it true, he said, the he'd pointed to pink stains on a wall in his Manhattan penthouse and claimed they were bloodstains he hadn't been able to remove. It was also a falsehood that he had referred to Bernard LeGeros as "my bodyguard" and "my executioner."

Attention also was being paid to Crispo by the city's gay press, especially *The Native*. In an April issue, the weekly newspaper reported on a man, "Thomas," who had answered a pay phone on a New York City street, "and was invited by Crispo to his 57th Street gallery. There, Thomas was held against his will and severely beaten by a parade of men, including LeGeros." The *Native* story was picked up by the *Daily News* and the *New York Post*. Two weeks later, *The Native* followed up its initial story with a report that "three individuals have come forward to report that they had been held by Crispo and terrorized by him and others in a sadomasochistic scene in his apartment," citing a source "close to the investigation" as basis. "Two of the three," the article continued, "had answered ringing pay phones on the street and were invited by Crispo to come to his gallery or apartment for sex. In the other case, Crispo met the man while cruising Washington Street." In these cases, said the newspaper, "cocaine played a major role in the evening's activities, and each of the three individuals was subjected to violence beyond his own definition of acceptable sex play."

In an article headlined THE MASK MURDER CASE: A SURVIVOR SPEAKS, *The Village Voice* expounded on the allegations cited in *The Native*.

The article suggested that at the root of the Vesti murder and the other allegations concerning Andrew Crispo was "homophobia combined with a craving for a victim." An unnamed "survivor" in the article told writer Brett Averill that "he had been invited to a small gathering" at Crispo's gallery where he was "joined by a man dressed in the uniform of a policeman or security guard; the 'guard'—who, he claims, turned out to be LeGeros—handcuffed and began verbally abusing him." At that point, the "survivor" said, "a group of strangers entered the room and joined LeGeros in the assault, taking turns beating, kicking, taunting and threatening him with a loaded pistol. They explained in detail the method they would use to kill him and, undetected, remove his body from the art gallery unless he showed a willingness to 'be a real man.'" The assailants, wrote Averill, still citing the source that he said was cooperating with police, "apparently toyed with their victims, allowing those who expressed remorse over their homosexuality to live and killing those who showed 'no hope of going straight.'"

These stories in the press and reports from individuals who came forward with similar ones led Manhattan District Attorney Robert Morgenthau to open an investigation. Five incidents in the Crispo gallery were being probed, Morgenthau said. One of these involved a young male art student who claimed that he had been held for six hours on September 22, 1984, and was whipped by three men acting on Crispo's orders. He'd been lured to the gallery on the pretext of going to a party, he said, and had been held at gunpoint by LeGeros. He was released, he said, only when he agreed to sodomize Crispo. He had waited so long before reporting the incident, he said, because Crispo had threatened to kill him. At a news conference announcing the indictment of Crispo, Morgenthau described him as a homosexual who hired straight men to beat up homosexuals. "It was strictly an anti-gay act," said Morgenthau.

At his arraignment on charges of kidnapping and abusing the student, Crispo denied the allegations and told reporters that he was "looking forward to a speedy and immediate trial and to being vindicated." His attorney, Robert Kasanof, said he would prove "by objective facts, that whatever happened was of a voluntary, social nature."

Shortly after Crispo's indictment and release on $100,000

bail, Southampton Detective Sergeant Anthony Olender confirmed for *New York Post* reporter Bill Hoffman that Crispo once propositioned a rookie cop by telephone. Crispo would call pay phones on Main Street, Olender said, and if a man answered, he would invite him to his estate. "He called the phone booth right in front of the police station. This rookie officer answered." The police considered setting a trap but the calls stopped.

With fresh allegations about Crispo appearing in the media and after hearing reports from other sources that there were bodies buried on Crispo's Gin Lane property, Southampton police swooped down on it with shovels and earthmovers, the focus of their immediate attention being the large black-and-bronze Oriental sculpture. Neither it nor any part of the property in the exclusive neighborhood produced corpses.

Other troubles were nagging Crispo at this time, including a federal income tax investigation based on an Internal Revenue Service claim that he owed eight million dollars. Artists were filing lawsuits. Landlords were suing for back rent. The artistic and social clubs he had begun to move in now turned a cold shoulder.

At this time I was pursuing him vigorously but, as one headline writer put it, Crispo was playing "the Artful Dodger." He had dropped out of sight, moving from his Greenwich Village apartment and the Southampton home and shuttering his gallery, although his attorney was in touch with me in early April on the subject of obtaining a grant of immunity from prosecution in the Vesti murder case in return for his testimony about what had happened in the smokehouse. Robert Kasanof told a New York paper, "My client is not going to give up his Constitutional rights. Without immunity, he will not testify."

To Harvey Eilbaum I said, "I wouldn't immunize him even if hell froze over."

With the cooperation of LeGeros and the hard work of DA detectives Christopher Goldrick and Ronald Taggart we were able to locate clothing Vesti had been wearing the night of the murder, discarded along the Palisades Parkway in New Jersey.

The AR-7 rifle that LeGeros said was the murder weapon was found precisely where he'd told us he had hidden it, in an air conditioner in Crispo's gallery.

A third piece of evidence eluded our searchers—the large dildo LeGeros told us had been used in the S&M rituals and at the time of the killing. In his confession, LeGeros said it had been thrown into a storm drain near a boat basin at the bottom of Dyckman Hill around Exit 1 of the Palisades Parkway. A search of the drain failed to locate it.

During the trial Thomas Ruby, a light equipment operator who worked for the Palisades Parkway Commission, explained why.

He had found it stuck in the drain. It was, he told the jury, "a big thing."

"How did you get it out?" I asked.

"Pulled it out."

"It was in there tight, that's correct?"

"Yes."

"What did you do with it?"

"I brought it down to show the fellows at work," he said as giggles rippled through the courtroom. "You never seen anything like that, you know."

"And how long did you keep it?"

"Long time."

The spectators' giggling was now stifled laughter.

"I'm not trying to be funny," said Ruby apologetically.

"That's all right. And did you ultimately give it over to a police officer?"

"Yes."

"Did you do anything to this particular item while it was in your possession?"

"Yes," he said nervously.

"Tell the jury. We're all mature."

"We drew a face on it."

Like water from a bursting dam, laughter flooded the court.

"What else did you draw on it?"

"Some guy put a bow tie on it."

At the defense table, LeGeros doubled over in his seat and buried his face in his hands in a futile effort to avoid laughing out loud.

"Was it given to your boss?"

"Yes."

There was no stemming the tide now. The courtroom was awash in unrestrained laughter—including mine.

Any effort by Judge Meehan to restore order was impossible because he, too, was chuckling.

Finally, as the hilarity ebbed, I now had to formally place the dildo into evidence, an act that I knew was going to bring down the house.

"I ask that we move it into evidence, Your Honor," I said as I lifted it and carried it to the desk of the clerk and placed it before him—eight pounds of latex penis, eighteen inches long and four inches thick.

No vaudeville sketch or burlesque comedy team's "courtroom" act ever got a bigger howl.

"This is serious business, really," pleaded Judge Meehan as he wiped tears of laughter from his cheeks.

"I have no further questions," I said, returning to my seat as quickly as decorum allowed.

"No questions," said Murray Sprung, wisely.

The raucous levity of that moment was a sharp contrast, however, to a clash earlier that day between the judge and Kenneth R. Marshall, an associate of Sprung, who made an attempt to have Vesti's sisters removed from the front row of spectator seats. "They are crying and staring at the jurors, perhaps influencing them from making a fair and impartial decision," he told Judge Meehan, suggesting they be seated in a back row.

Pointing out that there had been no overt outbursts of emotion from the women and rejecting the request, Judge Meehan stated bluntly, "This is a public, open trial and I am not going to tell anyone where they should sit." Fortunately, the Vesti sisters hadn't been present during the dildo testimony.

Two days later, the mood in court was grim as Dr. Frederick Zugibe took the stand as I asked about the gunshot wound that killed their brother. "Is it consistent with somebody being shot in the back of the neck where the victim is in a kneeling position and where the assailant is in a standing position?"

"Yes."

Billy Mayer testified, relating how LeGeros admitted shooting Vesti in that manner.

Bernard LeGeros' brother David also testified about having heard an admission of guilt from his brother, "He woke me up saying, 'I just shot somebody.'" Like Mayer, at first David had not believed Bernard's story of being with Andrew Crispo in Rockland County and killing Eigil Dag Vesti in the smokehouse. Especially hard to believe as Bernard spoke with him only a short time after the murder was a tale about using a knife and stabbing Vesti and then drinking his blood.

If you don't believe me, Bernard suggested, go and have a look in the smokehouse.

At first David ignored the suggestion that he investigate, but on a second occasion when he was at the country house he did look, "I looked inside and there was a lot of debris and what looked to be part of a skeleton."

"What did you do then?" I asked.

"I looked at it for a while and I said, 'That looks like a deer skeleton or Great Dane,' and figured my brother had found an animal in there and was trying to scare me. So I left and went home."

Eventually he believed.

Edo Bertoglio testified that on February 23, the night after the murder, he, Lynn Smith, Andrew Crispo, and Bernard were at dinner at Van Dam restaurant and Bernard whispered privately to Edo, "I killed a guy; don't tell Crispo I told you." He dismissed it as another of Bernard's macabre jokes. Two weeks later, Edo and Bernard had lunch together and when they finished went for a stroll. "We were walking down Sixth Avenue around West Fourth Street," he said, "and at one point Bernard noticed a poster and a picture of a blond guy, and he said, 'Oh, shit, this is the guy I did. This is the guy I killed.'"

"Then what happened?"

"He said that he and Crispo and the blond guy went to Rockland County where he roughed up the guy and then took him out and had him kneel down, and he told me that he shot this guy in the back of his head two times."

"Did he tell you anything else that he had done to this person with the blond hair that you had seen in the poster?"

"Well, he mentioned that he cut open his chest and took his heart out and then tried to burn the body."

That Bernard LeGeros killed Eigil Dag Vesti by shooting him twice in the head and that he attempted to destroy the body was not contested by his defense lawyer, Mr. Sprung. Their plea was that Bernard committed the crime because of mental disease or defect.

To support his contention that the crime was the result of Bernard's vulnerable and unstable mentality being taken over and taken advantage of, Mr. Sprung put members of the LeGeros family on the stand to testify concerning his troubled past and psychiatrists to testify concerning the state of Bernard's mind, all to underpin the defense claim that Bernard was vulnerable to and had been enslaved by Andrew Crispo.

"He was manipulated and exploited by a very clever man," argued Sprung. Andrew Crispo knew Bernard's mental and emotional weakness. "S&M games and a role which Andrew Crispo made Bernard play during these games and a role of being Andrew Crispo's bodyguard fed Bernard's needs for escape from reality, and his ego was fed." Cocaine was introduced and Bernard lost "critical judgment" and lacked "a substantial capacity to know or appreciate the nature and consequences of his acts."

Andrew Crispo's conditioning of Bernard's mind and body caused Bernard to react to Crispo's commands automatically, Sprung asserted. Maybe it had been Crispo himself who'd shot Vesti, but Bernard had been so conditioned by Crispo "that in his mind Bernard actually did it. Nobody knows who really did it except Andrew Crispo, who refuses to talk."

Summoned by the LeGeros lawyers, Andrew Crispo appeared in court on September 24. Dressed in a blue jacket, gray trousers, white shirt, and striped tie, he was flanked by his lawyer and a bodyguard and surrounded by photographers and reporters on the main stairway in the lobby of a courthouse that was bustling with extra sheriff's deputies checking packages and using hand scanners to screen the hundred or so spectators filing into a courtroom on the second floor.

The jury, however, was not present; it had been made clear in advance by Crispo's lawyer that Crispo would not respond to questions except to invoke his rights against self-incrimination granted by the Fifth Amendment to the Constitution.

Another LeGeros lawyer, Kenneth Marshall, began by asking, "Do you have a business? Where do you work?"

Crispo's reply was the Fifth Amendment.

Judge Meehan asked, "Do you know a person by the name of Bernard LeGeros?"

Crispo cited his right not to answer.

"I call your attention to the night of the twenty-second of February 1985," said the judge, "and ask you where you were on the evening of the twenty-second of February 1985."

Again, Crispo cited the Fifth Amendment to the Constitution as a basis for not replying.

"Have you ever been in Stony Point, New York, in your life?"

After Crispo again claimed the Fifth Amendment, Judge Meehan, with a clear appreciation that Crispo was not going to reply to questions except with a rote Fifth Amendment, announced, "The witness is excused."

Leaving the courthouse in a light rain, Crispo was talkative with reporters: "I think this whole affair is a tragedy. It's a tragedy for the family of Eigil Vesti and the family of Bernard LeGeros, and for myself."

In the glare of the lights of TV cameras, he was asked how he was handling the pressures of his assorted troubles. "I'm going to my acupuncturist to soothe my nerves," he replied. "It's a day at a time, like a baseball game. A baseball comes in and you bat it out, and that's the way I'll handle it."

Proceeding down the courthouse steps to a late-model station wagon waiting to whisk him away, a newsman asked what he thought of Rockland County. Sarcastically, he said "Charming."

Because the state of Bernard LeGeros' mind was central to the case and expert witnesses had been called by the defense, to rebut their testimony I put two phychiatrists on the stand.

First was Dr. Alan Tuckman, professor of psychiatry at New York University Medical School and chief forensic psychiatrist for the county of Rockland, who explained that LeGeros had demonstrated a trait common to individuals accused of a crime when he had attempted to blame someone else. But the true story comes out, eventually, he said, and that's what happened with LeGeros. "It is evident that he knew and appreciated what he had done," he testified. "He certainly knew the nature and consequence of the act, from my professional opinion, because he was able to hide it or he wanted to hide it."

"Doctor, during the course of my examination the defendant indicated he had no recall of his actual killing of Eigil Dag Vesti. To what do you attribute this so-called lapse of memory?"

"Well, because I reviewed other statements that he made to the police and to his friends after the crime, before he was arrested and after he was arrested, it is my opinion that he lied to me when he said that he didn't remember. I do know that people who do commit crimes at times try to push the crimes out of their minds, but they do to stop remembering weeks or months later after they are in custody."

My second expert was Dr. John Baer Train. LeGeros knew what he was doing, Train testified, and he was not psychotic. What was the state of Bernard's mind at the time of the murder? "He did not suffer from mental disease or defect at that time."

I asked Dr. Train about LeGeros' claim that he now could not recall the murder he had remembered so vividly in conversations with Edo Bertoglio, Billy Mayer, and his brother immediately after the crime.

"I think that his amnesia as presented to me was self-serving and consciously assumed."

"When you say self-serving, are you bluntly saying that he was lying?"

"In a sense."

The defense had not met their obligation to show that LeGeros was not legally responsible because he had been suffering from mental disease or defect, I argued in my closing statement to the jury. LeGeros knew exactly what he was doing that night, I said, and "in association with Andrew Crispo, intentionally planned and plotted the murder of Eigil Vesti."

After two and a half hours of deliberation, the ten men and two women of the jury returned a verdict of guilty.

On October 17 Judge Meehan sentenced LeGeros to twenty-five years to life for "a brutal murder."

Forty-three days later, Andrew Crispo pleaded guilty to evading four million dollars in federal income taxes, but he has not been prosecuted in the murder of Eigil Dag Vesti.

Why?

The answer lies in the Constitution of the United States and the laws of the State of New York. Unlike LeGeros, Andrew Crispo had made no incriminating statements. The only evidence connecting him to the crime was the statements of LeGeros and, under the law, those statements were inadmissible against anyone except LeGeros.

Moreover, even if LeGeros had agreed to testify against

Crispo at a separate trial, his testimony would have required independent corroboration because it would have been deemed accomplice testimony. Such corroborative evidence simply did not exist at the time of the trial.

Therefore the harsh reality in any consideration of legal action against Crispo was that there existed at that time insufficient evidence to corroborate LeGeros' prospective testimony.

In view of all this, in my considered judgment, there was not enough evidence to prosecute Crispo. I remained determined, however, to keep the case open as long as I was district attorney.

Crispo did go on trial in 1987 in New York City on a charge of kidnapping brought by District Attorney Robert Morgenthau growing out of his investigation of allegations made by a New York University student that he had been lured to Crispo's gallery and sexually assaulted. LeGeros testified as a witness against Crispo, but the jury was not persuaded that coercion had been a factor in the case and acquitted Crispo.

On January 6, 1986, the *New York Post* published excerpts of letters written in prison by LeGeros. It was the black mask that had driven him to murder Vesti, he said. "If he had never worn that mask, it never would have happened. It awoke my childhood fears. Anyone who wore that mask became a monster. Crispo used my childhood fears of the mask."

As for Crispo, LeGeros wrote, "He belongs in hell. The only thing is that he would enjoy it."

On February 10, twelve days short of the first anniversary of the murder of Eigil Dag Vesti, Crispo was sentenced to seven years in federal prison on tax charges.

Two months before, in an effort to raise money to help

settle his tax accounts, Crispo had sold Constantin Brancusi's famed sculpture "The Muse" for three million dollars to New York's Guggenheim Museum.

Asked if he has any reservations about dealing with Crispo, the museum director, Thomas Messer, retorted, "I wasn't purchasing Crispo, I was purchasing a Brancusi masterpiece."

18 | THE PERFECT MURDER

"TURN AROUND AND *close your eyes. I have a surprise for you,*" he said playfully with a smile like a little boy with a big secret, but when she turned her back to him, he grabbed a belt he'd prepared for this purpose, looped it around her neck, and jerked it tight.

"*It wasn't me,*" she gasped. Writhing against him, clawing her fingernails into his face, straining for breath, she muttered, "*I didn't do it.*"

The words gurgled in her throat.

At 6:15 on the morning of Wednesday, March 25, 1987, the bedside telephone in his home in Walden in rural Ulster County jolted Al Van Dam awake.

"Al, you've got to help me," Donald Mason said, sobbing. "Ruth didn't come home from work last night. I'm afraid something bad might have happened to her. Can you come over?"

Through his church affiliation, Van Dam knew Don and Ruth Mason very well and had often visited their home in a trailer park in Plattekill, half an hour's drive away. At twenty-seven, Don was a warehouse operator at the AT&T facility in Ramapo where Ruth also worked and was a highly valued and well-liked employee. But because of a recent hernia repair he hadn't been to work for a few weeks.

Six feet tall, 165 pounds slim, with receding black hair and a mustache, he looked drawn and tired—a combination of his recuperation and concern for his wife, Van Dam supposed.

Ruth's not returning from her job was unusual indeed, so Van Dam understood fully why Don was upset as he greeted him at the door of the trailer. He then proceeded to explain that the previous evening when his wife didn't come home from work he had called a friend, Bob Parks, and they'd driven around Rockland to see if they could locate her silver Chevrolet Sprint in the AT&T parking lot, at a shopping center, or perhaps abandoned in a wreck along a highway. They had found nothing.

"I just don't understand," he said to Van Dam, breaking into tears. "I talked to Ruth at her office in the afternoon and she told me that she'd be working overtime until 5:30 and would be right home after that. I had dinner waiting for her. When she didn't show up, I waited an hour and then called the police but they told me there was nothing they could do until twenty-four hours passed. I didn't sleep all night. Then this morning I thought of you, knowing that you've got friends who are with the police."

"I'll call Mike Demeo at home."

A sergeant with the Ramapo Police Department, Demeo spoke with Mason, taking down information regarding Ruth's car and telling Mason that he would be coming to pick him up to take him to Ramapo to help him file a missing-person report and that the two of them would then conduct their own search. "You just stay put, Don," he said, "and I'll be there as soon as I can."

It was 7:45 A.M.

At that moment in the Ramapo Police Department headquarters Sergeant Edward Dolan was taking a phone call from Joan Warbrick, an employee of the Shop-Rite supermarket in the Caldor shopping center directly across Route 59 from the police station. Understandably nervous, Warbrick was reporting that the body of a woman, apparently dead, had been found by a truck driver making a delivery at the rear of the store.

Police Officer Donald Hutta had arrived for work early and was putting on his uniform for his eight-to-four duty in a patrol car when Sergeant Dolan came in with an assignment. "A possible DOA next to a dumpster in back of Caldor's."

Lying on her back beside a huge blue steel trash container, she was an attractive young blonde with her head fully turned to the right. A raw red welt circled her neck and there were red blotches on her face. Her blue pullover sweater was pulled down, baring her left breast. No pulse. Cold to the touch. No shoes. Torn black pantyhose under a black-brown-beige-green-striped skirt.

Using his car's radio, Hutta called the station to request the medical examiner and homicide investigators.

At that moment, my chief of detectives, Peter Modaferri, was in the midst of his daily jog and, spotted by an Orangetown police officer passing in his patrol car, was informed of the likely homicide. Returning home, Pete telephoned Chief Assistant DA Harvey Eilbaum and arranged to rendezvous with him and detectives Ronald Taggart and Chris Goldrick at the scene.

Meanwhile, Mike Demeo had arrived at Don Mason's trailer home and in two telephone conversations with Ramapo police he described Ruth's car and the clothing she had been wearing and gave them the name of her supervisor at AT&T.

"If they hear anything, they'll call us," he said.

Hanging up, he noticed a long fresh scratch on Mason's worried-looking face.

Immediately upon his arrival at the crime scene, Pete Modaferri, conferring with Ramapo Police Chief Joseph Miele and Detective John Twoomey, noted that the dead woman's stockings were torn and that drag marks on the ground indicated she had been taken from a motor vehicle and placed there. Scratches on her face and neck also pointed to a struggle. A few of her fingernails had been broken, another indication that she'd resisted her killer.

Informed that Mike Demeo had called from Ulster County on behalf of Donald Mason to report that Mason's wife hadn't come home from her job at AT&T the previous night and also told that an AT&T supervisor who knew Mrs. Mason was being brought to the scene to make an identification, Pete waited and felt a growing uneasiness about this murder. He had a feeling that something strange was underlying all that he saw around him.

James Marinaccio of AT&T had no trouble verifying that the dead woman was Ruth Mason.

Now her car had to be located.

And her husband had to be informed, of course.

Mike Demeo took the call and broke the news.

Mason sobbed, "Was she raped?"

"I don't know," replied Demeo. "When you're feeling up to it," he said consolingly, "the police will be needing your help in finding whoever did this to Ruth."

"Yes," Mason said. "I want to help."

It was almost eleven o'clock when Ruth Mason's car was found in the parking lot of a King Kullen supermarket on Route 59 in Suffern. Both doors were closed but unlocked. The interior was neat and clean except that the ashtray was pulled out and was lying on the floor with a handful of coins scattered beside it. A pair of sunglasses also lay nearby.

Loaded on a truck, the car was hauled to the Bureau of Criminal Identification for a more detailed inspection inside and out.

A search of the area around the car failed to locate Ruth Mason's missing shoes and handbag.

In the detectives' minds the facts of the crime weren't adding up. What was the motive? Rape? Robbery? Rage? And why would a killer dump a body beside a trash bin outside a door that was used a great deal by employees of the Caldor store? Why such an open, heavily trafficked location? Where had Ruth Mason been and for how long between leaving work at 5:30 P.M. and the discovery of her body at approximately 7:40 A.M. a short distance from AT&T? Had she been abducted and held somewhere? Raped? The state of her clothing pointed to possible attempted rape, but had it taken place in her car? Her missing handbag and spilled coins in the car were evidence pointing more to robbery than to rape. If she had been killed while resisting rape, where had it occurred? Where the body had been found? If so, how to explain her being dragged? Why not just shove her out of the car? If she'd been attacked elsewhere, why had she been dumped behind Caldor's? Why not dump her body in a remote area where the likelihood of being seen getting rid of a corpse would have been far less than at a very busy shopping center along a main thoroughfare? How did she wind up at Caldor's and her car in a parking lot some distance away? The logistics pointed to the killer having needed a second car to effect a meeting with Mrs. Mason before the murder and the abandoning of her car after killing her. Had that fateful encounter taken place in the AT&T lot? If so, it had to have happened when people were leaving from work. Therefore they must have met elsewhere. Was it a chance meeting? Or had Ruth arranged a rendezvous? Had Mrs. Mason been her killer's lover? Or was she simply a random selection of a killer she did not know? What about the means of murder? It seemed obvious that she'd been strangled, but if abduction, robbery, or rape were the motive, it would seem likely that the killer would have brought a weapon, a gun or a knife. Why kill by strangulation?

Some clues that might lead to answers to some of these questions obviously might come from Ruth Mason's husband. Was she a faithful wife? If not, did Mr. Mason know of any men she might have known who would have a reason to harm her? Did she have any enemies capable of murdering her? Was there anything in her behavior that might suggest why someone murderous would be with her in her car? What was the status of the Mason marriage itself? Did Mason have any reason to harm his wife?

When Donald Mason stepped into the Ramapo police station shortly before noon, Modaferri and Twoomey immediately noticed what had attracted Mike Demeo's attention—a fresh scratch on Mason's right cheek. "How'd you get that?" Mason was asked.

"I don't know," Mason replied.

"How long have you had it?"

"I got it yesterday."

Letting the subject go for the time being, Twoomey spoke in a tone that was businesslike but sympathetic. "It's going to be necessary for you to identify your wife for us. It's tough, I know, but it has to be done. I'll drive you to the office of the medical examiner."

Arriving at the medical examiner's facilities in Pomona and discovering that Dr. Frederick Zugibe had not yet completed the autopsy, they waited until after three o'clock before Mason was allowed into Dr. Zugibe's morgue to identify Ruth's body.

Meanwhile, Dr. Zugibe had determined that she had not

been raped and that the cause of death had been asphyxiation due to ligature strangulation. A short piece of rope found next to the body had been compared with the marks around Ruth's neck by Dr. Zugibe and ruled out as the murder weapon. Something wide and smooth was a much more likely instrument of death—a belt, for example.

Still intrigued and troubled by the scratch on Mason's face, Peter suggested to Mason that Dr. Zugibe examine it and treat it if necessary. This would require a waiver of Miranda rights, he explained to Mason.

Agreeing to the waiver, he allowed the examination, in the course of which Dr. Zugibe determined that the scratch had to have been made by a fingernail. Present around the wound was a trace of cosmetic makeup. He'd applied it, Mason explained, so the scratch wouldn't be so noticeable.

After studying the wound, Dr. Zugibe examined an injury to Mason's elbow that looked like a burn caused by the coarse fibers of a rug. Discovering a few tiny strands embedded in the brush-burn, he removed them. It was from a carpet, Mason explained. Because of his operation, he said, he watched television while lying on the floor.

Suspecting that Mason not only knew more than he was saying about his wife's death but that possibly he had caused it, the detectives now wanted Mason to agree to submit to a polygraph test but expected that Mason would at last invoke his Miranda rights and refuse.

"Sure, I'll take it," said Mason unhesitatingly.

On such short notice a polygraph operator was not available immediately, a delay Peter Modaferri took advantage of, talking with Mason in a waiting room at state police barracks in Kingston and telling him bluntly that nobody believed the story he'd been telling. "We're checking out everything," he warned, "and I'm pretty sure it isn't going to add up to the way you've been telling it, so why don't you give me the whole truth now?"

Mason brooded for a moment, then blurted "I killed her. I did it in our trailer as soon as she came home from work."

The idea had been roaming around in his head for months, he said. A plan had jelled recently.

It was an intricate scenario that involved renting a car, making it seem as if his wife had been accosted on her way home from work and murdered, then an elaborate charade in which he would report her missing and search for her. It all had come together on Friday, when he thought she'd been flirting with another man. He knew then there could be no turning back, there was no other way. He would have to kill her.

All that he stood for, all that he'd learned in his boyhood Bible school and believed as a Christian ever since demanded he do it.

He'd been born in Rochester, New York, and was raised in the clean, clear country of Northern Michigan to do what the Bible and his Free Methodist father taught was right: no smoking, no cursing, no drinking, no dancing, and no sex before marriage.

He'd been very active in the church's youth movement and only dated girls affiliated with the church. One of them was a cheerleader named Susan. Finding nothing in the Bible that prohibited it, they kissed and petted, but he suspected that she might have allowed him to go too far. That she liked to dance and go to parties bothered him, as did the fact that her family permitted the drinking of beer, which he felt was contrary to church doctrine.

Before Susan he'd dated Ruth Ragatz, but his family moved away. After breaking up with Susan, he encountered Ruth again while attending a church convention and had hopes of renewing their relationship, but he was disappointed to learn that she was dating someone. This young man (named Steve) he believed unsuitable—partying, drinking, smoking, and not living in accord with the teachings of the Bible. Hoping to win her away from Steve, he kept in touch with her, seeing her at summer Bible camp, exchanging letters.

Ruth Ragatz was a beautiful girl—blond hair, bright eyes, vivacious personality, member of the "pompom squad"—but also a regular churchgoer.

At long last she ended her relationship with Steve, and in a courtship that was quite proper ultimately agreed to become Mrs. Donald Mason. Married in July 1983, they had their first sexual intercourse on their honeymoon, but to his dismay he discovered she was not a virgin. Soon he was obsessed with the idea that while he was making love to her she was thinking of Steve. In making love she was too good, too experienced, too practiced. She knew all about oral sex, and although he enjoyed it when she performed fellatio on him, he could not believe that she'd not done it previously.

Doubts about his wife's chastity before their marriage and about her fidelity after their wedding festered in his thoughts and soon he believed marrying Ruth had been a terrible mistake. Divorce? Out of the question! In his church, divorce would mean excommunication. What to do?

The question was weighing heavily on his mind in September 1986, when they were on vacation and rented a video cassette of the movie *Jagged Edge*, in which a man kills his wife and avoids prosecution by passing a lie detector test. Convinced that he could do the same, he decided to hire someone to actually do the killing and looked for such a person by approaching black men on the streets of Spring Valley and Newburgh.

Finding no takers, he made up his mind to do it himself.

On a ski trip in January 1987 he thought of pushing her off the slopes.

A few weeks later, he had his hernia operation and during that period of convalescence he came up with a scheme for the perfect murder.

"So during these past five or six weeks, you developed a plan?"

Called to the Bureau of Criminal Identification by Peter Modaferri after Mason's confession, Executive Assistant DA John Edwards was now doing the questioning.

"I knew I was going to choke her somehow," Mason said.

He decided to use a belt, catching her by surprise when she came home from work and then driving back to Rockland County to leave the body where it would appear that she'd been attacked on her way home. He would leave her car somewhere and have a rented car waiting in which to return to Ulster County.

"Turn around and close your eyes," he said playfully with a smile like a little boy with a big secret, but when she turned her back to him, he grabbed a belt he'd prepared for this purpose, looped it quickly around her neck, and jerked it tight.

"It wasn't me," she gasped. Writhing against him, clawing her fingernails into his face, straining for breath, she muttered, "I didn't do it."

The words gurgled in her throat.

He tightened the belt. She turned. Scratched his face. He threw her to the floor. His shirt ripped. One of her shoes flew off. Or maybe she'd kicked it off. He tightened the belt even more. His heart was pounding. Was hers? He listened, couldn't hear her heartbeat. He wanted to kiss her on the cheek but a trickle of blood oozed from her mouth. He yanked the belt harder. His hands were aching from pulling, so he loosened the grip and left her for moment to fetch a towel to press against her nose and mouth to cut off her air. Coming back, he smelled the sour odor of urine and saw a large wet spot on the carpet. And he smelled feces.

"What did you do after you strangled her?"

"I took her rings, her wedding band and her diamond, off her finger, tore a gold chain off her neck."

"Why did you do that?"

"I wanted the police to think that it was robbery. The necklace I was going to throw away, but the rings are worth twenty-five hundred dollars. I didn't take a pearl ring because it was on pretty tight and because I didn't think it was worth that much. I was going to take them into the city and sell them."

"After you took the jewelry off her body, what did you do?"

"I went out to the car and unlocked the passenger side, laid the seat all the way back in the reclining position. I took her by the wrists and dragged her out the door, down the steps, across the yard, and up to the driveway. I had a hard time getting her into the car because I couldn't lift her whole body weight. I was afraid I was going to tear out the stitches from my operation. I finally got her buckled into the seat as if she were reclining and asleep. I drove to Rockland County, down the Thruway."

"Did you go through the toll booths?"

"Yes."

"Then what?"

"I pulled in behind Caldor's, pulled in behind the dumpster and pulled her out of the car. Her head hit the ground hard. It upset me. I tried to break off her fingernails using the car's keys because I knew she had scratched me and I knew that some of my body fluid would be under her nails. I think I broke two or three of them but it was taking too long. There was a door by the dumpster and I was afraid somebody was going to come out to dump some garbage. I pulled her sweater partway down and I unlatched her bra, and that's how I left her."

His torn shirt, the necklace, the belt, and one shoe he discarded at various places in Rockland.

"What did you do with her coat and purse?"

"I threw them in the bushes on the left-hand side of the road going into our trailer park."

Then began his elaborate attempt to cover up the murder, his master plan to make it appear that Ruth had been abducted, robbed, and murdered while he, the loving husband, waited and kept her evening meal warm, then acting worried and frantically telephoning their friends, asking for advice and assistance, notifying the police his wife was missing, searching for her himself.

The valuable rings he had hidden in a film can and placed it in a gray metal strongbox under the bed. The strongbox also contained a $100,000 life insurance policy on Ruth.

"When did you take out the policy?" asked John Edwards.

"I took one out for each of us, probably six months ago."

"And that was at about the time you were formulating your plan to kill her?"

"Yes."

On March 28, after being indicted for second-degree murder, Mason pleaded not guilty. Although he was judged mentally competent to stand trial I expected him to adopt the familiar insanity defense. Indeed, in anticipation of it, he was examined by psychiatrists and psychologists for both the defense and prosecution, but in the end it was Mason's own conscience that ruled. Overswept by guilt and remorse and expressing a desire to avoid inflicting sorrow on Ruth's family, he overrode the advice of his public-defender attorney and made up his mind to plead guilty.

County Court Judge Robert Meehan asked Mason, "You think it is the right thing to do to plead guilty and not go to trial?"

"I am doing it voluntarily because I feel guilty for what I did," he replied. "I don't want to put my wife's family through any more than I already have."

Judge Meehan accepted the plea and sentenced Mason to a term of twenty-two years to life.

During the brief stroll from the courthouse to my offices after the sentencing, accompanied by detectives Pat Massi and John Casey, I paused for a moment upon a quaint wooden footbridge that spans a picturesque brook separating the courthouse from the Rockland County office building. My thoughts turned to the man who thought he'd planned and carried out the perfect murder.

"Mason actually believed he'd get away with it," I said incredulously. "He believed he'd planned the perfect murder, but in fact it was one of the most inept homicides on record. He stops people at random on the street and says, 'Hey, how'd you like to kill my wife for me?' Getting no takers, he goes to great pains to make it appear that his wife never arrived home from work that night and then casually throws pieces of her clothing in the bushes right outside their trailer. The body he leaves smack in the middle of a busy service area of a major shopping center, practically on the front doorstep of the Ramapo police station! He uses his own credit car for the car rental. And under his bed in a box is a brand-new insurance policy with himself as the sole beneficiary to the tune of one hundred thousand dollars!"

In dramatic contrast to this ill-conceived and blundered crime was the speed and efficiency with which it was solved—a period of less than twenty-four hours between Mason's brutal strangling of his wife and his formal confession to John Edwards, less then eleven hours after the discovery of Ruth's body. Within a few more hours, evidence and witnesses had been located so that a murder which had been committed on Tuesday evening was heard by a grand jury which handed up an indictment on Friday.

Justice may not always be so swift in coming but it is, as John Galsworthy wrote, "a machine that, when someone has once given it the starting push, rolls on of itself."

19 | THE SCARLET THREAD

"THERE'S THE SCARLET thread of murder running through the colorless skein of life," says Sherlock Holmes to Dr. Watson in "A Study in Scarlet," "and our duty is to unravel it, and isolate it, and expose every inch of it."

In this book I've attempted to describe extraordinary cases of murder that occurred during my current tenure as district attorney of Rockland County and the extraordinary professionals on police forces, in the office of the medical examiner, in the forensic laboratories, in the Bureau of Criminal Identification, and attorneys and detectives on my own staff who unraveled, isolated, and exposed every inch of them. They are modern-day sleuths who brought to each of these homicides their cunning and deductive reasoning plus the scientific and technological wizardry that has become part of criminology since Arthur Conan Doyle dreamed up his brainy detective over a century ago.

Of course, murder cases are a small part of the work of the police and of the office of district attorney, but it is murder that fascinates and holds people spellbound. In fiction, drama, movies, television shows, newspapers, and magazines throughout the history of humanity, murder has been right up there alongside love on our list of favorite topics.

It's been said that the detective story is the normal

recreation of the noble mind. And the best detective story is, of course, a tale of murder. We crave to know "who done it" and are delighted if we figure out the solution even before the detective gathers all the suspects into a room to, as Hercule Poirot puts it, "reveal all."

"Murder will out," warn Chaucer and Cervantes. "Other sins only speak," writes John Webster, "murder shrieks out." William Shakespeare makes much the same point: "Murder, though it have no tongue, will speak with most miraculous organ" (Hamlet). "Murder cannot be hid long" (The Merchant of Venice). In Hamlet, King Claudius promises his nephew "The murderer will be found. He will be brought to suitable punishment."

What is the suitable penalty for murder?

Today in America there is disagreement. Even though the Supreme Court of the United States has declared that the death penalty is permissible, a battle rages over its propriety. The dispute is probably one waged more according to one's own individual belief in the morality or appropriateness of government taking a life than in the validity of the arguments proffered by each side to support its own position. Whether there is any empirical data to back up the notion that the death penalty deters or does not deter further crime is an academic discussion, for proponents of the death penalty are content in the belief, founded or otherwise, that a human being cannot help but be deterred by the prospect of forfeiting his own life. Opponents, on the other hand, can always point to cases of murders being committed within hours of an execution.

I have always favored the death penalty. (My co-author, Mr. Jeffers, does not, taking the view that a government should not take life except in time of war.) I believe the death penalty does deter—perhaps not everyone, but surely some. Therefore, if it is instrumental in saving just one innocent life, albeit at the cost of another, then in my judgment it is worthwhile. Moreover, while I do not advocate its institution for a wide variety of offenses, I do believe that it is appropriate punishment for certain crimes.

I have no reservation about society's forfeiting the life of an individual who, out of greed or some other self-indulgent motive, was callously willing to take the life of another. So, for example, in the murders of the Sohns by Belton Brims and James Sheffield, or Richard LaBarbera and Robert McCain, who repeatedly stabbed and assaulted Paula Bohovesky, or Samir Zada, who within a period of ten days took two lives, I believe death at the hands of the state to be an appropriate—indeed, I believe, the only just— punishment.

The death penalty is not and never has been a cure for all of society's problems or a guaranteed deterrent to murder because there will always be those who give no thought to the possible punishment for their crime, or who believe the potential benefits are worth the risk. The existence of these individuals is not a sufficient reason to abandon totally that punishment that is the only one that fits the crime.

Some who believe the death penalty does deter the crime of murder have advocated its use to stem the gravest problem confronting law enforcement and society as a whole—drugs—by imposing it on the kingpins of the trade in narcotics. Whether it would have an effect remains to be seen.

Clearly, the way in which the drug problem is being addressed is woefully inadequate and ineffective. Illicit drugs have entered the United States in a flood, notwithstanding the involvement of the military in the air and on the sea to interdict the flow. A more concerted effort by the federal government to curb the traffic across our borders is required, as is a continuous effort to persuade the drug-producing countries to do more to help stamp out the narcotics business. Toward that end, the United States must be willing to offer economic incentives to these countries to encourage their cooperation. If such incentives fail, then more drastic "disincentives" will have to be employed even at the risk of straining relations with the governments of those countries. The problem is just that grave.

The federal government must also provide greater financial assistance to localities where the impact of drugs is felt most acutely, channeled in a manner that recognizes and addresses the broad nature of the problem.

In Rockland County we have created a narcotics task force that is wholly funded by the state and the county because, unfortunately, the federal government does not provide money for local narcotics task forces. However, despite this, our task force operating under director James V. Stewart has been very successful in grappling with street-level and middle-echelon dealers, removing hundreds of these predators from the county.

Prosecution and incarceration is not the answer to drugs, however. To wipe out this scourge, we must eliminate the demand. Drug use must become unacceptable. That means a dramatic reversal of past practice when "recreational" use was deemed acceptable.

I am appalled at suggestions that criminality associated with drugs can be eliminated by making drugs and their usage legal. To do so would be to surrender. It would be an abject declaration of defeat. Worse, it would condemn future generations to the eternal bondage of drug addiction.

The drug problem and its accompanying crime can be dealt with if we make a full commitment to the goal of ridding ourselves of the pestilence of narcotics, beginning with a realization that it is not merely a problem of law enforcement but a threat to our way of life as real and eminent as any enemy army.

The plague of drugs has contributed massively to the rise in this country's crime rate and the incidence of murder in particular, with many innocent victims caught in crossfire between drug gangs or simply murdered for their money or their valuable possessions.

That's what appeared to be the case of Cheryl Ickson, a twenty-two-year-old Rockland County resident who became enmeshed in the trap of drug abuse and wound up a victim.

On August 23, 1987, Cheryl was overdue at her job as a desk clerk at her family's motel in Stony Point. Because this was not typical of their daughter, her frantic parents contacted Sergeant Joe Liszack of the Stony Point police. Ordinarily, under state law action is not taken on a missing-person report for twenty-four hours, but this time Chief Stephen Scurti and Lieutenant Frank Tinelli decided to go ahead and send a teletype message about her car to regional police departments.

Within hours came a reply from New York City police reporting that the auto had been stopped in the Bronx for a traffic violation and the driver released for later court appearance. Driving the car was a man who identified himself as Dewayne Eurie. With him were another black man, a black woman, and a white woman who identified herself as Cheryl Ickson and told the police she would be in trouble with her parents if they found out she had been in New York City.

Refusing to believe this, the Ickson family persisted in asserting that Cheryl could not have left home under the circumstances described. Given a description of the woman who'd identified herself as Cheryl, Mrs. Ickson declared "That's not my daughter." Shown a photograph of the man who called himself Dewayne Eurie, she recognized him as a resident of the motel who had used the name Dwayne Johnson.

Advised of these developments, the Stony Point police put out a warrant for Johnson charging him with unauthorized use of a motor vehicle and set out to locate him. Working the case now were Lieutenant Tinelli, Sergeant Liszack, and Detective Joseph Denise of the Stony Point police and DA Detective John Gould, with the Ickson family members deeply involved by providing information on Cheryl's acquaintances and friends, most of them located in Haverstraw.

Based on conversations with persons there, the focus of the investigation centered on 33 Main Street, where Dwayne Johnson was reported to have been seen, but the woman who rented the apartment at that address said she had not seen Johnson.

Doubting the story, the police checked all parts of the building and located Johnson and Lori Ann Mitchell hiding on the roof.

An attractive eighteen-year-old with styled blond hair, dressed in pink slacks and a white jacket and insisting she'd done nothing wrong, Mitchell was soon telling the detectives what had happened to Cheryl Ickson.

It was around six o'clock on the twenty-third that Dwayne Johnson telephoned Cheryl and asked her for a ride to the city. They set up a meeting at a Grand Union market in Stony Point. When Cheryl arrived, Johnson, John Robinson, Nora Mann, and she, Lori Mitchell, got into Cheryl's car.

Johnson asked, "Can I drive?"

"No," said Cheryl. Did Johnson have anything for her? she asked, meaning cocaine.

He did, Johnson said, directing Cheryl to drive them to a secluded road in Mount Ivy and turn the car around. When she did so, he said he would need her keys in order to break down the cocaine, which was in the rock-hard form known as crack. Cheryl handed him the keys and he passed them to John Robinson in the back seat.

At that point, Johnson pulled out a gun; not a real one, but one made of plastic, although the toy was realistic-looking enough as he pressed it against Cheryl's head.

Resisting, Cheryl was forced into the rear of the car, where she was tied up with shoelaces, robbed, slapped, and beaten unconscious.

At a desolate construction site near Alpine, New Jersey, John Robinson dragged Cheryl into a wooded area and returned a few minutes later saying, "I took care of the bitch."

Detective Denise asked Mitchell, "Can you show us where the body is?"

"I think so," she said, nodding.

Because I had known Martin and Eleanor Ickson for nearly twenty years and because their children and mine had attended the same schools, they had come to see me in my capacity as district attorney about the mysterious disappearance of their daughter, expressing fears that she was dead and asking me to do whatever I could in helping to find her. Now, early in the morning of August 26 I was with Lieutenant Tinelli, Detective Denise, and Sergeant Liszack of the Stony Point police, Sergeant Wayne Dunn and Officer Jerry Sullivan of the Haverstraw Police, and Lieutenant Jim Stewart and detectives John Gould and Steve Colantonio of my own staff in a convoy of police cars heading into Bergen County, New Jersey, in the hope that

Mitchell could find the location where they'd left Cheryl's body.

Because of her uncertainty, we roamed the back roads of the area for some time until, at last, around 2:00 A.M. she spotted a large clearing which was being prepared for homes and expressed her belief that it was the place where Cheryl Ickson's body had been dumped.

With the predawn blackness pierced by flashlights and the beams of light cut by the crouching shadowy, silent, grim-faced figures of the searchers moving slowly into thick woods, the search scene took on aspects of a surrealistic horror film.

Then, an urgent voice pierced the stillness: "Over here!"

Beneath a thin blanket of branches and leaves lay Cheryl's body with the hands and ankles tied with shoelaces, the head face down but turned slightly, the bruised and lacerated skin blackened by exposure, the hair tangled and matted with blood, and the pulseless, cold, and clammy body acrawl with insects, flies, and maggots.

Because this apparent murder was in Bergen County, calls needed to be made on the radio to Rockland headquarters to alert them to notify the Bergen DA, the New Jersey police, and the medical examiner, a task in which I assisted after we had all withdrawn to our vehicles, leaving only Sergeant Dunn to stand guard at the shallow grave.

After a few minutes as we waited for the Bergen officials to arrive, Dunn pierced the air with a cry of alarm.

Instantly, those with guns drew them and raced into the woods, not knowing what they might find.

Possibilities flashed through my mind. Had John Robinson or someone else connected with the crime mysteriously appeared on the scene? Were there other accomplices who for some reason decided to return to the gravesite? Had

Sergeant Dunn stumbled upon other bodies? Had he himself been assaulted?

A few minutes later as I waited anxiously in the car with Lori Ann Mitchell, Jim Stewart dashed from the woods to exclaim breathlessly, "Boss, you're not going to believe it! The girl is alive."

Incredibly, after more than sixty hours in the shallow ditch, the person we'd seen a few moments earlier encrusted with dirt and blood and swarming with bugs had startled Sergeant Dunn by stirring in the shallow ditch and with an unearthly moan begun pushing herself upright.

Grabbing the microphone of the patrol car's radio, I now called for an ambulance instead of the medical examiner.

Although Cheryl remained semi-comatose for weeks and hospitalized for months, in due course she recovered sufficiently to identify her kidnappers and to assist in their prosecution.

Because the crime had been committed in Bergen County, it was tried there with assistance from Rockland County authorities.

Lori Ann Mitchell and Nora Robinson pleaded guilty in return for reduced prison sentences and testimony against Dwayne Johnson. "You ought to be ashamed of yourself," scolded Bergen County Superior Court Judge Charles Digisi as he pronounced a sentence of fifteen years for Mitchell and twenty for Robinson. "Isn't it a shame that you not only destroyed the victim's life but your own?"

Johnson refused to plead and was convicted, receiving a sentence of thirty-five years for attempted murder.

John Robinson decided to avoid trial for attempted murder by agreeing to plead guilty to kidnapping, aggravated assault, and armed robbery, an arrangement about which Cheryl Ickson was consulted and to which she agreed. His sentence of thirty years in prison made him ineligible for parole after fifteen years.

"This was just a cold-blooded, depraved, and heinous crime without rhyme or reason. The cruelty inflicted on this victim was worse than death. You just decided to take this young lady and snuff out her life—it's as simple as that," said Bergen County Judge Alfred Schiaffo, with Cheryl present in the court.

"I'm very happy with the sentence," she told reporters. "He'll just sit there and rot."

She had been very lucky. The warmth of her shallow grave, no rain in those sixty hours when she had been left for dead in a ditch in which she might have drowned in a heavy rainfall, the refusal of her family to accept the easy explanation that she had left home on her own volition, and diligent investigation and dogged detective work had produced a rare occurrence in the annals of crime . . . and a unique ending for this book—a case of murder with a happy ending.